Regions That Work

Globalization and Community

Dennis R. Judd, Series Editor

Regions That Work

How Cities and Suburbs Can Grow Together

Manuel Pastor Jr., Peter Dreier,
J. Eugene Grigsby III, and Marta López-Garza

Globalization and Community / Volume 6
University of Minnesota Press
Minneapolis • London

MINNESOTA

Published by the University of Minnesota Press
111 Third Avenue South, Suite 290
Minneapolis, MN 55401-2520
http://www.upress.umn.edu

Printed in the United States of America on acid-free paper

The University of Minnesota is an equal-opportunity educator and employer.

Library of Congress Cataloging-in-Publication Data:

Regions that work : how cities and suburbs can grow together /
    Manuel Pastor, Jr. . . . [et al.].
        p.   cm.—(Globalization and community ; v. 6)
    Includes bibliographical references and index.
    ISBN 0-8166-3339-8—ISBN 0-8166-3340-1 (pbk.)
        1. City planning—California—Los Angeles Metropolitan Area. 2. Regional
    planning—California—Los Angeles Metropolitan Area. 3. Urban policy—
    California—Los Angeles Metropolitan Area. 4. Suburbs—California—
    Los Angeles Metropolitan Area. 5. Los Angeles Metropolitan Area (Calif.)—
    Economic policy. 6. Los Angeles Metropolitan Area (Calif.)—Social policy.
        I. Pastor, Manuel. II. Series.
    HT168.L6 R44   2000
    307.76'09794"94—dc21
                                                                00-044717

11 10 09 08 07 06 05 04 03 02 01 00   10 9 8 7 6 5 4 3 2 1

Contents

Figures and Tables

Tables

Acknowledgments

This book grew out of an ongoing dialogue between various community leaders and the authors regarding the future of the Los Angeles economy. For urging us to develop a new understanding of the region and the poor, and to create a new policy framework that could both challenge preconceptions and build common ground, we thank especially three Los Angeles–based organizations—the Multicultural Collaborative, the New Majority Task Force, and the Coalition of Neighborhood Developers—as well as Ed Ochoa of Cal Poly Pomona, Stewart Kwoh of the Asian Pacific American Legal Center, and Joe Hicks, Cyndi Choi, Ruben Lizardo, and Gary Phillips (currently or formerly with the Multicultural Collaborative). Special thanks go to Goetz Wolff, who worked with Eugene Grigsby and the Multicultural Collaborative to develop earlier iterations of the conceptual framework used in chapter 3.

Thanks also to those who provided comments on various parts of this work in various stages of development, including Scott Bernstein, Rick Cole, Denise Fairchild, George Galster, Paul Gottlieb, Ben Harrison, Madeline Janis-Aparicio, Dennis Judd, Bruce Katz, Julia Lopez, Peter Olney, Anthony Thigpenn, Joan Walsh, and Linda Wong. Thanks, too, to those who were so cooperative about providing data and interviews in various neighborhoods and agencies throughout Los Angeles, as well as those who provided information and interviews in Boston, Charlotte, and San Jose.

Through the course of this research, we were blessed with an extraordinary crew of research assistants, including Yadira Guardado, Lucia Chairez, Joseph Whitfield, Talin Jemjemian, and Eddie Jauregui from Occidental College; Stephanie Babb from the Urban Planning Program of the University of California, Los Angeles; Enrico Marcelli and Steven Conroy from the Economics and Political Economy programs at the University of

Southern California; and Rachel Rosner, John Hipp, Melissa Reyes, and Alex Armenta from the University of California, Santa Cruz. Marta López-Garza also thanks her research classes at both Occidental College and California State University, L.A. for their fieldwork on the informal economy in L.A. as presented in chapter 2. Five assistants played especially critical roles. Karina Ramos of Occidental College stepped in as research coordinator at a critical time and brought some degree of order from our happy but unproductive chaos; she also helped design and implement the San Jose case study. Lezlee Hinesmon-Matthews from UCLA's Urban Planning Department coordinated and wrote up the interviews in low-income communities in Los Angeles. John Pike from Occidental College was our data savior, understanding the nuances of MSAs and GIS and happily cooperating with endless requests for different cuts at the underlying data. Albert Carlson from UCLA Planning joined us in the final stages and helped update our analysis of alternative strategies. Maya Bendotoff from UC Santa Cruz brought together the final drafts of the book, gently and patiently offering queries to busy authors using different word processors, referencing styles, and sometimes theoretical frameworks.

The research team (Pastor, Dreier, Grigsby, and López-Garza) jointly conceptualized the initial research design, interview instruments, and data requirements, as well as the chapter structure and order of this volume. Chapter 1 was written by Pastor and Dreier. Chapter 2 was primarily written by Pastor, with López-Garza providing the analytical frame and ethnographic analysis of the informal sector, and contributing to the overall regional history, conclusion, and chapter editing. The initial draft of chapter 3 was written by Grigsby, with Pastor providing supplemental research on both L.A.'s development history and the various initiatives; Pastor and Lezlee Hinesmon-Matthews were also responsible for the neighborhood profiles at the end of that chapter and in appendix A. Chapter 4 was written primarily by Dreier, with portions (particularly on Los Angeles) contributed by Pastor. Chapter 5 was written by Pastor, with John Pike providing portions of the literature review and part of the empirical discussion. For chapter 6, Pastor and López-Garza wrote the section on San Jose, Grigsby wrote the section on Charlotte, and Dreier wrote the study of Boston; Pastor and Pike provided the empirical work for case selection, and Pastor wrote the introduction and threaded the cases together. Chapter 7 was discussed thoroughly by the whole team, who all contributed portions; the final version of this framework was written primarily by Dreier, Pastor, and Grigsby. Pastor edited and reworked the various pieces into a single manuscript, and provided all the statistical analysis in chapters 2, 3, 5, and 6. Copyediting of the whole manuscript was provided by Michelle Miller in an earlier draft and, as noted above, by Maya Bendotoff in the final draft.

This project would never have happened without the financial assistance of the John Randolph Haynes and Dora Haynes Foundation. Foundation leaders showed remarkable insight when they created a Solutions Research Program in the wake of the L.A. civil unrest, hoping to steer academics in the direction of real-world policy recommendations. It was not an easy charge, but it was one from which we have learned a great deal. We thank them for their support.

The New Regionalism and the New Community Building

In April 1992, the City of Los Angeles suffered three days of the worst civil disorder in American history. While the immediate cause was a verdict in the Rodney King case, many laid the blame on the economic wreckage left by both persistent poverty and a decade of regional restructuring.[1] Subsequent analysis gave credence to this view: in the areas of Los Angeles that experienced property damage, poverty and unemployment rates were twice as high, and home ownership and per capita income only half as high, as in the rest of the city.[2]

Many observers hoped that the Los Angeles unrest would catalyze a major national commitment to revitalize American cities—an urban Marshall Plan. The timing seemed perfect: the riots occurred in the midst of a national election for president and Congress, and with the Berlin Wall felled and the Soviet Union in collapse, a "peace dividend" to address long unmet domestic needs was possible. Newly elected president Bill Clinton proposed a $19.5 billion "stimulus package" based on a list of projects presented to the administration by the U.S. Conference of Mayors, and Henry Cisneros, a dynamic former mayor of San Antonio, took over as secretary of Housing and Urban Development (HUD).

Yet the plight of the cities quickly fell off the agenda as Congress rejected the spending package and slashed the budget for HUD. Such a slippage of policy attention was in keeping with America's attitude toward its urban areas: no other major industrial nation has allowed its cities to face the type of fiscal and social troubles confronting large U.S. municipalities. While violent crime rates in urban areas have declined in recent years, other indicators of social stress have remained unconscionably high. Moreover, the problems of cities, such as chronic fiscal problems and deepening

1

poverty, have "spilled over" into surrounding areas, including the older inner-ring suburbs. As a result, some have wondered whether the central cities are showing the suburbs their frightening twenty-first-century future.

The Urban Dilemma and the Regional Connection

Many Americans believe that America has tried to save its cities but that the cities resist being saved. Since the New Deal, various efforts at central city revitalization, such as urban renewal and Model Cities, have fallen victim to political backlashes. Many Americans believe that even if there were ample money, we would not know what to do with it, or at least could not guarantee that it would be spent wisely or efficiently to solve the nation's urban problems. They believe that more than thirty years after the urban unrest of the 1960s and the War on Poverty, the condition of America's cities is in many ways worse than ever. Why waste our tax dollars throwing more money at cities or at the poor that live there?

Countering this view requires a two-step strategy.

The first step involves helping decision makers understand the urban dilemma. While cities are the *location* of many of our nation's problems, they are not necessarily the *cause* of them. The larger driving forces of global competition and corporate business strategies have, for example, increased the ranks of the structurally unemployed and the working poor;[3] while a disproportionate share of those affected live in the city, this does not mean that the city itself is the reason for falling wages. Moreover, federal subsidies to cities—whether to revitalize downtowns, attract private business and jobs to inner cities, stabilize and improve poor and working class neighborhoods, or provide fiscal assistance to local governments—have been only a drop in the bucket compared to those federal policies that promoted suburbanization. Highway spending and low gas taxes have encouraged long commutes while tax deductions for mortgages and property taxes have induced consumers to buy large suburban homes. These and other subsidies have disproportionately favored sprawl and encouraged the abandonment of the central city.[4]

The second step to creating a new urban agenda involves building a broader political constituency for revitalizing cities. Today, two-thirds of Americans living in major metropolitan areas (amounting to about half of the nation's population) reside in suburbs. In every region of the country, even where city populations are increasing, the fastest-growing parts of the metropolitan areas are the surrounding suburbs.[5] The 1992 presidential election was the first in history in which an absolute majority of voters came from suburbs. Even more important, the number of Congress members who represent cities is declining, while the number who represent suburbs is increasing (Wolman and Marckini, 1998).[6] Thus, any success at addressing the problems of cities will necessitate appealing to some segment of the suburban electorate.

But why should suburbanites care about cities? Some leaders invoke an appeal to compassion or what cynics might call "do-gooderism" or charity. Much of the early War on Poverty effort tapped into this spirit. However, this altruistic strategy loses appeal when a majority of Americans feel economically insecure and policy choices begin to seem more like trade-offs. Some instead suggest that suburbanites should support urban policy as a form of "riot insurance." While fewer people now live, work, or shop in our cities, many suburbanites still use their nearby cities and want to know that they'll be safe. Unfortunately, this approach views cities as dangerous war zones that need to be contained before the problems spread, which leads to harsh and punitive policies and a failure to understand the dynamic community-building efforts underway in many poor neighborhoods.

A more compelling argument, the one we develop here, suggests that the fate of cities and their suburbs is increasingly linked. In this view, two trends are important: (1) central cities and many suburbs are becoming more alike, and (2) their futures are inextricably interdependent.

While the disparity between the median incomes of cities and suburbs has widened over the last twenty years, the image of the suburb as an upper-class lily-white enclave is more and more a thing of the past. Suburbs, particularly older inner-ring suburbs, are becoming more diverse ethnically and economically. While the percent of Anglos remains much higher in suburban areas, the suburbanization rates for blacks and Latinos are rising faster than for whites.[7] Poverty rates are still twice as high in central cities but 30.5 percent of the nation's poor do live in suburbs. Thus, although the most severe pockets of concentrated poverty tend to be in central cities, a growing number of suburbs are not immune from the problems of crime, fiscal strains, and unemployment confronting our urban centers.

Perhaps more important, cities and suburbs have become interdependent parts of shared regional economies. A number of recent studies have indicated that problem-ridden cities and declining suburbs go hand in hand. In other words, suburban islands of prosperity cannot exist in a sea of poverty (see chapter 5). This interconnection across the metropolitan landscape is partly because both city and suburb are affected by region-level economic restructuring, such as the downsizing of the auto industry in Detroit and its surrounding environs. But an even newer strand of research has uncovered an intriguing set of alternative causal arrows: poverty in the central city and inequality across the region can actually drag down the whole region.

Why the Region? Why the Poor?

The New Regionalism

Regionalism is an old idea. During the 1930s, 1940s, and 1950s, city planners and political scientists (such as Lewis Mumford and New York's Regional Plan Association) promoted the notions of regional planning and metropolitan-wide government, either to promote government efficiency or to promote a sound environment (such as greenbelts surrounding cities). Robert Wood's 1961 book *1400 Governments* made a compelling case that the fragmentation of metropolitan areas by jurisdictions—cities, townships, villages, boroughs, counties, and special districts for everything from parks to water to transportation—was irrational and inefficient. In the late 1960s, the federally sponsored Advisory Commission on Intergovernmental Relations recommended ways to broaden the tax and service base of cities.[8]

Most of these ideas fell on deaf ears. Local politicians preferred to exercise their influence within the narrower boundaries of their own municipalities. As people sought to "escape" troubled cities, the proportion of Americans living in suburbs grew. Asking these new refugees to share their local taxes, schools, and other public services with central-city residents was a hard sell indeed.

The most recent revival of regional thinking, what we term the "new regionalism," has been premised more on economic factors.[9] Neal Peirce (1993), for example, has argued that the key economic entities in the competitive global economy are "citistates," a new moniker for metropolitan regions that "market" their areas to outside businesses in ways that single municipalities cannot, identifying sites for job creation, helping train the workforce, and devising future growth plans that minimize traffic gridlock, pollution, ugly sprawl, and environmental devastation. A recent volume by William Barnes and Larry Ledebur (1998) even argues that the U.S. economy should not be looked at as a single entity but rather as a "common market" of local economic regions that compete with each other as with regions in other parts of the world.[10]

The emergence of the region as a central organizing unit of economic activity may seem paradoxical: in the current globalized business environment, manufacturing and design can occur anywhere and indeed may be separated by time and space. Many firms and industries are free to roam the planet in search of the optimal, or cheapest, location. The result, some argue, is the increasing irrelevance of local government as regulations and wages are eroded to a low but uniform standard.[11]

But if low labor costs and unfettered opportunities for business were the only issues that mattered, Haiti would be one of the most rapidly expanding economies in the world. What actually attracts business is the entire geographically based infrastructure of skills, markets, and expertise. These are the assets that make it worthwhile for businesses to accept higher labor and community standards in return for access to an educated, skilled, and enthusiastic pool of workers, supportive business suppliers, and the "intangibles" of sound public policy.[12]

Increasingly, these private, public, and community assets are constituted at the regional level. Indeed, when one asks which areas are doing well in the new global economy, the answer is frequently not countries per se but regions: northern Italy and its linked manufacturing networks; the Silicon Valley and its flexible chains of technology-based firms; and Monterrey, Mexico, and its allied industrial firms. Even in Japan and East Asia, certain industrial valleys stand out as the true competitors in the world economy.[13]

While the reasons behind the emergence of regions are still the subject of research, some preliminary investigations suggest that regions are the smallest economic unit at which interrelated industries and firms can cluster in production groups of integrated suppliers. The density of these relationships means that if the demand or supply of a particular product is not forthcoming from one firm, another will likely step up to the plate; in such an environment, individual firms feel the security necessary to expand design and/or production facilities to a size where each can achieve the lowest possible costs. Not surprisingly, regions become known by their industrial clusters. In Los Angeles, for example, the multimedia and entertainment sectors include sets of interacting firms working in both collaboration and competition to meet the needs of Hollywood's dream factories as well as other entertainment-related ventures.[14]

Regions, then, may offer the minimum size at which markets and business networks achieve the low-cost economies of scale necessary to compete in international markets. At the same time, they may offer the maximum size at which working relationships can be crafted and sustained. As Annalee Saxenian argues in her influential study of the Boston and Silicon Valley electronics industries, the "geographic proximity [of firms in a region] promotes the repeated interaction and mutual trust needed to sustain collaboration" (Saxenian, 1996: 161).[15] Collaboration, in turn, leads to joint efforts and the continual transmission of new technologies and industrial innovation. It can also lead to a generalized sense of the "commons," and therefore a recognition of the need to provide public goods and infrastructure that can lower costs for all businesses. In Silicon Valley, for example, the business sector has sometimes led the way in urging government to provide improved public transportation and affordable housing—even at the cost of higher taxes and various building restrictions.[16]

Stated more formally, as the scale of an economic unit grows, average costs may decline, but the ability to craft relationships based on trust declines as well. The reason for the latter flows directly from theories of collective action: the smaller the group, the more likely are people to find common interests; the larger the group, the more likely it is that individuals will "free ride" and groups will subdivide into factional and competing interests. Determining the optimal size for nimble industrial clusters and effective governments in the new economy involves weighing the benefits of expansion against the increasing difficulties of organization.[17] The appropriate balance is often found at the regional level; there, face-to-face relations among business partners, business and government, and communities and business can be maintained and trust built.[18]

Social Capital, Poverty, and Community Building

In essence, then, regions are defined and often constituted by what Robert Putnam (1993) has called "social capital": the dense set of relationships, such as business collaborations and labor market networks, that allow individual producers and workers to enhance their own individual outcomes.[19] But if social capital is the crucial glue that holds regions together and leads to enhanced economic performance, then inequality and poverty may be counterproductive. Inequality, after all, can breed distrust and social tension, leading to conflicts over public policy; poverty can lower the skill base, or human capital, necessary for a competitive economy.

Strikingly, a focus on social capital is also crucial to what we term the "new community building." This framework begins with a recognition of the changing nature of poverty: even more than in the past, the poor are highly concentrated in certain geographic spaces. This phenomenon stems in part from regional dynamics that have changed the terrain for workforce and community development. Manufacturing jobs with decent salaries have moved away from cities, to be replaced by service sector jobs with lower salaries (Wilson, 1996). Meanwhile, housing segregation has prevented minorities, especially African-Americans, from moving in pace with suburbanized employment opportunities (Massey and Denton, 1993). This "spatial mismatch" between jobs and residents leads to deepening pockets of poverty.[20]

The resulting concentrated poverty is self-reproducing: not only are residents distant from employment, but most of one's neighbors have either no jobs or bad jobs and therefore do not offer social networks that are helpful in connecting to available employment.[21] Geography also affects small business formation: those who save and invest in their own homes in poorer areas may find that "contagion" dampens any appreciation in value, subverting the major way most Americans accumulate wealth and thereby diminishing the possibilities for business start-ups.[22] As a result, successful residents often choose to escape the drags of neighborhood on income, wealth, and personal security by departing to outlying suburbs.

This new poverty—more concentrated and more self-reinforcing—requires a new set of solutions. Previous efforts have tended to break down into either place- or people-based approaches. In the place-based approach, real estate development and the elimination of physical blight are seen as key; attention is therefore focused on "bricks and mortar" in the neighborhood. In the people-based approach, connections to employment are essential and therefore more attention is paid to individual skills and opportunities. The risk in the place-based approach is that it may affect the physical but not the social landscape. The risk in the people-based approach is that economically successful individuals may exit the neighborhood, leaving even more concentrated poverty and worsened social problems as they depart.

In *Stories of Renewal,* Joan Walsh (1997) observes that some community development corporations (CDCs) and other community-based organizations have tried to resolve these tensions with a new community-building approach. This model starts from the premise that the traditional community development strategy of revitalizing housing and retail has been insufficient. The emphasis instead is on the relationships between people, albeit in a specific geographic place: the notion is that one must help build the social capital of poor communities, recognizing that improving this capital will, like improving access to physical capital (machines), financial capital (credit), or human capital (education), enhance individual economic outcomes.[23] As Walsh notes, places like Baltimore's Sandtown-Winchester neighborhood have been revitalized by this new combination of patient work by organizers and innovative public-private community partnerships. What is crucial is recognizing that the social fabric matters: an area dense with community organizations and social networks is less likely to slide into poverty and remain there.

With their common focus on social capital and the potential mutual interest in both antipoverty efforts and regional growth, one would imagine that the new regionalists and the new community builders would have developed deep connections. While there are a few positive cases of connection (see chapter 7), for the most part, regional leaders and community developers have been like ships passing in the night.

Three Variants of Regionalism

The gap exists in part because the proponents of regionalism, both new and old, often have different motives and therefore different approaches to regional cooperation. Some support regionalism because they believe it will foster *efficiency*.[24] They argue that public services can be delivered more cost-effectively if one takes advantage of economies of scale and insist that allowing each municipality to have different regulations, fees, zoning laws, and tax rates makes it difficult to do business in a region. Many business leaders, particularly those with facilities in many municipalities, have led the way in this latter arena, forging cooperative arrangements across municipal boundaries in the same region (through Chambers of Commerce or industry associations) and helping to set more uniform rules among cities. A stellar example is Joint Venture: Silicon Valley Network, a business-led effort based in San Jose, California; it persuaded twenty-seven cities across two counties to agree on a uniform building code that has made it easier to rapidly develop facilities for the ever-changing high-tech industry.[25]

Others support regionalism because of its ability to protect the *environment*. The notion here is that the competition of municipalities for new residents and hence tax dollars has produced suburban sprawl. With the distance between home and work growing, traffic congestion and pollution rise. Meanwhile, open space and often agricultural land are consumed by outwardly radiating housing construction. The solution is a combination of urban land boundaries, infill development, and regional planning. This is a version of the efficiency argument, but one focused on quality-of-life or "livability" issues, such as pollution, transportation, and land use, rather than on cost-effectiveness.[26] A stellar example here is Portland, an area that has actually developed a form of metropolitan-level government that steers development and protects the natural habitat.

The third variant of regionalism, one that is still emerging, stresses that regional analysis and policy may be beneficial for *equity*. The emphasis here is on how greater regional cooperation can deconcentrate poverty, promote a broader tax base, and provide for a more equitable distribution of resources for schools and other public services. Possible policies to improve the geographic mobility of the poor could include portable vouchers for rent subsidies and scattered-site affordable housing; both would reduce concentrated urban poverty and relieve the burden such concentration imposes on particular municipalities.[27] Other equity-oriented strategies might include region-level job connection programs and "reverse commuting," as well as regional tax-sharing schemes that can more fairly spread the social costs of whatever poverty pockets remain.[28] Minneapolis–St. Paul has been a leader in such regional revenue sharing and in Milwaukee, labor and community groups have been able to craft a far-reaching set of programs that have included a Central City Workers Bureau and efforts to redirect transit dollars to facilitate inner-city commuting to suburban jobs (for more examples, see chapter 7).

While the efficiency and environmental variants of regionalism have solid support in the business and environmental communities, the political calculus of equity-oriented regionalism is more complex. There are at least four main potential constituencies for the equity-oriented approach: big-city mayors who may see regionalism as a way to bring the urban agenda to the fore; residents of the inner-ring suburbs who are frustrated that new infrastructure spending is heading outward as their older communities disintegrate;[29] leaders of community-based organizations (CBOs) and community development corporations (CDCs) who worry that they are "managers of decline" as the region passes them by (Nowak, 1997); and labor unions, particular metropolitan-based central labor councils, that see the fates of their (often immobile) workers tied to the fortunes of the regional economy.

Crafting a coalition from these divergent interests is difficult. Urban mayors have often alienated their own inner-city communities with schemes of urban renewal that seem to provide little benefit to the poorest residents. Inner-ring suburbanites often feel lucky to be one step away from the worst neighborhoods and may hesitate to form alliances with those "left behind" in the cities. Community activists are sometimes suspicious of those who have moved one municipality away, and they also resent being asked to divert attention from what seems like the more immediate need to address neighborhood poverty. Labor unions have formed some innovative alliances with community groups, but a legacy of exclusion, particularly in the building trades, makes establishing trust with low-income minority residents a slow process. Moreover, some union leaders question whether a regional approach is really the right strategy for workers challenged by globalization and large-scale industrial transformations.

What makes the equity-oriented version of regionalism even more challenging is the nature of the policy agenda likely to surface. For regionalism to have any impact, local governments must cooperate. Typically, this involves sharing revenues and/or service provision, often by creating special authorities for parks, water, transportation, major infrastructure projects, or air quality.[30] Yet metropolitan jurisdictions seem to find it easier to share the provision of "neutral" public services like sanitation, parks, and transportation than to agree to share their tax base, coordinate land use planning (especially with regard to housing and economic development), or consolidate public education. In other words, regional efforts to promote efficiency are the least difficult to enact, efforts to contain urban sprawl and unplanned development are more problematic, and efforts to address concentrated poverty and economic inequality are the most difficult. Thus, while David Rusk (1999) may be correct that a regional approach is a precondition for addressing the concentration of poverty, there is no guarantee that regionalism will, on its own, address this issue.

Indeed, the two issues that bear most directly on poverty and inequality, schools and housing, are among the biggest obstacles to regional cooperation. Since schools are largely funded by property taxes, wide disparities in real estate values can generate great regional variation in per capita funding for public education (Kozol, 1991). Suburbanites seek to protect control over and funding of their public schools and efforts to equalize funding usually require litigation or the threat of litigation.[31] In exceptional circumstances, cities and suburbs have unified their school systems to promote efficiency and/or equity goals. But economic and racial inequities remain even in these districts because schools serve neighborhoods that remain economically and racially segregated (Orfield, 1993).

Similarly, middle-class suburbs can use zoning laws to restrict the construction of low-income housing, avoid racial integration, and stop "threats" to property values. Here, too, litigation is often required to overcome suburban resistance to scattering assisted housing across regions. The Mt. Laurel decision in New Jersey and the Gautreaux decision in metropolitan Chicago reflect two efforts at promoting regional housing mobility; the first involves constructing low-income housing in suburbs and the second emphasizes provision of Section 8 housing vouchers so low-income inner-city families can move to market-rate housing in the suburbs.[32]

The complex political dynamics—and the fact that equity solutions are sometimes driven by negative litigation rather than political coalition-building and compromise—make a new community-based regionalism challenging. Given this, it might seem easier to push forward with the other variants of regionalism, particularly since efficiency and environmental concerns can be indirectly supportive of efforts to reduce poverty. After all, poorer communities are not likely to make progress if the overall regional economy is shrinking, and environmental measures, such as the urban growth boundaries in Portland, can help promote infill development and hence neighborhood revitalization in central-city communities (Rusk, 1998:22).

Still, we worry that those who emphasize the economy and the environment have often dominated the regional debate while those who emphasize distribution have sometimes posed equity as a zero-sum conflict between haves and have-nots. In our view, equity, the environment, and efficiency are actually three interrelated pillars of a healthy and sustainable region: combining all three makes sense for both the poor and the larger region. To do this, however, requires further elaboration of an equity case for regionalism, one that will bring new regional leaders to the antipoverty agenda even as it convinces neighborhood-based community builders to add regional issues to their already overcrowded plate. This book seeks to do just that, providing an intellectual and policy bridge between those who focus on urban neighborhoods and those who focus on metropolitan regions.

Origins and Organization of the Book

We came to this vision of linking the new regionalists and the new community builders in what may be an unusual fashion. In the wake of Los Angeles's 1992 civil unrest, several of the coauthors helped organize a series of discussions for a group of three community organizations in Los Angeles. One, the New Majority Task Force, consisted of African-American, Latino, and Asian community leaders and urban planners who had been meeting since 1987 on issues of economic development in poorer communities. The other organizations, the Coalition of Neighborhood Developers and the Multicultural Collaborative, arose from the ashes of the unrest and sought to define a new agenda for economic policy.[33]

Our initial discussions naturally focused on traditional community strategies, including how best to leverage some of the postriot local, state, and federal resources geared toward deprived communities. Yet participants increasingly felt that the real policy conversation was passing them by: while we were talking about reinvesting in South Central Los Angeles or the Central American community of Pico-Union in Los Angeles–area business leaders were focused on surviving the recession and jump-starting the regional economy. There was, in short, another important game in town and we knew much too little about it.

The three organizations therefore hosted a series of monthly meetings for community leaders that covered both the dynamics of the regional economy and an evaluation of the initiatives business and the public sector were proposing. As the series closed in mid-1994, three things were clear: (1) the regional economy had had an important effect on the economic problems affecting poorer neighborhoods, (2) the new regional initiatives being proposed did not pay sufficient attention to the problems of the poor and poor neighborhoods, and (3) we would need to know much more about both Los Angeles and the rest of the country if we intended to recommend a new approach that might better link regional and community development.

This volume is the product of that intellectual journey. Fortunately, it was a trip with prepaid tickets: just as we were defining this new intellectual and policy challenge for ourselves and our community collaborators, the John Randolph Haynes and Dora Haynes Foundation issued a call for "solutions research" into the problems affecting Southern California. With the luxury of support, we began a search that took us far away from Los Angeles. We did this because we hoped to learn from others. We soon realized that while Los Angeles might excel at fragmentation and disconnection, other regions were not far behind. In short, the challenge of connecting the new regional thinking and the new community building is a national one.

Our central argument is simple. First, regional economies would benefit from a better incorporation of the concerns of the poor. Many suburbanites believe that living in a separate jurisdiction will shield them from the problems of the central city. Businesses, seeking to minimize immediate costs, often hope that they can avoid the immediate costs of policy attention to the poor. But, as we show in an econometric study of seventy-four different regions in the United States, eventually poverty and inequality will drag you down. In a new economy in which collaboration matters, you are only as strong as the team to which you belong.

Second, poor communities would benefit from better integration into the regional economy. This can be a frustrating message to community developers who have felt ignored by regional leaders and now hope to promote their neighborhood base. But our research, both in Los Angeles and in the rest of the country, suggests that individuals and communities that are better connected to regional opportunities experience higher incomes and increased efficacy.

Third, it is possible to do better. While Los Angeles and other regions were wracked by widening inequality in the 1980s, some areas were able to make progress on multiple fronts: they raised per capita income, reduced central city poverty, and slowed the concentration of poverty in the 1980s. Key elements of their success included a committed business leadership, strong community organizations, city-suburb linkages, informal public-private partnerships, and the willingness of local governments to use public policy creatively. In recent years, a new set of experiments has emerged that builds on these factors and points to creative ways to link the poor and the region, combining neighborhood and regional strategies to bridge the geographic and racial chasms that often divide us.

We explore these three points in the order in which we came to them: in essence, the plan of the book follows the path of the research we have undertaken over the last six years. We begin in chapter 2 with an analysis of

Los Angeles County.[34] We note there how the patterns of urban poverty, the importance of which was underscored by the Los Angeles civil unrest, have often had regional roots: the overall shrinkage of L.A.'s basic industries and the emergence of low-wage industrial clusters in the county had deep impacts on the poor, especially on those living in communities of color. What is perhaps most striking about Los Angeles is the presence of the working poor: many families living in poverty have at least one household member engaged in full-time or nearly full-time work. We argue that this reflects economic energy waiting to be tapped for improved regional growth, suggesting a possible synergy between efforts to tackle poverty and strategies to revive the regional economy.

Chapter 3 analyzes efforts by key decision makers in the mid-to-late 1990s to address regional issues in Los Angeles. We develop a list of the most important regional initiatives that unfolded in that period and examine them with regard to their connections to, and possibilities for, economic development in the region's low-income neighborhoods. As it turns out, most of them were lacking: while the initiatives often embraced innovative theories of industrial clusters and built on the region's comparative advantages in technology and trade, including the poor in the economic calculus often seemed like an afterthought.

This "disconnect" is revealed in the second main section of chapter 3: a review of ten lower-income neighborhoods and their leadership in Los Angeles County. Examining the patterns of growth and development, we find that these neighborhoods have been deeply affected by regional restructuring and that those best able to weather the changes have had some method of connecting with regional economic opportunities. We also find that leaders in these communities were often able to identify the emerging industries in Los Angeles, but were frequently less informed about the regional initiatives, partly because they had not been invited to the appropriate policy discussions. As with our example of the working poor, this represents underutilized resources: a community leadership with much to contribute still needs to be incorporated into the sometimes informal, often public-private dialogues that constitute regional planning in Southern California.

Of course, this "failure to communicate" is a two-way problem. As we note, most of L.A.'s corporate leadership has weak connections with the community sector of the county. Regional planners have typically focused on increasing overall growth rather than dealing with poverty and equal access to opportunities. But it is also true that many community developers —tired of being slighted, pressed by other concerns, and worried that their antipoverty agenda might be subsumed in "larger" issues—have tended to shy away from regional debates. Both sides, then, need a rationale to begin discussions that can foster common ground.

The rest of the book tries to offer this rationale, building the case for linking regional and community development. Chapter 4 offers one side of the argument, starting with a national-level examination of the history of past community development and antipoverty efforts. We suggest that the traditional place-based strategies that focus on developing housing and bringing jobs to the community may have helped spawn a vibrant group of community development corporations (CDCs), but they have often been less effective at arresting economic decline. We argue instead for combining such neighborhood-focused efforts with an emphasis on people-based strategies that connect individuals to job opportunities wherever they might exist in the region. We especially stress how this is consistent with the emerging community-building movement that focuses on neighborhood social organization and networks.

Indeed, the nascent community builders have already begun to recognize the importance of the metropolitan region: while community-based organizing can create "bonding" social capital within a neighborhood, equally important is the construction of "bridging" social capital that can connect the poor and their advocates to new sources of employment and arenas of decisionmaking. We examine various places around the country where, in fact, community organizations have been able to form strategic alliances with business and the public sector and suggest how this may enhance the success of neighborhood development.

Chapter 5 tries to build the case from the other direction, emphasizing how tackling poverty might be helpful to regional prosperity. We examine past work on the correlation between central-city poverty and metropolitan economic expansion; while much of it tends to be supportive, the literature is plagued by various methodological challenges. We then contribute our own statistical analysis, which seeks to control for other factors that cause growth (or poverty) and to deal with the simultaneous relationship between the two (for example, while lowering poverty might build trust and promote growth, faster growth will also tighten labor markets and allow some residents to work their way out of poverty). Using a sample of seventy-four metropolitan regions in the United States, we find that, even controlling for the fact that growth itself lowers poverty, targeted antipoverty efforts can improve regional performance and benefit city dwellers and suburbanites alike. We conclude by illustrating a new way of conceptualizing the growth-poverty relationship, emphasizing that regions can improve their performance by stressing growth, poverty reduction, or a combination of the two.

In the next chapter, we draw on this modeling and data to select and analyze what we term "regions that work," places that combined rapid growth and relative improvements in equity during the 1980s. The three areas selected—the greater Boston area, the San Jose metropolitan area, and the metropolitan region anchored by Charlotte, North Carolina— were in the top ten of seventy-four major metropolitan areas measured by a multidimensional criteria that includes growth, change in central city poverty, and residential integration of the poor. For each case, we prepared extensive background research and conducted on-site interviews with policy makers, businesspeople, and community leaders about their views of what made the difference for these regions in the period examined.

As it turns out, San Jose boasted a high level of regional consciousness, particularly on the part of its dynamic business sector, but had done little specifically to help the poor. While the city hosts one of the most interesting job training centers in the country, San Jose's improvement on the poverty front came mainly from a rapidly growing economy. Boston, on the other hand, combined growth and antipoverty policy: while its labor markets were tight in the 1980s, it put in place a series of policies to ensure that some of the fruits of development would accrue to lower-income residents and communities. Charlotte's positive record seems to have emerged in part because of a conscious effort to keep the city and suburb linked jurisdictionally, thereby preserving their common interests. This, in turn, led to a series of targeted antipoverty efforts even as the city sought to activate and become the center of a vibrant regional economy. These varying illustrations of the growth/poverty relationship suggest that there is no one single route to success but rather a multiplicity of strategies, each of which may work best in different regions.

The final chapter contains our own prescriptions for a better and more inclusive set of regional and community development strategies. We suggest that there should be three guiding principles for what might be termed "community-based regionalism."[35] The first is simple: to "reconnect" the region, we must reconnect its people, bringing together business and government decisionmakers with community leaders around key policy discussions. The second and third principles are concerned with what specific strategies might emerge from those discussions. On the one hand, we argue that regional planning should pay special attention to low-income communities; on the other, we suggest that community development must acknowledge the importance of the region.

Drawing on "best practice" examples from around the nation, we offer concrete suggestions on how best to encourage the participation of poor and working people in local economic growth. We go on to discuss how external incentives, such as federal and state policies, might be reconfigured to encourage a new, and more equity-oriented, regionalism. We conclude by returning "home," focusing on the new strategies and social movements for community-based regionalism that have emerged in the complex, dynamic mix that is Southern California.

In our view, the moment may be ripe for such a connection of city and suburb, neighborhood and region. The economic rationale is increasingly clear: industrial clusters are rooted in, and define, regional production systems, and regional policies will be increasingly important to encouraging the growth of employment and income.[36] The new regionalism also offers distinct political advantages: linking central cities with nearby suburbanites may be especially attractive to a Democratic Party eager to align its minority base with middle-class white voters who swung right during the 1980s, then shifted toward Clinton in the 1990s, and remain uncertainly in the middle as the new millennium dawns. In keeping with this, Vice President and presidential contender Al Gore began emphasizing city-suburb connections in 1998 with a series of Smart Growth and livability ideas designed to both contain suburban sprawl and promote inner-city development.[37]

But the rationale for reconnecting across our regions goes beyond a simple political calculus. Behind suburban gates and within the hearts of our country's ghettos and barrios, social fragmentation by space and race has caused not just economic damage but also a profound sense of isolation. Those who recognize and marry the three pillars of the new regionalism —efficiency, environment, *and* equity—may be happily surprised. Americans have become frustrated with "zero-sum" solutions and "wedge issue" politics. They are tired of being driven apart; they may be ready to try growing together.

2

When Work Doesn't Pay

Poverty and Employment in Los Angeles

In the wake of the 1992 civil unrest, local low-income communities in the Los Angeles region enjoyed what Andy Warhol once described as fifteen minutes of fame. Then-mayor Tom Bradley announced the formation of Rebuild LA (soon rechristened RLA), a nonprofit corporation intended to promote corporate investment and encourage job and neighborhood development in South Central Los Angeles, the scene of some of the worst rioting. As the mayoralty passed to Richard Riordan in 1993, city officials labored to have several Los Angeles neighborhoods designated a federal empowerment zone. Low income communities mobilized, often with foundation support, giving rise to groups like the Coalition of Neighborhood Developers, a citywide grouping of community development corporations (CDCs) committed to promoting comprehensive neighborhood development and to creating a unified policy voice for diverse CDCs.

This welcome upsurge of attention to the poor soon faded. Attempting to overcome deep suspicions of its activities by residents of poorer communities, RLA created an unwieldy governance structure involving four co-chairs and an excessively large board. Increases in corporate and public investment were disappointing relative to the need, and RLA's own assessment of its impact on private investment was criticized as inflated.[1] Meanwhile, the city's application to the U.S. Department of Housing and Urban Development (HUD) for designation as an empowerment zone was rejected despite the fact that the federal legislation providing for such zones had been prompted specifically by the Los Angeles urban unrest. The city instead received the consolation prize of a Community Development Bank, a promising initiative that nonetheless required several additional years to organize and capitalize.[2] The Coalition of Neighborhood

Developers produced a hopeful planning document for the city's neighborhoods but then confronted external funding cutbacks, internal tensions, and the departure of its professional staff.[3]

Why were the poor displaced from the top of the city's agenda? First, business and political leaders typically have short attention spans when it comes to cities in general and the inner-city poor in particular. Previous waves of policy efforts—the War on Poverty, the Model Cities program, the Urban Development Action Grant efforts—have been exactly that: waves of attention that soon receded as policy makers became frustrated by the difficulty of alleviating poverty and overwhelmed by the need to appeal to middle-class voters.[4] In their wake, inner-city joblessness and concentrated poverty worsened, exacerbating the problems confronting the next generation of community development practitioners (Wilson, 1996).

The second reason for the shift in policy attention away from L.A.'s poorer communities was one of timing. Just as Los Angeles began to target its "neglected" areas and people in 1992 and 1993, the regional economy hit the depths of an economic slump. Unemployment remained above 9 percent through 1994, even as the rest of the nation began to climb its way out of the national recession (see figure 2.1). Policy makers began to recognize that the Southern California region faced not a simple downturn but a more fundamental economic restructuring. Gone was the defense spending that had propped up local industry for forty years; here was the new international competition that dragged down local wages and consumer demand. Declining were the large, vertically integrated firms that had comprised the backbone of the region's industrial economy; emerging were the new niche firms, smaller and often lacking unions or union-scale pay and benefits. The L.A. region was experiencing a sea change, one that required the city and region to define a new role for itself in the national and international economy.

In short, the deep problems of the regional economy eclipsed the concern with poverty and community development. The Southern California Association of Governments (SCAG) unveiled a new regional program focusing on the possibilities of aggregate economic development. The New Economy Project (initiated by the New Vision Business Council of Southern California and sponsored by various city agencies; see chapter 3) celebrated the potential for emerging small businesses to steer the local economy out of its doldrums and thereby seized the attention of the new Republican mayor, Richard Riordan. Other business and policy leaders focused on the opportunities presented by the Metropolitan Transportation Authority's (MTA's) plans to spend over $70 billion to expand the area's transportation infrastructure, a project whose economic impact would surely be felt regionwide.

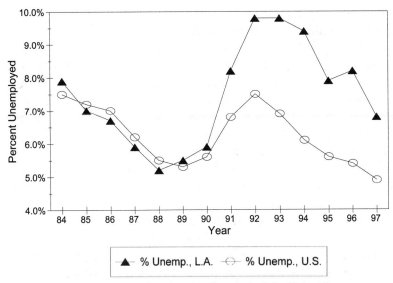

Figure 2.1. Unemployment in Los Angeles County and the United States, 1984–97.

The disconnect between these emerging regional initiatives and community development efforts was both striking and seemingly paradoxical. After all, the processes of regional change—deindustrialization (the loss of basic industry) and reindustrialization (the attraction of new low-wage jobs)—had contributed significantly to the poverty problem. And while poverty is certainly a drag on the regional economy, the poor are potential assets for regional development. As the data below indicate, over 50 percent of poor households in Los Angeles County had at least one member who was working and over 30 percent of these working poor households included someone working full time, suggesting economic energies waiting to be tapped for regional revitalization.

In this chapter, we discuss how underlying economic trends transformed Southern California, casting the shadow of low wages and poverty across lives of thousands of households. We then examine the nature of poverty in Los Angeles, emphasizing the importance of working poverty and the emergence of an informal sector characterized by contingent labor and unregistered enterprises. We conclude by noting that the central challenge facing both regional policy makers and community groups in the mid-1990s was how best to utilize the energies of the poor to improve the prospects for both regional and community economic well-being.

The Region and the Poor
Deindustrialization, Reindustrialization,
and Poverty in Los Angeles

In recent years, social scientists have bemoaned the shrinkage of what might be termed the "working middle class," that is, nonprofessional workers who enjoyed a middle-class lifestyle involving home ownership, economic security, and continually improving prospects for their children.[5] Since 1973, workers' real wages have been in more or less steady decline, rising only briefly when the economy hit the peak of a business cycle.[6] Firms have scrambled to restructure, often abandoning manufacturing activities in the United States in favor of locations elsewhere. Jobs have been lost, communities abandoned, regions shattered.

Not surprisingly, the nation's shifting economic structure contributed to a worsening problem of poverty. Yet as Jargowsky (1997: 185) stresses, the problem was not simply an overall increase in the poor but also an acceleration in their geographic concentration. As older industries abandoned central-city areas, racial segregation in housing impeded the ability of minority residents to follow jobs outward. Partly as a result, the number of (poor and nonpoor) persons living in high-poverty ghettos, barrios, and slums in the United States grew by 92 percent between 1970 and 1990, with the number of poor people living in these locations increasing by 98 percent. The resulting "neighborhood effects"—a lack of strong social networks, low levels of local purchasing power, and problematic access to employment—make conditions even worse than for those poor people who live in more dispersed fashion. And, as Jargowsky also argues, one of the primary determinants in this increasing geographic concentration is the changing structure of metropolitan regional economies (Jargowsky, 1997: 161).

Because of its role as the major industrial center of the western United States (Soja, 1989; Wolff, 1992), Los Angeles was especially vulnerable to these general processes of economic change. Industry in Southern California has a long, if often unrecognized, history. Steel, metal fabrication, and other heavy industries were developed at the beginning of the twentieth century and, by the 1920s, major U.S. automobile and rubber tire companies had added their production facilities to the local manufacturing mix. Workers employed in these industries, in turn, created consumer demand that prompted the growth of nondurable/light industries (such as apparel, furniture, etc.) and gave rise to a thriving service sector.[7]

World War II lifted the local economy out of the Depression and ushered in a dramatic growth of the defense-related industry, which continued through the postwar years. Aerospace soared, as did related industries such as fabricated metals, machinery, and electronics (Wolff, 1992). Federal expenditures on research and development, channeled through local universities and institutes, led to positive secondary spin-offs for civilian production, including the development of high technology "clusters" or industrial ensembles (Scott, 1993).

By the late 1970s, Los Angeles had emerged as the nation's largest industrial center (Soja, 1989; Ong et al., 1989). While manufacturing-related employment peaked in 1979 and then fell along with that of the rest of the country in the recession of the early 1980s, the region's drop in employment was smaller than for the rest of the nation, partly because of continued federal spending on defense and the ongoing expansion in the nondurable goods sector.[8]

The strength in defense and nondurables, however, masked an underlying decline in basic heavy industries such as autos, steel, and machinery. Since the workers in these industries comprised the heart of the local labor movement, union membership in Los Angeles County declined from 34 percent of manufacturing employment in 1971 to 19 percent in 1987 (Wolff, 1992: 16). With union protections down and international competition on the rise, wages and income slumped. Partly as a result, regional real per capita income growth was sluggish: between 1972 and 1988, real per capita income increased by only 11 percent, then fell for six consecutive years, bottoming out in 1994 at only 3 percent over the 1972 figure.[9]

This bleak tale of "deindustrialization" of the older manufacturing sector is, however, only half the story.[10] With the ebbing of traditional industry, new high-tech industries emerged in electronics, aerospace, and the media, while, at the same time, employment in the service sector and in relatively low-skill assembly work expanded dramatically. From 1972 to 1996, service sector employment more than doubled; indeed, except for during the recession of the early 1990s, service industry employment rose in each of these years. While some of the new service jobs provided high wages and secure benefits, many did not. Meanwhile, between 1972 and 1992, as countywide employment in higher-wage industrial sectors such as transportation equipment and machinery fell dramatically, employment actually grew in lower-wage industries such as apparel, textiles, and printing, and held steady in such sectors as food processing (Southern California Edison, 1995).

This "reindustrialization" of L.A.'s low-wage manufacturing base was not entirely expected.[11] By the rules of international trade theory, "Fordist" mass production industries such as apparel should have migrated south to Mexico in search of even cheaper labor. Yet the makeup of the garment business itself illustrates why some industries remained. First, labor migrated north from Latin America and west from Asia to meet the demands of firms, dampening wages and thereby slowing the relocation of the plants. Second, garment assembly is "networked" to fashion design, a higher-skill operation that involves clusters of designers working as both collaborators and competitors. By keeping assembly operations in close proximity to design centers, the fashion industry can provide "just-in-time" marketing responses. This avoids the high costs incurred when offshore assemblers produce excessive amounts of a product line that later becomes unpopular or too little of one that is received warmly by consumers.[12] Of course, this type of reindustrialization, which couples high-end fashion design and low-wage assembly, disequalizes the labor market over time. By the late 1980s, many observers were worried about the "widening divide" by class and race in Los Angeles.[13]

It was on this uneven structure—with joblessness resulting from deindustrialization and low wages from reindustrialization—that the recession of the late 1980s and early 1990s hit.[14] The downturn, particularly acute in aerospace due to defense cutbacks (Scott, 1993), spread quickly to nearly all manufacturing and service industries. As a result, Los Angeles County was the epicenter of the state's recession. The county suffered up to 84 percent of California's job losses between 1991 and 1993.[15] Not until 1995, several years after the rest of the country had emerged from recession, did Los Angeles experience growth in employment. Even as the recovery proceeded, the area's unemployment rate remained two to three percentage points above national trends, and poverty rates continued to be much higher than state and national averages. In short, the wreckage left by economic restructuring and wage cuts left a scarred social landscape, one that contributed to the unrest of 1992 and continued to plague the region through the mid-1990s.

Ethnic Transition and the Reconfiguration of Los Angeles

In tandem with the region's longer-term economic restructuring was an ongoing demographic transition. Between 1970 and 1990, the Anglo share of the population of Los Angeles County declined from 68 percent to 41 percent. Making up the difference were rapid increases in the minority population. The Latino population, which grew from 18 percent to 38 percent of the total between 1970 and 1990, accounted for the largest increase. The Asian population increased from 3 percent of the regional population in 1970 to over 10 percent by 1990. African-Americans, meanwhile, held steady at around 10 to 11 percent of the population throughout the period.[16]

This shift in ethnic composition was accompanied by an even more dramatic change at the city and neighborhood level. While the City of Los Angeles is commonly perceived as a complex multiethnic mosaic, by 1990 this characterization applied to the rest of the county as well. In 1970, four of the seventy-eight cities that comprised Los Angeles County had a "majority minority" population; by 1990, forty-two had become "majority minority." Some cities had gone through tremendous transformations in just ten years. Compton's population, for example, evolved from 75 percent African-American and 20 percent Latino in 1980 to 53 percent African-American and 44 percent Latino in 1990. Pomona saw its Latino population jump from 31 percent to 51 percent from 1980 to 1990. Cities arrayed along the industrial belt often termed the Alameda Corridor, such as Bell, Bell Gardens, and Huntington Park, went from a slight majority Latino population to percentages in the high eighties and nineties. Areas within Los Angeles also experienced tremendous change; for example, South Central Los Angeles shifted from 77 percent African-American and 20 percent Latino in 1980 to a near balance between these two ethnic groups by the mid-1990s.[17]

How did these demographic changes intersect with the ongoing shifts in the economy? While deindustrialization affected all residents, it had an especially severe economic impact on minority residents, in part because they were often the last hired in the growth of manufacturing prior to 1989.[18] Meanwhile, reindustrialization—the growth of low-wage nondurable manufacturing and service industries—was made possible by the availability of the Latino immigrant population. Thus, the largest impacts of restructuring, higher unemployment and reduced wages, generally were felt most sharply in those populations and neighborhoods that were the least able politically and economically to influence regional policy.

The ethnic and geographic character of the resulting poverty are shown in figures 2.2 through 2.5.[19] Figure 2.2 shows the correlation of color and poverty in Los Angeles by contrasting the ethnic composition of the county's poverty population with those living in households enjoying an income at least 200 percent above the poverty line. Individuals of color constitute nearly 82 percent of the poverty population while they constitute only 48 percent of those who fall in the category of "middle and above." The poverty pattern for Latinos is especially striking: while they make up 57 percent of the poor, they account for only 27 percent of the "middle and above" economic strata. African-Americans are also overrepresented among the poor (15 percent versus 10 percent of the middle and above), while Asians are represented almost equally in both categories.

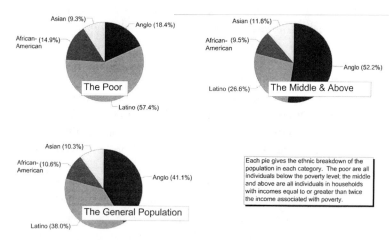

Figure 2.2. The color of poverty in Los Angeles County, 1990.

Figures 2.3 and 2.4 illustrate the geographic concentration of poverty and unemployment in Los Angeles County.[20] Note that the highest levels of both measures of economic distress occur in the central parts of the city with a concentration of economic difficulties elsewhere, including Pacoima in the San Fernando Valley and Pomona in the San Gabriel Valley. As figure 2.5 shows, most of these areas suffered plant closings (that is, deindustrialization) in the early through mid-1980s, and minorities generally lived where most of the jobs disappeared. A similar comparison of the residential locations of African-Americans and Latinos suggests a high geographic overlap of poverty and ethnicity in the county (see figures 2.6 and 2.7).

Yet, as stressed above, the disappearance of jobs due to deindustrialization is only part of the story. Figure 2.8 plots "job density," the number of jobs in a census tract divided by the number of residents in that tract, for Los Angeles County. Although many low-income areas are jobs-poor (for example, South Central Los Angeles), many of the poorest parts of Los Angeles are, in fact, quite jobs-rich. This is particularly true in the industrial belt along the Alameda Corridor (i.e., from the ports of San Pedro and Long Beach through Compton to Huntington Park and eastward).

The fact that some high-poverty areas actually had a significant base of employment became evident when RLA, the post-riot effort initiated by Mayor Tom Bradley, began its attempt at rebuilding. Charting the location of industrial clusters in Los Angeles County, RLA analysts found that over half of the county's metalworking and machinery firms were located in areas in

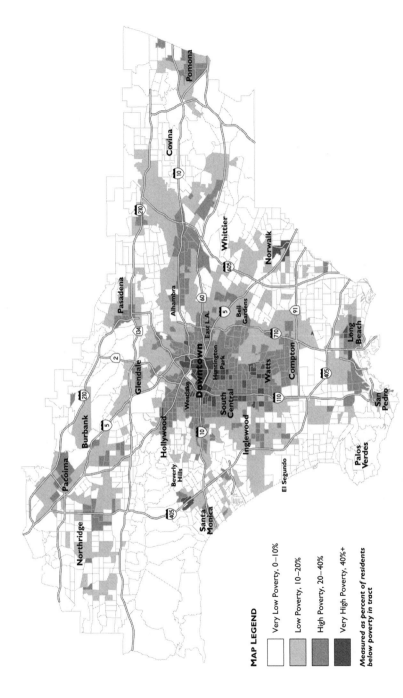

MAP LEGEND

Very Low Poverty, 0–10%

Low Poverty, 10–20%

High Poverty, 20–40%

Very High Poverty, 40%+

Measured as percent of residents below poverty in tract

Figure 2.3. The geographic distribution of the poor, metropolitan Los Angeles County, 1990. Population Data: 1990, U.S. Census Bureau STF3A. Geospatial Data: 1990, U.S. Census Bureau Tiger Line Files.

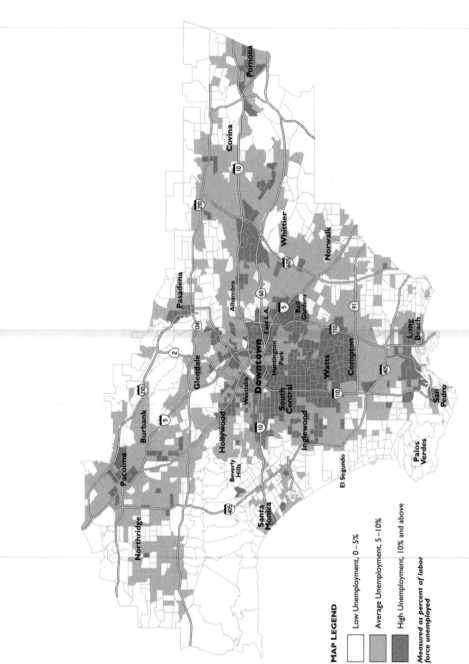

MAP LEGEND

Low Unemployment, 0–5%

Average Unemployment, 5–10%

High Unemployment, 10% and above

Measured as percent of labor force unemployed

Figure 2.4. The geographic distribution of unemployment, metropolitan Los Angeles County, 1990. Population Data: 1990, U.S. Census Bureau STF3A. Geospatial Data: 1990, U.S. Census Bureau Tiger Line Files.

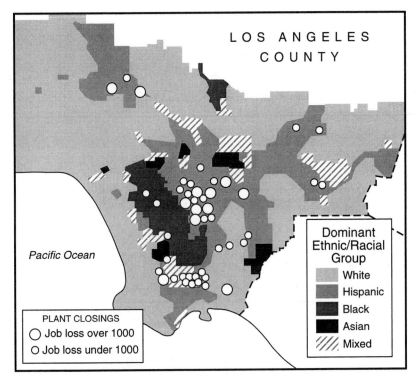

Figure 2.5. Plant closings in Los Angeles County, 1978–82. Source: U.S. Census, 1990; Plant Shutdown Directory, 1978–1982; U.S. Department of Commerce, 1991. Thanks to Melvin Oliver, Ford Foundation, and Chris Langford, UCLA, for supplying this figure.

which more than 20 percent of the residents lived below the poverty line. These firms alone generated $7 billion in sales and employed more than 65,000 workers. Over 60 percent of the county's food-processing firms were also located in these high-poverty areas and these firms enjoyed about $5 billion in sales and employed over 30,000 workers. About 75 percent of the textile/apparel industry was located in poorer tracts—and this industry was actually the single largest source of manufacturing employment in the county, with an aggregate sales total of over $10 billion and an employment base of nearly 100,000 workers.[21]

In short, one of the usual explanations for inner city poverty—spatial mismatch, or the physical distance between central-city residents and increasingly suburbanized job opportunities (see Wilson 1987, 1996)— does not fully fit the Los Angeles case. Of course, inadequate public transportation remains a major impediment to employment for some residents and this has been one focus of community organizing efforts, such

MAP LEGEND

☐ Low, 0–5%

▨ Average, 5–20%

▨ High, 20% and above

Tracts by percent African-American

Figure 2.6. The geographic distribution of African-Americans, metropolitan Los Angeles County, 1990. Population Data: 1990, U.S. Census Bureau STF3A. Geospatial Data: 1990, U.S. Census Bureau Tiger Line Files.

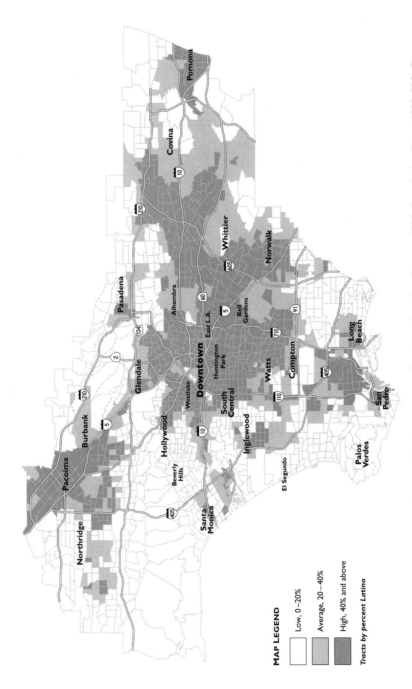

MAP LEGEND

☐ Low, 0–20%

▨ Average, 20–40%

▦ High, 40% and above

Tracts by percent Latino

Figure 2.7. The geographic distribution of Latinos, metropolitan Los Angeles County, 1990. Population Data: 1990, U.S. Census Bureau STF3A. Geospatial Data: 1990, U.S. Census Bureau Tiger Line Files.

MAP LEGEND

☐ Jobs-Poor, 0–30

▨ Jobs-Adequate, 30–75

▧ Jobs-Rich, 75 and above

Measured as jobs per 100 working-age residents in tract

Figure 2.8. The geographic distribution of jobs, metropolitan Los Angeles County, 1990. Population Data: 1990, U.S. Census Bureau STF3A. Geospatial Data: 1990, U.S. Census Bureau Tiger Line Files. Employment Data: Southern California Association of Governments.

as the Los Angeles–based Bus Riders Union (see chapter 3). Still, neighborhood poverty also occurs because residents fail to connect to existing jobs due to limited social networks, lack of skills, and continuing discrimination. And, as we will see, the jobs individuals do obtain quite often pay poverty-level wages, a phenomenon deeply rooted in the reindustrialization process.

Neighbors, Networks, and Wages

Although much of the current political discourse attributes poor economic outcomes to a lack of training and other human capital characteristics, discrimination, networks, and geographic location matter. For example, recent job market tests involving nearly identical applicants indicate that racial discrimination persists and, in confidential interviews, employers openly admit to preferring one ethnic group over another in their hiring decisions.[22] Moreover, individuals with better social network connections or more jobs-rich spatial locations tend to secure a higher wage even when they have the same low-level skills and experience as a less well-connected or well-placed job seeker.

To test for the relative impacts of location and networks in the Los Angeles County labor market we drew a sample of approximately 11,000 male workers from the U.S. Census Public Use Microdata Sample (PUMS). Individuals were linked with summary data identifying key locational characteristics, including the poverty level and the distance from employment in their immediate and adjoining area.[23] These locational variables were included in a regression analysis that also took into account individual skills and racial discrimination (for details, see Pastor and Adams, 1996).[24]

While other researchers have focused on the impacts of locational factors on employment probabilities, we focused on wages for two reasons. First, it allowed us to better examine the effects of location on the working poor, and second, we would be better able to match a continuous dependent variable (wages) with continuous independent variables (such as level of poverty in one's area). The base regression included standard explanatory factors such as education, years of work experience, marital status, English-language skills, era of immigration, and ethnicity to capture any remaining discrimination against minority workers.[25] All the basic variables were signed as expected and the coefficients (or size of the impact on wages) and explanatory power were consistent with studies done in other cities and at the national level.[26]

We then added the distance from employment (measured by commuting time) and the poverty level in one's area as a proxy for the "quality" of social networks. The latter variable reflects the notion that most individuals secure employment through networks of family and neighbors and that such networks are often spatially constrained, especially for the poor. The basic premise here is that when most of one's local contacts are poor or low income, it will be harder to connect to high-quality employment and wages despite one's own skill level (see O'Regan, 1993; Ihlanfeldt and Sjoquist, 1990a, 1990b; Ihlanfeldt, 1992; Oliver and Lichter, 1996; and Sexton, 1991).[27]

As it turns out, both spatial mismatch and concentrated poverty had a statistically significant dampening impact on wages, but the concentrated poverty (or network effect) was more important than the mere fact of living far from where jobs were located.[28] We estimated, for example, that moving an individual with exactly the same human capital and demographic characteristics from high-poverty Compton to the more middle-class city of Glendale would raise wages by fifteen percentage points. Fourteen of these points were attributable to Glendale's lower poverty rates, which provided superior connections to employment possibilities. We then focused on the possible effects of commuting from a high-poverty to a low-poverty community. Using the same Compton-Glendale comparison, we found that an individual who lived in Compton and worked in Glendale made 8 percent more than a Compton resident who worked in his/her own high-poverty neighborhood.[29] These estimated improvements in income parallel the results of an actual experiment in mobility conducted under the Chicago Gautreaux program, in which public housing residents were allocated rent vouchers so they could move to the suburbs and saw their employment prospects brighten as a result (see Rosenbaum et al., 1993; Rosenbaum, 1995; Peterson and Williams, 1994; and Polikoff, 1995).

Of course, encouraging such mobility is a mixed blessing. Like most urban planners, we are concerned about the costs posed by long commutes in terms of the environment, loss of family time, and alienation from one's neighbors. But if some people can live in the far-flung suburb of Agoura Hills and work as high-wage professionals in downtown Los Angeles, why should residents of South Central be confined to seeking employment in their neighborhoods? Broadening the range of options by connecting those in areas of concentrated poverty to dynamic regional enterprises, wherever they may be, could help resolve the problem of working poverty that has plagued contemporary Los Angeles.

Work and Poverty in Los Angeles

The Working Poor as an Untapped Resource

William Julius Wilson (1996) has recently noted that a key feature of today's high-poverty neighborhoods is the increasing lack of employment. When work disappears, he argues, social order and the community fabric break down. However, Los Angeles tells us another story. Even when work is available, if it doesn't pay adequate wages, the community fabric may still be torn asunder.

To get at the work-poverty nexus, we turned to the Census Bureau's Public Use Microdata Sample (PUMS), a database that records the individual answers to census questionnaires for nearly five hundred thousand individuals in Los Angeles County.[30] Drawing on this data, we created sixteen categories of work experience for those of working age, then grouped these into four larger and mutually exclusive groups (see table 2.1): full-time work (more than fifty weeks a year and more than thirty-five hours a week); significant work (more than thirty-five weeks a year and more than twenty-five hours a week); part-time work (more than ten weeks a year and more than ten hours a week); and little or no work (less than ten weeks a year or less than ten hours a week). Note that our definition of year-round, full-time work (in concert with that of the Census Bureau) is rather restrictive. For example, an individual who works over forty hours a week for forty weeks of the year would be considered engaged in "significant" but not "full-time" work. Similarly, a year-round but very part-time employee (one who works less than ten hours a week) is labeled as experiencing "little or no" work, while a worker who has held a full-time job for half the year would be labeled "part-time."

We confined our attention to households whose head of household was sixty-five years old or less at the time of the census and, thus, not likely to have retired in the prior year from which income and work figures are taken. As it turns out, nearly 25 percent of poor households in Los Angeles County were headed by individuals engaged in either full-time or significant work (see figure 2.9).[31] The degree of labor market attachment is even stronger if we consider whether anyone in the household was employed. As indicated in figure 2.10, over half of poverty households had at least one member engaged in at least part-time work; and nearly 30 percent had one or more members engaged in full-time or significant work.

Figure 2.11 broadens our analysis to households where wages hover near the poverty line (i.e., incomes ranging between 80 and 120 percent of the federally defined poverty level for their respective family size). Strikingly, well over half of these households have some member engaged in full-time

Table 2.1

Categorizing Work Experience

	Weeks Worked per Year			
Hours of Work per Week	**50 or more**	**Less than 50; 35 or more**	**Less than 35; more than 10**	**Less than 10**
35 or more	Full-time work	Significant work	Part-time work	Little or no work
Less than 35; more than 25	Significant work	Significant work	Part-time work	Little or no work
Less than 25; more than 10	Part-time work	Part-time work	Part-time work	Little or no work
Less than 10	Little or no work	Little or no work	Little or no work	Little or no work

The categories above become:

Full-time work	Worked at least 50 weeks a year *and* at least 35 hours a week
Significant work	Worked less than full-time but more than 35 weeks a year *and* more than 25 hours a week
Part-time work	Worked less than significant worker but more than ten weeks a year *and* more than ten hours a week
Little or no work	Worked less than ten weeks a year or less than ten hours a week

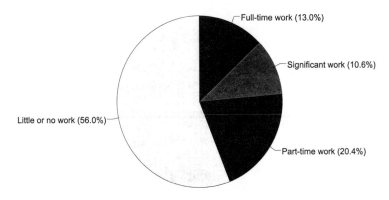

* Households where householder is less
than 65 years old. Work experience refers
to householder.

Figure 2.9. Work experience of heads of poverty households, Los Angeles County, 1990.

or significant work and only 25 percent do not have anyone involved in at least part-time work. Of course, a job remains one effective antidote to poverty: 74 percent of those households with incomes above 120 percent of the poverty line have at least one household member working full-time. Still, being employed is not enough: poverty results from both "no" jobs and "bad" jobs, with the former connected to the processes of deindustrialization and the latter linked to the economic reconfiguration wrought by reindustrialization.

As many authors have stressed, these processes of deindustrialization and reindustrialization have had disparate racial impacts. African-Americans have often seen their prospects diminished by the reduction of mainstream manufacturing jobs while Latinos, particularly immigrants, have tended to secure employment in emerging low-wage industries. As a result, joblessness is more characteristic of low-income African-American households while working poverty is more characteristic of low-income Latino households.

Figure 2.12 explores this issue by looking at the ethnic composition of households living below the poverty line. As it turns out, Latino households comprise nearly 47 percent of all poor households in Los Angeles County but 74 percent of those households with at least one member with full-time work; African-Americans comprise nearly 18 percent of all poor households

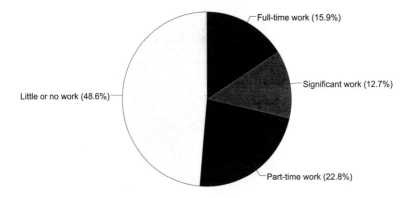

* Sample is households below the poverty line headed by someone of working age; work experience defined as: full-time work by at least one household member; significant work by at least one household member; part-time work by at least one household member; little or no work by any household member.

Figure 2.10. Work experience of poverty households, Los Angeles County, 1990.

in the county but account for only 5 percent of those households with at least one full-time worker and 26 percent of those households where no member has more than little or no work.[32]

Poverty and work experience also vary by immigration status. For example, the poverty rate for households headed by immigrants who arrived in the 1980s is three times higher than that for those households headed by U.S.-born individuals. However, only 13 percent of the poor U.S.-born working-age household heads enjoy either full-time or significant work, while more than 30 percent of poor recent immigrant household heads work either full time or significantly (see figure 2.13).[33] If we examine the working poor—those with either full-time or significant work—in terms of race, ethnicity, and immigrant status, we find a striking result: fully 60 percent of the working poor households in Los Angeles are headed by Latinos who immigrated in the 1970s or 1980s (see Figure 2.14).[34]

While we have made much above of the presence of working poverty in Los Angeles, there is also substantial evidence indicating that the "welfare poor," who are ostensibly unemployed, often supplement inadequate government aid with "irregular sources."[35] Such sources consist of financial help from social networks (i.e., family, friends, neighbors), as well as "off-the-books" employment.[36] This off-the-books or irregular employment is often undertaken in the informal economy, a topic we take up in the next section.

In short, work is an important part of the poverty experience. Given this evident activity and energy, incorporating the poor and their concerns into

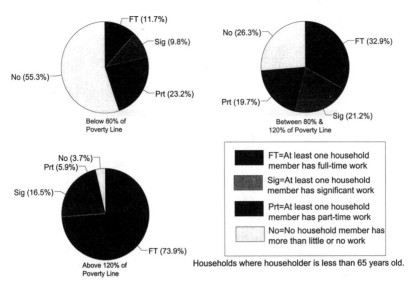

Figure 2.11. Composition of household poverty by work experience, Los Angeles County, 1990.

regional planning could serve as a way to improve the overall economy. That such inclusion has not always been a part of regional planning efforts represents a waste of resources. It also leads to the alienation of potential allies among low-income advocates who have begun to recognize the importance of the regional economy in structuring the life-chances of the poor.

Poverty and the Informal Economy

Many of L.A.'s working poor, and some of those officially labeled jobless, participate in the informal economy. Before the 1980s, economic informality—that is, unregulated and highly contingent work—was considered a phenomenon limited primarily to Third World countries. By the mid-1980s, however, Los Angeles had become a high-profile site of street vending, sweatshops, home maintenance, and other manifestations of informal work. The expansion of such marginal employment paralleled the increase in, and to a large extent absorbed, the growing Latino and Asian populations in Southern California.[37]

While debate remains about how exactly to define this sector, most experts agree that some key characteristics include intermittent and fluctuating work hours; wages paid in cash; and generally lax labor, health, and safety regulations, all of which are also associated with very small enterprises of ten or fewer workers (Portes and Sassen, 1987; Portes, Castells, and

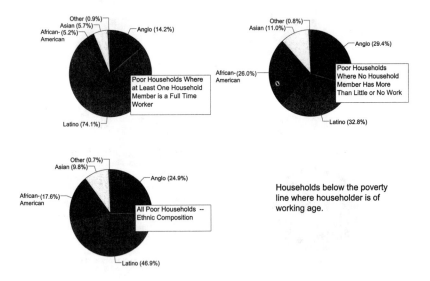

Figure 2.12. Poor households by work experience and ethnicity, Los Angeles County, 1990.

Benton, 1989; Sassen, 1994a, 1994b; Zlolniski, 1994). What distinguishes informality in these definitions is not the illegality of the *product* but rather the illegality of, or lack of regulations over, *working conditions.* For this reason, most analysts make a sharp distinction between the informal and illicit economy (which is composed of drug sales, prostitution, and other criminal activities).[38]

Certain activities performed in the formal (regular) sector can also be found in the informal (underground) sector of the economy. For example, work for the garment industry is often conducted simultaneously by both formal and informal sectors of the labor market. The formal sector includes garment firms that generally meet building safety codes, pay workers at least minimum wage, sometimes provide benefits, and are occasionally even unionized. The informal sector, particularly in Los Angeles, includes garment workers earning below minimum wage (at times paid by the piece), without benefits, and laboring under sweatshop conditions or as a part of a cottage industry structure in their own homes.

Indeed, the formal and informal economies are often intertwined. In August 1995, for example, inspectors discovered a sweatshop in El Monte (located minutes east of Los Angeles) that had held 72 Thai garment workers in virtual indentured servitude. However, contracting with this sweatshop were dozens of formal sector firms, including labels (e.g., Tomato, Clio,

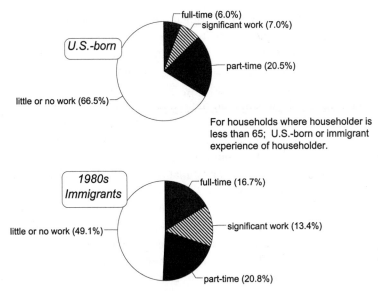

Figure 2.13. Composition of Los Angeles County poor (U.S.-born and recent immigrants) by work experience, 1990.

B.U.M., High Sierra, Cheetah, Anchor Blue, and Airtime) that were owned either by major retail chains (Mervyn's, Miller's Outpost, and Montgomery Ward) or sold at major department stores (e.g., Macy's, Nordstrom, Sears, and Target).[39] Such a combination of informal sweatshops and high-tech fashion design and marketing is deeply connected to the region's economic restructuring, constituting a local version of a "global assembly line" in which the least rewarding ends of the production chains have become the province of the most vulnerable sectors of the population, including immigrants, women of color, and other politically disenfranchised groups.

While we assume that informal economic activities are associated with poverty, and spectacular cases like the Thai workers in El Monte add to this presumption, it is difficult to directly document the relationship. After all, entrepreneurs operating "under the table" are not likely to advertise that fact, or reveal the minuscule wages they pay, in any census of manufacturing. To uncover the relationship between informality and poverty, we instead built a proxy for each economic sector based on the percentage of unauthorized (or undocumented) workers in that sector. We assumed that those employers most likely to avoid the law in hiring the unauthorized are also likely to avoid the sorts of labor and other regulations that distinguish the formal from informal economy.

Of course, this proxy is itself difficult to measure. To do it, we built on a database created by the University of Southern California and El Colegio de la Frontera Norte (COLEF) that contains information on immigration status and key demographic characteristics for a group of Mexican-born residents (Marcelli and Heer, 1997).[40] The demographic characteristics were regressed against documentation status and the resulting coefficients were then applied to the PUMS sample to predict the probability of an individual foreign-born Mexican being an unauthorized immigrant.[41] These individual-level probabilities were then summed across a range of industry and occupation categories, thereby yielding estimates of the number of unauthorized Mexican workers in each grouping.[42]

The results, depicted in tables 2.2 and 2.3, show the occupational and industrial patterns. For example, undocumented workers account for a significant portion of farmworkers, food service employees, construction laborers, and nonprecision machine operators, and a high percentage of employees in industries such as textile/garments, agriculture, furniture manufacturing, and private households. This pattern squares with general impressions regarding the economic locations of the undocumented. Moreover, the approximately 279,000 undocumented working-age immigrants (both male and female) in Los Angeles County yielded by the procedure is safely below other reputable estimates, including that of the U.S. Census Bureau.[43]

What is most important for our analysis of the relationship between informality and poverty is the relative ranking of the industries and occupations with regard to the degree of unauthorized workers and, hence, the probability of informal labor relations.[44] To check the rankings yielded by our indirect procedure, we asked several experts on the informal sector to review a full census listing of occupations and rank them as "probably formal" or "probably informal." We then reworked their answers into the more compact occupational and industrial lists shown in tables 2.2 and 2.3.[45] As it turns out, the correlation between the expert determination and our proxy is very strong (.688) and highly significant (at the .001 level) for occupations, and is nearly as highly correlated for industry.

We then compared our informality proxy with the poverty rate for those identified in the various professions and industries. Here we focused on occupation rather than industry since some industries are segmented into formal and informal conditions (construction, for example, has both day laborers working with a high degree of informality and tradespeople who may work under unionized and regulated conditions).[46] Figure 2.15

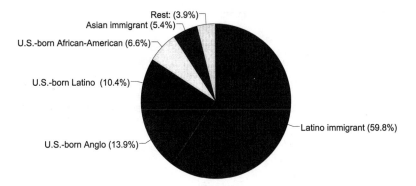

Refers to households living below the poverty line where householder is less than 65 and has either full-time or significant work. The householder is considered an immigrant if s/he immigrated in the 1970s or 1980s; pre-1970s immigrants are included with the U.S.-born.

Figure 2.14. Immigration and ethnicity in working-poor households in Los Angeles County, 1990.

illustrates the relationship between informality and poverty by occupation (males only), showing both a scatterplot and a fitted regression line to make the trend clear. As is apparent, informality and poverty go hand in hand: statistical tests reveal that the correlation between the two is .894, with a significance level of .001.[47] Moreover, the pattern holds (albeit with a lower correlation) even when we exclude all foreign-born workers—and thus, all the undocumented workers—from the poverty calculation (see Figure 2.16).[48] The results suggest that informality and low wages are characteristics of the jobs, not the people.

Is the informal sector important in terms of its overall impact on the economy and labor force? Assuming that an occupation is considered to be significantly affected by informality when more than 10 percent of its workers are undocumented Mexicans (and therefore the likely percentage of unauthorized or informal employees, including non-Mexicans, is likely to be higher), informal-affected occupations contain over 30 percent of the county's labor force and account for almost 20 percent of the county's earned income.[49] The parallel results for industry suggest that over 26 percent of the county's labor force works in industries affected by informality. These industries account for nearly 20 percent of the county's earned income.

Table 2.2

Undocumented Mexicans as Percent of Labor Supply in Industry

Industry (ranked by % undocumented)	Undocumented Mexican males as % of all male workers	Undocumented Mexican females as % of all female workers	Undocumented Mexicans as % of all workers
Textile mill & finished textile products	26.4%	22.2%	23.9%
Agriculture	24.6%	10.3%	22.1%
Furniture, lumber, & wood products	21.7%	15.4%	20.4%
Eating & drinking places	19.1%	9.7%	15.3%
Food manufacturing	15.3%	14.3%	15.0%
Other durable goods	14.1%	14.4%	14.2%
Private households	13.9%	14.2%	14.2%
Other nondurable goods	12.7%	15.8%	13.7%
Primary metal industries	13.6%	9.1%	12.7%
Fabricated metal industries	12.6%	10.9%	12.2%
Chemical & allied products	11.0%	12.7%	11.7%
Construction	11.8%	4.7%	11.2%
Repair services	11.1%	5.3%	10.6%
Other personal services	8.8%	7.9%	8.3%
Machinery, except electrical	8.2%	8.1%	8.2%
Food, bakery, & dairy stores	8.7%	6.8%	8.0%
Electrical machinery	6.6%	9.1%	7.6%
Wholesale trade	7.3%	6.2%	7.0%
Forestry & fishing	6.9%	3.8%	6.1%
Trucking service & warehousing	6.2%	4.1%	5.9%
Business service	6.6%	4.7%	5.8%
Automotive dealers & gasoline stations	5.9%	3.5%	5.5%
Printing, publishing, & allied products	5.7%	4.2%	5.1%

Table 2.2 (Continued)

Undocumented Mexicans as Percent of Labor Supply in Industry

Industry (ranked by % undocumented)	Undocumented Mexican males as % of all male workers	Undocumented Mexican females as % of all female workers	Undocumented Mexicans as % of all workers
Mining	5.5%	0.8%	4.5%
Other retail trade	5.4%	3.5%	4.5%
General merchandise stores	5.2%	3.1%	4.1%
Social service, religious, membership organizations	2.3%	4.1%	3.6%
Transportation equipment	3.0%	1.8%	2.7%
Railroads	3.0%	0.2%	2.6%
Hospitals	3.5%	1.8%	2.3%
Health services, except hospitals	2.0%	2.2%	2.1%
Utilities & sanitary services	2.4%	1.3%	2.1%
Entertainment & recreational services	2.6%	1.3%	2.1%
Other transportation	1.7%	1.3%	1.5%
Insurance, real estate, & other finance	1.9%	1.2%	1.5%
Elementary & secondary schools & colleges	1.2%	1.3%	1.3%
Banking & credit agencies	1.3%	1.1%	1.2%
Other educational services	1.5%	0.7%	1.0%
Communications	1.4%	0.6%	1.0%
Legal, engineering, & professional services	0.9%	0.8%	0.9%
Public administration	0.7%	0.9%	0.8%

Source: Author estimates using raw data from Marcelli and Heer (1997) and Public Use Microdata Sample.

Table 2.3

Undocumented Mexicans as Percent of Labor Supply in Occupation

Occupation (ranked by % undocumented)	Undocumented Mexican males as % of all male workers	Undocumented Mexican females as % of all female workers	Undocumented Mexicans as % of all workers
Farm workers & related occupations	24.9%	14.9%	23.7%
Machine operators except precision	20.9%	23.5%	22.0%
Construction laborers	21.0%	26.7%	21.1%
Forestry & fishing occupations	21.4%	12.5%	20.6%
Other handlers, cleaners, helpers & laborers	20.9%	8.8%	20.0%
Fabricators, assemblers, inspectors, samplers	16.1%	19.4%	17.4%
Food service occupations	22.0%	9.6%	17.0%
Freight, stock, & material handlers	15.0%	18.0%	15.7%
Private household occupations	15.1%	14.8%	14.8%
Cleaning & building service occupations	13.2%	15.5%	14.0%
Construction trades	11.1%	10.2%	11.1%
Material moving equipment operators	10.2%	11.8%	10.3%
Precision production occupations	9.4%	12.3%	10.1%
Farm operators & managers	9.8%	2.9%	8.4%
Cashiers	6.1%	8.1%	7.4%
Motor vehicle operators	7.5%	3.8%	7.1%
Mechanics & repairers	7.0%	3.8%	6.8%
Extractive occupations	7.3%	2.8%	6.6%

Table 2.3   (Continued)

Undocumented Mexicans as Percent of Labor Supply in Occupation

Occupation (ranked by % undocumented)	Undocumented Mexican males as % of all male workers	Undocumented Mexican females as % of all female workers	Undocumented Mexicans as % of all workers
Health service & personal services	3.7%	5.1%	4.8%
Other sales occupations	4.2%	2.7%	3.5%
Other administrative support occupations	4.2%	2.0%	2.8%
Other protective service occupations	2.2%	0.9%	2.0%
Supervisors & proprietors, sales occupations	2.1%	1.7%	2.0%
Rail & water transportation occupations	1.1%	9.3%	1.9%
Sales representatives, commodities & finance	1.8%	1.8%	1.8%
Mail & message distribution	1.8%	1.3%	1.6%
Financial records processing occupations	2.6%	1.3%	1.5%
Computer equipment	1.0%	1.7%	1.4%
Secretaries, stenographers, & typists	1.8%	1.4%	1.4%
Health technologists and technicians	1.6%	1.3%	1.4%
Officials & administrators, other	1.4%	1.1%	1.3%
Technologists & technicians, except health	1.4%	0.8%	1.3%
Other professional specialty occupations	1.4%	0.8%	1.2%

Table 2.3   (Continued)

Undocumented Mexicans as Percent of Labor Supply in Occupation

Occupation (ranked by % undocumented)	Undocumented Mexican males as % of all male workers	Undocumented Mexican females as % of all female workers	Undocumented Mexicans as % of all workers
Teachers, elementary & secondary schools	0.8%	0.9%	0.9%
Management-related occupations	1.0%	0.7%	0.8%
Other teachers, librarians, & counselors	0.7%	0.7%	0.7%
Officials & administrators, including public administration	0.3%	0.8%	0.5%
Health assessment & treating occupations	0.9%	0.4%	0.4%
Architects, surveyors, & scientists	0.3%	0.4%	0.3%
Police & firefighting	0.3%	0.0%	0.3%
Health diagnosing occupations	0.2%	0.3%	0.2%
Engineers	0.2%	0.1%	0.2%

Source: Author estimates using raw data from Marcelli and Heer (1997) and Public Use Microdata Sample.

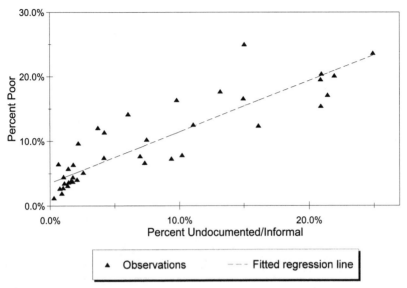

Figure 2.15. Relationship between informality and poverty by occupation (males), 1990.

An Ethnographic Study of the Informal Sector

To go beyond the useful but indirect estimation techniques above, we explored a sample of 106 workers in the informal sector collected over a three-year period in the mid-1990s.[50] Using standard ethnographic techniques, student research teams directed by Marta López-Garza drew the sample by targeting likely locations of informal sector workers, including the Pico-Union, Boyle Heights, South Los Angeles, and Echo Park neighborhoods of Los Angeles. Additional respondents were then selected through established contacts with immigrant-rights and community-based organizations. Other respondents were approached by researchers while in the field conducting observations, and still others were referred by various social networks. Of the respondents, 48 percent hailed from Mexico, another 31 percent came from the Central American countries of El Salvador, Guatemala, and Honduras, and the bulk of the remainder were U.S.-born.

Many of the characteristics of the respondents in this more focused study parallel those in the indirect estimation techniques above. While nearly a third of those in the sample were street vendors, primarily because their visibility and accessibility led to some oversampling, the ranking of other occupations held by those in the sample were similar to our indirect estimates, with domestic work, garment assembly, and construction leading the way (see table 2.4).

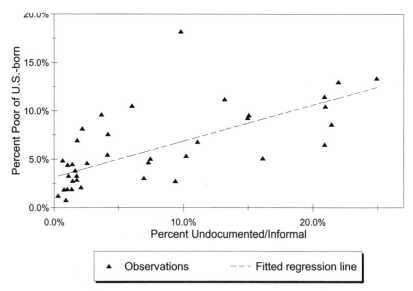

Figure 2.16. Relationship between informality and poverty of U.S.-born males by occupation, 1990.

As is typical in the informal sector, payment methods were irregular. Seventy-eight percent of our Latino respondents and 83 percent of all the respondents were paid in cash, personal check, or a combination of the two. Those respondents working for others consistently reported difficulties with occupational safety and health conditions, such as violations of overtime pay, minimum wage, and tax laws, performing industrial homework, and working within unregistered commercial and manufacturing operations. Given these conditions, it is perhaps not surprising that very few of the workers (and none of the Latinos) in the study received any form of work-related benefits, medical or otherwise.

As might be expected, these conditions led to low incomes. Unfortunately, income comparisons were difficult to calculate given the lack of uniformity of payment schedules for many of the workers: some were paid daily, some by the hour, and some by the piece, while street vendors had erratic revenues. Still, the correlation of informality with poverty can be seen when we overlay respondents' residences on poverty conditions in Los Angeles (see figure 2.17). Moreover, respondents themselves conveyed a sense of economic instability and precariousness and often expected little, if any, possibility of upward mobility.

Table 2.4

Respondents by Occupation and Gender

	Women	Men
Street Vending	16	15
Domestic	16	0
Garment	8	1
Domestic/Nanny	6	0
Construction	0	5
Service/Sales	3	1
Arts and Entertainment	0	4
Gardener	0	3
Day Laborer	0	3
Janitor	1	1
2+ Jobs	8	2
Other	6	9
Total	64	44

Our results reveal the informal sector as one locus of poverty in Los Angeles County. As we stress in chapter 7, policy efforts addressed to the informal sector must realize that individuals who work under informal conditions generally fall into one of two groups: entrepreneurs who are proprietors of a small business (e.g., vendors) and employees of unregulated enterprises. As a result, the policy approach must also be dual: while entrepreneurship should be promoted and regularized, informal employees should be shielded from the worst labor abuses. Either way, the overriding point here is that any attempt to reduce disparities, improve opportunities, and strengthen the regional economy should take account of the social and occupational locations of the poor—and in Los Angeles and several other major urban areas one such location is the informal sector.

The Poor and the Region

By the middle of the 1990s, an economically battered Los Angeles was finally greeted by good economic news. After four straight years of decline in employment, 1995 saw a modest improvement in employment figures. The decision reached in December of that year to locate DreamWorks Studios, the first new movie studio built in more than fifty years, in Los Angeles sig-

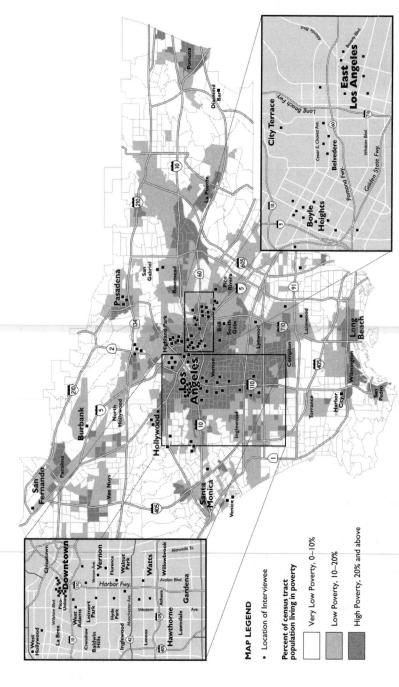

MAP LEGEND

■ Location of Interviewee

Percent of census tract
population living in poverty

▢ Very Low Poverty, 0–10%

▨ Low Poverty, 10–20%

▨ High Poverty, 20% and above

Figure 2.17. Residence of informal sector interviewees and population living below poverty level, metropolitan Los Angeles, 1990. Population Data: 1990, U.S. Census Bureau STF3A. Geospatial Data: 1990, U.S. Census Bureau Tiger Line Files.

naled the strength of the region's multimedia and entertainment industries.[51] In 1996, the federal government, driven in part by election-year concerns, chipped in with a $400 million loan to help build a high-speed rail line in the Alameda Corridor designed to aid the development of L.A.'s role as an international trade center.[52]

Despite the hopeful rebound in employment, one that continued through the rest of the decade, Los Angeles remained plagued by persistent poverty and higher-than-national levels of joblessness.[53] In part, this was because the recovery was occurring on a social landscape wounded by the ravages of longer-term regional restructuring. Through the previous decades, deindustrialization, or the loss of basic manufacturing jobs, had resulted in the increasing social isolation and detachment from the labor force of many inner-city residents. Meanwhile, reindustrialization—the creation of a new set of manufacturing and service industries that often rely on low-wage, immigrant, and informal labor—yielded a class of individuals who engaged in full- or nearly full-time work but still earned too little to provide their households with an acceptable standard of living.[54]

The presence of a strong work ethic among the poor presents a challenge to a system that values but often does not reward labor. Stereotypes of the poor, which have helped fuel the punitive "welfare-to-work" strategies of recent years, are based on the notion that low-income individuals prefer to rely on public assistance rather than work for wages. The research presented here about Los Angeles demonstrates that a large number of individuals are playing by the agreed-upon rules: they are working hard every day and pursuing dreams of progress for themselves and their children, but continue to live in poverty. While there are some whose commitment to work was eroded long ago by the difficulties of a changing economy, racial discrimination, and hopelessness, studies demonstrate that even those on public assistance often find creative forms of informal or supplemental work to help their families.

This emerging picture of the poor in Los Angeles and throughout the nation calls for rethinking of traditional views. The documented level of attachment of low-income individuals to the labor market suggests that what has dragged many regions down is not the poor but rather the failure of policy makers to ensure that this admirable labor force participation translates into more equitable incomes and benefits. It is essential that this energy be harnessed and upgraded, lifting working households above poverty, promoting new sources of consumer demand, and encouraging additional work effort. To do this, labor standards must be raised and enforced, and job training, education, and child care must be provided to help individuals to move up the employment ladder to better jobs and a better family life.

As we will argue, business has clear incentives to support targeted antipoverty efforts in order to improve the overall economy. By the same token, community advocates must understand that the fate of the region is critical to the fate of the poor. Many inner-city activists seek to build local solutions for their ravaged neighborhoods and are concerned that attention to the region may, as in the early 1990s in Los Angeles, divert policy efforts away from a community development agenda. Meanwhile, the geographic and ethnic character of poverty can make some middle-class residents feel that they are insulated from the worst effects of regional restructuring and therefore should pay little attention to problem areas and populations.

Yet we are all in the same economic boat, and creating common ground across the spatial and social distances that characterize Los Angeles and other metropolitan economies could make for both good ethics and good business. As we see in chapters 6 and 7, examples for "win-win" scenarios exist and by the end of the 1990s, new and hopeful voices for community-based regionalism began emerging in Los Angeles and elsewhere around the country. But before we focus on these efforts, let us turn to the regional efforts that emerged in Los Angeles in the mid-1990s and evaluate whether they addressed the economic inequities that both dragged the region down and pulled its citizens apart.

3

Disconnected Futures

Regional Strategies and Urban Revitalization in Los Angeles

California has long been a focal point for the American Dream. Blessed with a striking natural environment, a strong and often pacesetting economy, and a fluid and changing population, it has been the place where migrants from other states and other countries come in search of their own piece of the future. Los Angeles, a place where the motion picture and music industries literally have made dreams come true, has been at the center of the state's sense of hope and transformation. And after the 1984 Olympic Summer Games, in which the diversity and potential of the city were on international display, Los Angeles could boast of having it all. With "I Love L.A." booming in the background, the city was forging a new multicultural identity and economy.

A decade after the Olympics, Angelenos were far less optimistic about the future. The national recession of the early 1990s hit Southern California a bit late, giving an initial false impression that the diversity of the region's economic assets would allow it to ride out any negative national trends. But when the economic downturn came, it came with a vengeance. Total employment shrank by 3.6 percent in 1991 and by another 4.5 percent in 1992.[1] The dynamics of deindustrialization and reindustrialization (outlined in chapter 2), became increasingly evident: while manufacturing employment had been declining since 1988, it fell nearly 8 percent in both 1992 and 1993, far outpacing the more modest recession in services. Indeed, manufacturing employment did not begin to tick upward until 1996, and most of the business clusters that led Los Angeles forward through the 1990s were service-oriented activities such as motion pictures and multimedia, tourism and entertainment, transportation and international trade, and health (see figure 3.1).[2]

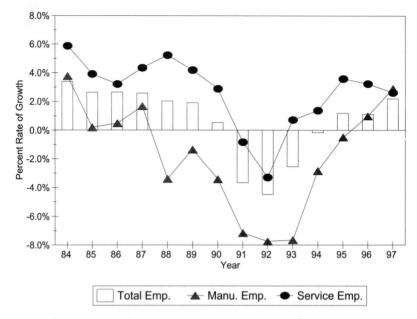

Figure 3.1. Employment growth in Los Angeles County, 1984–97.

In the worst moment of the economic downturn came the 1992 civil unrest. While the specter of a city under siege by its own citizens shocked the nation, it was a special blow to Los Angeles's self-image. The riots called into question the multicultural harmony portrayed during the 1984 Olympics, making clear that many in the region were suffering economic deprivation. With the embers still cooling, the image of Los Angeles as a *Blade Runner*-style dystopia captured the national imagination. Not surprisingly, business confidence eroded.

Extraordinary times required extraordinary measures—and the early 1990s saw a plethora of proposals to restructure Los Angeles' ailing regional economy. Some saw hope in the transport sector, counting on the stimulus to be provided by an ambitious program of subway and light rail development coordinated by the Metropolitan Transportation Authority (MTA). Others suggested that a consortium of downsizing aerospace companies could capitalize on the Southland's environmental challenges by developing an electric car industry. The notion of promoting new industrial clusters or business networks captured the attention of many policy makers; the Southern California Association of Governments (SCAG) tried to use this concept in its Regional Comprehensive Plan. So did the New Economy Project (NEP), which also emphasized the critical role of smaller businesses as the engine of economic growth. Finally, many argued that massive infrastructure improvements along the port-to-downtown Alameda Corridor could help overall regional employment growth by better linking the region to growing international trade.

Because the Los Angeles unrest occurred during an economic downturn, one might have expected that the new initiatives would address the economic and geographic inequities that drove the unrest. Unfortunately, regional strategists and community developers were moving in different worlds: few of the regional initiatives held promise for the poorest neighborhoods and residents, while few advocates in low-income communities were aware of, or participating in, the proposals for economic growth.

In this chapter, we analyze this "disconnect," beginning with an analysis of why the revitalization of poor areas has traditionally been divorced from regional efforts, both nationally and in Los Angeles. We then examine the specific initiatives proposed for the Los Angeles region in the mid-1990s through the prism of the needs of low-income neighborhoods. We suggest that while some elements of these strategies addressed the problem of poverty and inequality, most were limited in their ability to improve conditions for poorer residents and communities. We then report on our analysis and interviews with community development practitioners in ten poor areas of Los Angeles County. The results are striking: while community leaders were frequently able to identify emerging areas of the regional economy, they were much less likely to identify new regional initiatives, partly because they had not been invited to the various tables of regional and business decision making.

In some sense, this gap between the region and communities was not surprising. Looking at the boards of directors of the forty largest corporations in Los Angeles in the mid-1990s—a key place where decisions affecting the region were being made—we found that less than 10 percent of their members also served on the boards of community or youth organizations. This impeded the sort of relationship building between business and community that is necessary to establish trust and mutual engagement. Building these relationships is a key first step in developing a new regional approach that links growth and equity concerns, a point we emphasize in the policy recommendations of chapter 7.

Urban Revitalization and the Region

The National Picture

The disconnect between community and regional strategies has deep roots. While urban revitalization efforts have historically tried to reposition the central city as the heart of a metropolitan region, many critics have noted that urban renewal has frequently ignored or displaced the poor. As Mier and Fitzgerald (1991) observe, urban policy prior to the 1960s centered on (1) development practices that offered tax abatements, loan packaging, infrastructure and land development, and other efforts to reduce the costs of production and entice firms to locate plants and create jobs in designated areas in or adjacent to urban centers; and (2) housing construction, often implemented by redevelopment agencies that declared areas "blighted" and took property for housing and commercial revitalization purposes.[3] The hope was that the resulting burst in employment, housing, and retail would restore the competitiveness of the central city and thereby reduce local poverty.

By the late 1960s and early 1970s, these approaches to urban revitalization came under attack by planners and the public alike. The practice of luring production facilities with fiscal incentives produced a proliferation of industrial parks, but it also convinced firms that there were benefits to being, or pretending to be, footloose. Many city officials were dismayed to see already subsidized firms relocating to other jurisdictions, often within the same region, when public officials in those areas offered even better inducements. Since costs were often lower one suburb away from the traditional central city, employment radiated outward. Regions grew, but their central-city cores experienced increasing economic difficulty, often with fewer fiscal resources to confront new problems because of the revenue loss incurred from previous giveaways.

Meanwhile, urban neighborhood activists began to challenge the bulldozer approach to urban renewal. As Frieden and Sagalyn (1989) note, urban revitalization programs of the 1950s and 1960s created two separate and conflicting interest groups: one serving as advocates for low-income housing, and another consisting of lawmakers, developers, business leaders, and the local media interested primarily in downtown commercial rejuvenation. In the ensuing political conflicts over redevelopment funding and strategies, developers and their allies had disproportionate influence. As a result, many community groups became convinced that low-income residents within renewal areas were being summarily removed, deriving few if any tangible benefits from federally sponsored programs.

The administration of President Lyndon B. Johnson (1963–69) responded to such criticism by shifting from a straightforward attack on physical blight to a more comprehensive approach involving job training, social services, housing rehabilitation, and sometimes neighborhood organizing for the residents of depressed areas. Unfortunately, this rethinking of urban policy occurred a bit late in the game: jobs, shopping centers, and middle-class (mostly Anglo) residents had begun their exodus to the suburbs even as urban mayors faced tremendous demands from newly mobilized low-income (often predominantly African-American) neighborhoods.

Desperate to meet these demands, as well as to prevent their cities from hollowing out, many big-city mayors adopted what Carla Robinson (1989) has termed a "corporate-center" approach: they gambled that stimulating growth in the central business district would eventually "trickle down" to disadvantaged residents. Fewer city administrations used what Robinson terms an "alternative" framework, promoting economic development activity that flowed to disadvantaged residents.[4]

This shift toward a corporate-centered approach intensified in the 1980s when the Reagan administration decided to sharply cut or eliminate the core elements of the federal funding system for poorer areas, including Urban Development Action Grants, Community Development Block Grants, new construction financing, small business assistance, and housing assistance funds.[5] In response, many local governments looked for ways to generate more private sector growth. One mechanism was tax increment financing, a strategy that became particularly popular in California where local governments also faced the fiscal constraints imposed by Proposition 13.[6] Under these conditions, money-generating commercial projects were preferred to housing and large-scale commercial projects were preferred to smaller, neighborhood-oriented development activities since only the former could generate sufficient tax increments to meet the financial tests required of a redevelopment project area. In short, trickle-down economics became the centerpiece of urban revitalization efforts.

The election of Bill Clinton to the presidency in 1992 led many big-city mayors and urban activists to hope that the federal government would reverse the neglect of America's cities. But, as noted in chapter 1, the president's initial $19.5 billion "stimulus package," based on a list of projects presented to the administration by the U.S. Conference of Mayors, failed to make it through Congress. While the U.S. Department of Housing and Urban Development (HUD) managed to introduce some new initiatives—including the renovation of public housing, an increasing reliance on mobility strategies, and stronger enforcement of the anti-redlining Community Reinvestment Act—the HUD budget was unable to promote more than token "pilot" programs.[7]

In the context of continuing fiscal and social problems for cities, there was a "revival of interest in regional solutions to urban problems" (Swanstrom, 1996: 5). Mayors and others realized that with federal support continuing to erode, they had to attach the goal of meeting their cities' needs to the broader task of regional recovery. Central-city mayors, in short, tried to position themselves as regional actors in order to form alliances of mutual benefit with suburban leaders.[8] After a long period of decline, the idea of regionalism had come back in vogue.

Urban Revitalization in Los Angeles

Urban development in Los Angeles parallels this general history. The city's initial revitalization projects, like those across the nation, combined downtown renewal with the development of affordable housing. Soon, however, commercial developers gained the upper hand. For example, the Bunker Hill project in downtown Los Angeles, launched in 1961, eliminated housing for over 7,000 low-income residents and removed many small businesses. While the project eventually yielded over 1,000 affordable housing units, the most prominent and immediate outcomes of Bunker Hill's revitalization were luxury housing, corporate skyscrapers, and a center for the performing arts. Partly as a result, the Community Redevelopment Agency (CRA) became a favorite target for community-based opposition (Light, 1987).[9]

The 1965 Watts riots made evident the problems of inequality and poverty in Los Angeles and led to the creation of redevelopment projects outside of downtown. These included the Hoover, Watts, Beacon Street, and Normandie sections of South Central. At the same time, L.A.'s downtown-centered redevelopment strategy was consolidated in two ways. First, the 1965 riots forced businesses to recognize that the center of the city was vulnerable and needed the policy and development attention that had been lacking in this sprawling, low-density city. Second, the social upheaval paved the way for a new political alliance led by Jewish and African-American leaders and supported by moderate business interests. The result was the election of a liberal African-American city councilman, Tom Bradley, as mayor in 1973.[10]

The Bradley administration embodied an ongoing tension: while it provided opportunities for the political advancement of African-Americans and other minorities in the city, its major economic development thrust focused on the corporate center rather than on lower-income neighborhoods. As the 1970s turned into the 1980s, the central business district (CBD) took off, with land values skyrocketing in pace with the construction of new corporate headquarters and office buildings.[11] Potential critiques from minority and other communities were muted, in part because of political gains under Bradley but also because the financial success of the downtown allowed the CRA to fund infrastructure, public improvements, parks, and social service projects in 17 other redevelopment projects throughout the city, as well as to create over 16,000 subsidized housing units throughout the city (Grigsby and Caltabiano, 1998).

By the late 1980s, however, the image of Los Angeles as a "tale of two cities"— a booming downtown and decaying minority neighborhoods— led critics to call for an alternative strategy that would link neighborhood renewal to downtown growth.[12] These calls came a bit late: the slide of the regional economy in the early 1990s meant that the city's central business district was no longer a recipe for generating jobs and revenues to fuel neighborhood development. Like other major cities around the country, Los Angeles began to look for new and broader regional solutions in the 1990s.

Regional Strategies for the Los Angeles Economy

The turn to regionalism in Los Angeles had important historical roots and antecedents. Throughout this century, publicly supported regional infrastructure projects, such as the man-made Wilmington–San Pedro Harbor, the Owens and Colorado River aqueducts, and the Department of Water and Power's hydroelectric plants, have been essential pillars for the city's economic development (Erie, 1992). Los Angeles's key regional organization, the Southern California Association of Governments (SCAG), was formed back in 1965. In the late 1980s, Mayor Tom Bradley helped launch "L.A. 2000," a joint public-private effort that stressed the need for growth management at a regional level and even called for the creation of new regional governmental authorities, including a Regional Growth Management Agency to set policy for land use, housing and transportation, and the merger of the regional antipollution agency with agencies that manage water control and solid waste (see Los Angeles 2000 Committee, 1988; Fulton, 1997).

The regional efforts that emerged in the mid-1990s focused almost exclusively on economic matters. At least seven major regional strategies entered into public arena, including the following:

- The Los Angeles County Metropolitan Transportation Authority (MTA) Long Range Transportation Plan
- The Alameda Corridor Project
- CALSTART
- The Southern California Association of Government's (SCAG) Regional Comprehensive Plan
- The New Economy Project (NEP)
- Rebuild LA (RLA)
- The Los Angeles Community Development Bank

To assess the relevance of these initiatives to poor communities, we conducted our own assessments and interviewed community leaders in ten selected high-poverty neighborhoods regarding their views on both regional economics and these seven specific initiatives. While we evaluate all seven here, partly because this was the list used in our community-based surveys (conducted from 1994 to 1996), we should note that some of these regional initiatives have since declined in importance. CALSTART, for example, was hurt by the California Air Resource Board's decision, apparently under pressure from Governor Pete Wilson, to eliminate the requirement that 2 percent of vehicles sold in California in 1998 be zero-emission. The New Economy Project's ideas were more or less folded into the city's economic development strategy after Richard Riordan became mayor. And RLA ended its operations in 1997, with its technical resources moving to the Los Angeles Community College District.[13]

Below, we outline the general approach of each strategy, then focus specifically on how well it was linked to neighborhood economic development. The framework for this type of assessment was initially developed by Wolff and elaborated in Wolff and Grigsby (1995). Wolff's work there included a complicated matrix for evaluation; our approach here is simpler. We draw below on Wolff's assessment of the New Economy Project.

Metropolitan Transit Authority

For over two decades, Los Angeles has been engaged in an ambitious comprehensive program of highway expansion, traffic management, and subway and light rail development. The effort, funded through a combination of federal and local resources, has been coordinated by the Metropolitan Transportation Authority (MTA) and guided by the MTA's Long Range Transportation Plan (LRTP).[14] Adopted in 1995, the LRTP established the agency's integrated long-term strategy, including the sequencing of project implementation, to address the transportation challenges facing Los Angeles County.[15]

The most obvious economic impact of the MTA's plans involved its projected $72.4 billion in spending over twenty years—and the resulting scramble of developers, consultants, and companies for contracts was testimony to the economic opportunities being generated. Of course, spillovers from new construction-related employment, as well as retail and housing developments near key station locations, were likely to benefit some lower-income communities. Additionally, MTA's ongoing operations, such as maintaining and driving its fleet of buses, have provided steady jobs for a predominantly minority workforce.

Still, given the low density of much of the Los Angeles area and the actual physical layout of the transit lines, the emphasis on rail construction disproportionately benefited suburban middle-class commuters. Indeed, to the extent that job opportunities have drifted to the suburbs or been scattered through the region, MTA's fixed-rail strategy, which focused on accessing downtown from outlying areas and initially had few trains scheduled for "reverse commutes," was unlikely to meet the pressing needs of low-income residents.[16]

This emphasis on subway and rail construction was especially striking given the fact that Los Angeles has what is said to be the nation's most overcrowded bus system. A civil suit filed in 1994 against the MTA by the Bus Riders Union, an organization initiated by the Labor/Community Strategy Center, argued that bus fare increases intended to relieve the fiscal burdens of rail construction discriminated against the largely low-income and minority ridership of bus lines. In its public protests, the group noted that rail commuters, who represented only 6 percent of the system's total ridership, were receiving 70 percent of the MTA's spending.[17] In September 1996, the suit was settled by a consent decree in which the MTA agreed to reduce the price of a monthly pass, lower the off-peak cash fare, and put more than 150 new buses on the road in the following two years.[18]

The MTA was slow to improve bus service and comply with the consent decree, worsening the lot of thousands of transit-dependent low-wage workers. With problems in subway construction, rotating executive leadership, and a politicized board contributing to a negative public image for the MTA, in November 1998, voters overwhelmingly (68.1 percent) approved a proposition to prevent the agency from using sales tax proceeds to plan, build, or operate new subway lines.[19] The MTA still enjoys some public support in low-income areas hungry for construction and other jobs. But the fundamental critique remains: while the MTA's infrastructure spending was likely to generate aggregate benefits to the region, it might have more effectively met the mobility needs of the region's poor by developing a more adequate bus system and limiting fixed-rail projects to those that prioritized the needs of poor and working-class residents.[20]

Alameda Corridor

A second regional strategy, still underway, was premised on the importance of international commerce to the Los Angeles area. Trade is indeed crucial to the region: the transshipment of goods through the ports of San Pedro and Long Beach increased 16 percent annually between 1976 and 1995 and some analysts claim that upwards of 25 percent of Southern California's GDP is dependent on foreign commerce.[21] Given this pattern, business leaders and policy makers felt that facilitating the movement of goods could spur economic growth and perhaps have positive effects in many communities.

The Alameda Corridor Transportation Authority (ACTA) was formed in 1989 for just this purpose. The corridor refers to the area running from the ports to the downtown, an industrial swath of the Southland that includes the cities of Vernon, Huntington Park, South Gate, Lynwood, Carson, Compton, Wilmington, and San Pedro, as well as parts of Los Angeles and Long Beach. The corridor project will take the current rail lines, on which traffic is slowed by 200 at-grade roadway crossings, and create a single twenty-mile, high-capacity, and fully grade-separated transportation corridor linking the regions' two ports with key transcontinental rail yards near downtown Los Angeles.[22] As a result, Los Angeles will be better able to move freight to various distribution centers throughout the country. Proponents claim that by 2010, corridor activities will, at a minimum, create 70,000 new U.S. jobs in international trade and add $2.5 billion in federal revenues.[23]

The Los Angeles and Long Beach Ports have been the two driving agents behind this $1.8 billion project, with additional support coming from the Southern California Association of Governments (SCAG) and various business organizations. The federal government has also been supportive, providing $59 million to leverage a $400 million federal loan for construction.[24] The corridor cities, some of the poorest in Los Angeles County, generally favored the project, but also worried that they would not receive their fair share of benefits. Of special concern was the distribution of the 10,000 construction and engineering jobs to be generated during the building period (1998–2001).

This worry about fairness was exacerbated by the authority's decision to place the corridor's spending power in the hands of a small finance committee in which the ports and port cities held 80 percent of the votes. As a result, a number of the smaller corridor cities, including Compton, Lynwood, South Gate, and Vernon, filed a lawsuit that sought to address the governance issue and increase their influence over spending, jobs, and economic benefits.[25] While the specific issues of legal contention were environmental, traffic, and other concerns, the lawsuit also reflected an underlying concern that, in the words of one knowledgeable observer, there were "no explicit linkages between the construction of the corridor and actual job creation and business development in the corridor cities."[26]

Indeed, while the debate has often focused on the construction jobs — a challenge to which the Corridor Authority responded with aggressive attempts to include minority firms and local employees — the real issue is the permanent effect on employment in the region.[27] As Steve Erie, a University of California, San Diego, expert on Southern California infrastructure, noted in early 1996, "what is missing is a development plan for the cities along the corridor."[28]

That this concern might have some merit is demonstrated in an extensive study of trade "winners" and trade "strugglers" in Los Angeles (Pastor, 1998). Taking national level export and import patterns by industry and mapping them onto the economic structure of Los Angeles, Manuel Pastor found that nearly all of the areas along the corridor had actually been negatively impacted by trade trends in the early 1990s. As a result, while enhancing the capacity to move imports through the region will benefit businesses in the distribution and freight transportation sectors, it may weaken the industrial enterprises (such as metalworking and garments) along the corridor itself. Indeed, the very design of the train system, which passes though one of the most job-dense areas in Los Angeles County but leaves only one of the three projected lines available for local train stops, is likely to create a "drive-by" development strategy that will not help local firms put their own export-oriented products onto the trade train.

The underlying assumption of most observers was that increased rail capacity would result in tremendous economic gain for the corridor cities, the Southern California region, and the nation as a whole. Yet poor residents may be relative losers. While the resulting port employment will be high-wage, it will also be limited in scale, even as the accompanying increase in warehousing downtown will use up significant amounts of land per job in an area (the downtown industrial district) that is already land-scarce. For benefits to really trickle down, more attention needs to be paid to encouraging export activities by those hard-hit businesses along the corridor itself; if not, this project will represent a linkage between the region and the nation but not one between the region and its poor neighborhoods.[29]

CALSTART

A third regional strategy that emerged in the early 1990s was CALSTART. Founded in 1992, CALSTART is a nonprofit consortium that has grown to include over 200 Southern California–based transportation, defense, and other companies seeking to apply the skills and technology of downsized defense sector firms and employees to develop an advanced transportation industry centered in Los Angeles County.[30] The direct impetus for this effort, apart from a general desire to reemploy aerospace workers and engineers, was a 1990 decision by the California Air Resources Board mandating that 2 percent of the cars sold in the state by 1998 be zero-emission vehicles

(ZEVs)—a requirement that, given technological constraints, essentially meant the production and sale of electric vehicles.[31] In essence, CALSTART formed on the belief that the sea change being forced in Southern California by environmental concerns might actually help create a new industry. And as local industry learned to meet state mandates, it was argued, Southern California manufacturers would gain a competitive advantage in electric vehicle production and therefore be well-placed to satisfy any additional regulation-induced demand in other states and countries.[32]

Unfortunately for CALSTART, the California Air Resources Board, apparently under pressure from Republican governor Pete Wilson, relaxed its requirements in March 1996. In their place came voluntary production goals.[33] The board did leave a mandate requiring that 10 percent of vehicles sold in the state in 2003 be zero-emission; even if this mandate is also relaxed, however, the worldwide market for zero-emission vehicles will probably grow over the next half decade as the Japanese and the Europeans also seek to reduce pollution. The introduction of all-electric cars by General Motors, Chrysler, Ford, Toyota, Nissan, Mazda, and Honda in 1996 and 1997 is evidence that a market may exist, albeit still in gestation. In short, CAL-START responded to a real opportunity and reflected a good match between the region's skill base and national and international opportunities.

CALSTART was a promising initiative: it built on existing skills, responded to the downsizing of a key industry, and tried to transform the regulations that some think inhibit new industries into an opportunity to develop a competitive industry. It also managed to secure significant financial support from numerous sources. In 1992, for example, CALSTART received start-up funding of $4 million from the Intermodal Surface Transportation Efficiency Act of 1991 (ISTEA), $1.8 million from California's Employment Training Panel, and an additional $14 million from consortium members (including large firms such as Hughes Aircraft, GM, IBM, Lockheed, and Southern California Edison).[34] With more funding arriving in subsequent years from the Department of Defense, the Department of Transportation, and others, by July 1998, CALSTART reported that it had spent over $90 million on 50 different technology development programs.[35]

There was, however, little involvement by community-based groups in either planning or participating in CALSTART, and the effort had an extremely low level of recognition in poor and minority communities.[36] While CALSTART did initiate some meetings and seminars designed to encourage minority- and women-owned firms to contribute to the development of the electric car industry, there was little thought about supplemental programs that could insure that the low-wage workers located in largely minority communities would gain the requisite skills to be employable within this new industry. CALSTART had great potential as a regional growth program, but the linkage to community development was a not a major concern or strength.[37]

New Economy Project

The New Economy Project (NEP), originally proposed by the New Vision Business Council of Southern California, produced a report on economic strategy sponsored by the Community Redevelopment Agency, the Community Development Department, and the Department of Water and Power of the City of Los Angeles.[38] The report identified policy changes that could help stimulate economic activity in a set of industrial "clusters"—metalworking, computer hardware and software, textile, biomedical, entertainment, and environmental engineering—that were thought to be the key engines of economic growth in a region experiencing sharp declines in aerospace and traditional heavy manufacturing. Using an industry audit approach, the initial report stressed the impressive reliance on self-financed expansion in these industries. It suggested that past economic development policies, which had been mainly concerned with the Fortune 500–type industries, neglected the smaller, entrepreneurial, and often immigrant-owned businesses that constituted the basis of the new economy.

The strategic themes of this report were picked up by Mayor Richard Riordan's Office of Economic Development as well as by other organizations, including SCAG and RLA (see below). Some of these ideas were typical of any probusiness framework: first, that regional economic development requires a strong political commitment from the private sector; second, that regional decision makers need to avoid "negative images" that deter investment; and third, that regulatory burdens should be streamlined, particularly by eliminating overlapping regulations (Friedman, 1994).[39]

But the key contribution of the New Economy Project was its emphasis on the importance of industrial clusters. Arguing that economic development in Los Angeles was hindered by a "one-size-fits-all" assistance program, the NEP stressed the need to create industry focus groups to provide government with information necessary to create "customer driven nuanced strategies." Such focus groups would also increase opportunities for intra-sectoral business collaboration and networking that is typical of successful industries and regions. The Fashion Roundtable, organized in part by Riordan's office, was the first official expression of the report's recommendation to form industry focus groups, although less visible pilot efforts, such as the Southern California Edison's Apparel Roundtable, already existed.

While the sectoral focus was welcome, the celebration of entrepreneurial, smaller businesses in new industrial clusters left little explicit room for community development. Certainly, minority residents can benefit from the growth of certain sectors: in the emerging industries identified by the New Economy Project (representing 10 percent of the county workforce), minorities occupied 32 percent of the management positions and 85 percent of the production positions.[40] Yet this racially bifurcated structure of labor and management also suggested the potential for perpetuating inequalities. Moreover, the NEP envisioned helping local firms, not local communities. Indeed, the NEP failed to identify linkages between growth industries and their location in poorer neighborhoods, paid no attention to increasing the mobility of the labor force in disadvantaged areas, and neglected the key role of human resource and skill development in addressing problems faced by both firms and their workers. In short, the NEP was a business-oriented approach with an implicit reliance on trickle-down economics that failed to condition subsidies and other government help on economic improvements in low-income communities.

Southern California Association of Governments Regional Comprehensive Plan

One of the agencies that embraced the cluster concept was the Southern California Association of Governments (SCAG), Southern California's regional planning agency. While it lacks any real enforcement mechanisms, SCAG's purpose is to coordinate governmental activity among its 152 member cities in a six-county region (Los Angeles, Orange, San Bernardino, Riverside, Ventura, and Imperial Counties).[41] In February 1992, SCAG's General Assembly adopted new bylaws requiring that "future SCAG planning be comprehensive, and directed that such planning be undertaken in a 'bottom-up, interactive' mode" (Southern California Association of Governments, 1996: 2). SCAG's Regional Comprehensive Plan (RCP), eventually finalized in March 1996, was designed to serve as a general guide "to the growth and changes that can be anticipated during the next 20 years" (Southern California Association of Governments, 1996: 2).

The RCP provided a regional framework for addressing concerns such as transportation, air and water quality, housing, growth, and hazardous waste management in Southern California. However, the RCP was also SCAG's first plan to propose an economic strategy for the entire region.[42] Following the New Economy Project, SCAG adopted a language and strategy based on industrial clusters and business networks, stressing the positive externalities of information sharing and close cooperation.[43] Its list of promising clusters—including the entertainment and tourist industries, advanced transportation systems and related technology, the biomedical equipment industry, environmental technology, the apparel industry, and aerospace and defense (even though they were actively downsizing)—was parallel to those identified by other efforts.

In order to promote regional competitiveness, SCAG proposed a Regional Economic Strategies Consortium (RESC) to promote the entire region, encourage industry clusters, and help small and medium-size firms with financial assistance. The RCP proposed that this consortium include the 2000 Regional Partnership (an outgrowth of the earlier L.A. 2000 regional effort), SCAG, and the Los Angeles Area Chamber of Commerce. Because industrial clusters are inherently multijurisdictional, cities were urged to cooperate and coordinate their economic strategies. Since it was difficult to do this at a broad regional scale, SCAG first concentrated on having identifiable subregions form alliances and develop joint economic strategies. This effort has helped, for example, to evolve a consortium of "Gateway Cities" that surround the Alameda Corridor.[44] Still, the overall regional approach embodied in the RESC was slow to develop momentum. In the meantime, other alternatives, including the New Los Angeles Marketing Partnership (NLAMP), grabbed the attention of policy makers (NLAMP developed out of the mayor's office and worked primarily on improving L.A.'s image both within the region and in the rest of the country in order to attract and retain business).[45]

SCAG's RCP was innovative: even as it tried to reinforce more traditional "macroeconomic" regional initiatives such as the MTA and Alameda Corridor projects, it stressed that new economic policies should focus on promoting industrial clusters and business networks. The RCP was less novel on issues of equity and poverty.[46] While the plan stressed that economic development should be gauged by both improvements in real personal income levels and enhancements in the distribution of income, there were few specific policy suggestions to close the equity gap (except for the notion of an Enterprise Trust Fund to provide capital to small businesses in high-poverty communities and vague admonitions regarding the need for training and skill development that would match the needs of specific populations).[47] Indeed, while the key sixty-five-page economy section of the Regional Plan noted the need to develop investment strategies for "communities-in-need," it devoted a scant three pages to the topic and instead confined most of the discussion of what might be done in lower-income neighborhoods to a separate Human Resources chapter focused more on service delivery than on community development.

This relative lack of attention to the poor reflected the very nature of SCAG: it is a membership organization of elected officials with no logical way for representatives of poorer neighborhoods to be involved systematically except as spectators in publicly held forums or conferences.[48] Many leaders we interviewed in poorer communities were only vaguely aware of SCAG's activities and sensed that SCAG, as is typical of many regional councils, had little authority or clout to carry out its initiatives, particularly in the economic arena.[49] Thus, while SCAG's RCP offered a unique and powerful economic vision, it fell short on incorporating the concerns and participation of low-income communities in its agenda.

Rebuild LA

Three days after the 1992 civil unrest, Los Angeles mayor Tom Bradley called Peter Ueberroth, a prominent Orange County businessman and organizer of the 1984 Olympic Games, to persuade him to develop a private sector initiative that would spark a Los Angeles "renaissance." RLA (originally known as Rebuild LA) was launched one day later.

The very formation of RLA—that is, the fact that a sitting mayor essentially acknowledged that an entirely new organization was needed to promote development in the poorer communities of his city—signaled an admission that prior federal and local efforts to stimulate urban revitalization had largely failed. Given this, Ueberroth argued that private sector business leaders would have to assume the lead. As Ueberroth put it, "RLA's job is to get private sector business to invest in people and jobs."[50] Of course, some objected to this very mission, worrying about the implications of placing the restoration of Los Angeles's economy and public future in private hands. Moreover, the turn toward business leadership and a strategy of attracting corporate investment was curious: after all, the same corporations that had supported the downtown focus and ignored the neighborhoods were unlikely saviors of the city's ghettos and barrios.

RLA established six main objectives: creating more jobs, enhancing access to capital, increasing the number of business owners, improving workforce skills, engaging the public sector more actively in solving problems in the impact areas, and building community pride.[51] After five years, RLA was to "sunset"; in the meantime, it was slated to attract $500 million in development donations and encourage major corporations to invest in what came to be called "neglected" areas.[52] With these ambitious objectives, RLA quickly grew to have a staff of some sixty people and 1,200 volunteers. The organization also wound up with four co-chairs and a board of over ninety members, with the unwieldy size resulting partly from suspicions regarding Ueberroth's business-oriented leadership and partly because of concerns about the representation of different ethnic groups.[53]

RLA's initial approach was neither well-conceived nor well-received. As noted, some observers were wary of relying on big-business largesse to rebuild areas that business previously had abandoned. These concerns were exacerbated after a major controversy erupted about the amount of investment RLA claimed was forthcoming and the investments firms were actually making.[54] The size and fragmentation of RLA's board also limited organizational coherence and led to more squabbling. A year after the unrest, Ueberroth stepped down and RLA was left in the hands of four co-chairs. In March 1994, RLA was again restructured and Linda Griego, a former deputy mayor for economic development in the Bradley administration and a successful small business owner, became the new president.[55]

Griego helped streamline governance, creating an executive committee of fifteen, replacing the co-chair structure with a single chair, and taking over as the full-time chief executive officer. More significantly, she shifted RLA's focus from an approach reliant on big business to a strategy that sought to encourage economic activity by working with small companies, community-based organizations, and others. A community-needs assessment conducted in 1995 indicated that residents' top priority for retail was high-quality grocery stores. RLA therefore sought to attract grocery facilities to the properties that remained vacant following the civil unrest.[56] Drawing on the analysis of the New Economy Project, RLA also focused on employment creation and wage improvement by beginning to identify and build networks of existing small- to medium-size manufacturing companies already located in neglected neighborhoods. However, just as these efforts were gaining ground, RLA ceased operations, turning its activities over in 1997 to L.A. Prosper Partners, which is in turn managed by the Community Development Technologies Center based at a local community college.

The record RLA left was mixed. Its initial thrust to have major corporations lead the way in reinvesting in South Central Los Angeles largely failed. While it did play a role in the redevelopment of some of the more than one thousand buildings damaged during the unrest, it is not clear how important its intervention was in the bulk of the cases.[57] It lured some grocery stores into the agency's "focus area" in South Central, but the numbers were not large—six new chain stores and two smaller nonchain stores in the focus area.[58] RLA's shift toward helping small business enterprises under Griego was helpful, albeit modest. The organization targeted biomedical production, food processing, household furniture manufacturing, metal, textiles, and toy manufacturing/wholesale; as noted in chapter 2, each of these industries had a significant number of firms in high-poverty areas. After conducting extensive industry audits, including both data analysis and interviews, it went on to help facilitate the creation of several industry-based business networks. It also worked in collaboration with neighboring community colleges and universities to provide job training and education programs for workers in these emerging industries and in the neglected areas in general. Finally, RLA helped various nonprofit community development corporations obtain other funding for economic and housing development purposes.

This post-Ueberroth approach to business development was received much more favorably, as was RLA's assistance to nonprofits and its attempts to attract grocery stores and other retail amenities to poorer neighborhoods. The "clusters" and networks strategy implicitly recognized the importance of regional dynamics and the need to connect the poor to dynamic sectors of the economy; it specifically sought to help those clusters that had the most potential to hire low-income residents. One wonders how much more could have been accomplished if this had been the strategy for RLA's whole five years and not just the last two of its existence.

Los Angeles Community Development Bank

Federal authority and support for the Los Angeles Community Development Bank was granted in 1995 in the wake of Los Angeles's failed application for a federal empowerment zone. The bank's purpose was to provide loans to business enterprises that otherwise would not be eligible to receive funds from traditional lending sources. In addition, it was granted authority to pay for land to ease physical development, make equity investments in emerging firms, and assist community organizations in providing housing and pursuing economic development objectives.[59] All activities were to occur in "poverty" neighborhoods (defined as those in which over 20 percent of residents live in households with incomes below the poverty line), and a majority of any jobs created were to go to residents of these neighborhoods.[60] The bank's specific target zone (labeled a supplemental empowerment zone) encompassed a geographic area of nineteen square miles including communities such as Pacoima, Boyle Heights, and parts of downtown and South Central Los Angeles.

While this was a federally sponsored initiative, the private sector was also supposed to participate in the lending process. The bank's initial capitalization included $115 million in Los Angeles City and County Economic Development Initiative (EDI) funds, and $315 million in HUD loan guarantees. However, private institutions, who were to act as co-lenders to the bank, were expected to contribute up to $310 million, giving the bank a total capitalization of over $700 million.

The bank was slow in getting started, making only $2.3 million dollars in loans in 1996. The delay partly reflected an attempt to maintain community involvement: a number of advisory meetings were held with various community-based organizations prior to finalizing the structure and functioning of the bank, a fact that led to a high level of receptivity in many of the low-income communities profiled below. Lending progress subsequently stepped up: by the end of 1997, loans totaled $25 million and by the end of 1998, an additional $43 million in loans had been approved. Still, at the end of 1998, the bank admitted that it had reached less than 40 percent of its lending goals and critics labeled its performance as disappointing.[61]

In some sense, the bank began as a traditional urban revitalization strategy rather than a regional initiative. But its geographic scope was different from the beginning: it was empowered to serve many poor neighborhoods simultaneously rather than a particular subarea and indeed was featured in HUD's 1996 *Report on Metropolitan Economic Strategy* as a key regional effort in the Los Angeles basin. In 1998, it actually became more regional in its framework, announcing that it was shifting away from financing isolated enterprises and toward funding industrial clusters. While it is too early to tell what impact this shift might have on strengthening businesses within depressed neighborhoods, it was clearly in keeping with the analyses offered by the RLA, the New Economy Project, SCAG, and others.[62]

Of all the initiatives we examined, this was the one best-received by residents and most clearly designed to benefit low-income residents and neighborhoods. It included community participation in its planning, and its goal of lending to enterprises in the hope of securing employment expansion in poor neighborhoods was consistent with the themes of community development. Moreover, while the bank recognized that the primary engine of economic growth was the private sector, it imposed regulations to ensure that most jobs created by borrowers actually accrue to low-income residents.[63] Still, the bank's poor record in lending and community development should give supporters reason for caution.

The Initiatives and the Neighborhoods

Many of the foregoing strategies were quite forward-looking: the Alameda Corridor tied into internationalization, CALSTART tied into the environment, and both SCAG and RLA built on the notion of industrial clusters. Yet each had its gaps in addressing the problem of a Los Angeles divided by race, class, and opportunity. RLA's initial corporate strategy was shelved in response to tepid investment, and it wound up with little time left in its mandate to reap the fruits of its new small business–based approach. The transportation-oriented program of the MTA provided construction jobs and business contracting but it did little to link low-income communities via transit to appropriate job opportunities. The cluster strategies were consistent with the changing economy but generally failed to include specific strategies to prepare low-skilled workers for emerging job opportunities. The Alameda Corridor appeared to benefit Southern California and the nation as a whole, but there was little guarantee that it would either create a significant number of permanent jobs in the cities adjacent to the corridor or that the lower-income residents of those cities would occupy those jobs. And while the Community Development Bank seemed promising, its initial performance was uninspiring and its meager resources guaranteed a small impact.

How did leaders in low-income communities view these strategies and their likely effects? To examine this, we analyzed a sample of low-income communities in detail. Since our primary objective was to determine the awareness of regional issues among community development leaders in poor areas, we did not simply select the poorest tracts in Los Angeles on a random basis. Instead, we selected identifiable "neighborhoods" in which there was a sense of community, even if the neighborhood was not defined juridically as a separate city or council district. Relying primarily on the neighborhood definitions available from the Los Angeles County Department of Regional Planning, we generated a list of about twenty candidate "poverty" neighborhoods. We then narrowed our focus to ten: Belvedere, Boyle Heights (born in East Los Angeles), Huntington Park, Inglewood, Northwest Pasadena, Pacoima, Southeast Pomona, South Vermont, Watts, and Westlake/Pico-Union (see figure 3.2).

As the detailed description in appendix A makes clear, these areas represented a good geographic mix and some diversity with regard to economic experience. What stood out was that all the neighborhoods had been deeply affected by regional economic trends. The Belvedere area of East Los Angeles offered a particularly poignant reflection of the region's shift from manufacturing to service: after the Uniroyal tire plant there closed down, the site was converted into a factory outlet shopping center called "The Citadel" that actually employs more people than did the tire plant but at lower wages and less regular hours. Manufacturing remained critical for Belvedere and other Latino neighborhoods such as Pacoima, Huntington Park, and Boyle Heights, but most of the residents were engaged in the low-wage end of industry. Some areas, including Boyle Heights, Pacoima, Southeast Pomona, and South Vermont, had also lost major employers, increasing both joblessness and working poverty in the process.[64] Watts and Northwest Pasadena were economically stagnant. Those neighborhoods that had successfully connected to regional opportunities, such as Inglewood, Huntington Park, and

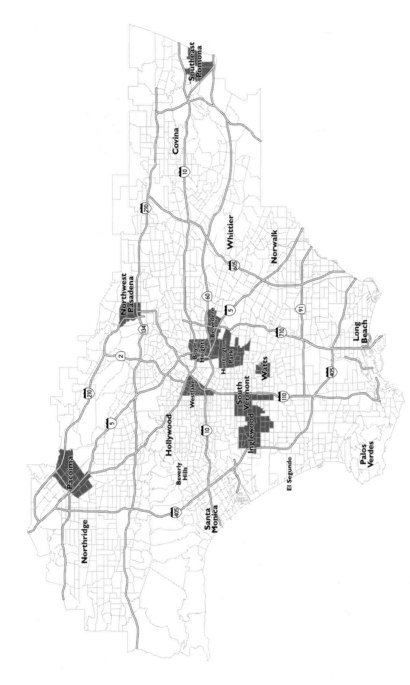

Figure 3.2. Selected areas in Los Angeles County. Geospatial Data: 1990, U.S. Census Bureau Tiger Line Files.

Pomona, were faring relatively better. Pomona, for example, had been hard-hit by the defense cuts, shedding thousands of jobs when General Dynamics shut, but by 1996 had largely made up for the employment losses with gains in medical services, high-tech equipment, and other dynamic regional sectors.[65]

To assess community leaders' awareness of regional trends and initiatives, we first conducted background research on each area. We then developed a list of local institutions, such as community development corporations (CDCs), major employers, and community leadership groups, and catalogued current development efforts by these groups and by city/county agencies. Based on this analysis, we selected and interviewed key leaders in the ten communities, asking them two broad sets of questions: first, where was the regional economy heading and what was the relationship of their own neighborhood to expanding sectors of that economy; and second, what did they know about the seven key regional strategies outlined above.[66]

The community leaders interviewed had a good sense of where the regional economy was headed and which sectors were important.[67] For example, respondents most frequently identified film/entertainment and technology/telecommunications to be key emerging industries in the Los Angeles area. Following behind these were industrial/manufacturing and port/trade businesses, with garment-making appropriately viewed as an expanding, albeit low-wage, sector. Health care, ethnic food products, business services, and aerospace were also considered important. Transportation was mentioned, but respondents rightly believed that the economic benefits once associated with the transportation sector would soon be reduced in scale as federal support declined. All of these views were consistent with results obtained from a smaller round of interviews with regional experts and economic decision makers.

Significantly, our respondents knew much less about the major policy initiatives underway to restructure the Los Angeles regional economy. We queried whether their neighborhood had been affected by institutions such as RLA or SCAG, or planning efforts such as the Alameda Corridor Project or the New Economy Project. A surprising number of people had not heard of certain policy efforts or institutions. For example, while nearly 90 percent of respondents had heard of RLA, the MTA, and the Alameda Corridor Project, only 70 percent had heard of SCAG. More than 70 percent had heard about the Community Development Bank, even though it had not yet begun operations at the time of the interviews, a reflection of the bank's outreach. The least well-known initiatives by far were CALSTART and the New Economy

Project (NEP), with the latter drawing less than 20 percent awareness among our community leader respondents, even though this was a main basis for the mayor's economic strategy.

No one who ventured a guess about the impact of the more well-known regional initiatives associated them with a negative impact, suggesting an essential optimism that could be useful to future community-regional planning efforts. The spending plans of the MTA were viewed as having, or being likely to have, the most favorable impact, with the Alameda Corridor a close second. These answers, however, reflected a focus on immediate construction expenditures rather than the long-term mobility or employment implications explored above. While RLA was the most well-known institution, it was also identified by 60 percent of the respondents as having had no effect on local neighborhood development. Slightly less than half of those respondents who had heard of SCAG indicated that it had no impact, and the bulk of the rest suggested that any positive impact was negligible.

We then asked these leaders about their involvement with the various regional initiatives. Respondents in only half the neighborhoods reported a direct involvement with RLA. In these neighborhoods, RLA had assisted community-based organizations (CBOs) on special projects such as finding vacant land for development (South Vermont), helping to paint a fire station (Inglewood), or providing RLA staff help in the development of a CBO's business plan (Westlake).[68] As for the Alameda Corridor Project, only two of the ten neighborhoods, Huntington Park and Watts, seemed to have any direct involvement: one organization in Huntington Park was going to furnish job training for work created as a result of the project, while a Watts organization was hoping to provide video-conferencing and other communication services for industries that might develop in the corridor. Many wondered whether the project would bypass the neighborhoods under study (our concern above), and leaders along the corridor itself were worried that they would not have the political and economic clout to shift some of the corridor's benefits in the direction of their residents.[69]

Despite the challenges and concerns regarding mobility and the overburdened bus system, community leaders tended to have a positive impression of the MTA because of the opportunities presented by its rail construction program. Respondents had actively advocated for metro rail stations in their neighborhoods (Inglewood and Pacoima), sought to implement innovative commuter programs (Huntington Park and Watts),[70] and worked to ensure that local residents were hired, and local firms contracted, for MTA projects (Boyle Heights, Belvedere, and Pacoima). One Northwest Pasadena respondent also felt that the Blue Line, which was designed to connect downtown Pasadena with downtown Los Angeles, would give residents access to a wider employment base; indeed, this line, which has since been delayed because of financial problems, is one of the few rail projects running through high-density areas with significant numbers of low-income residents (Pasadena and Highland Park).

As for SCAG, respondents from five neighborhoods (Huntington Park, Watts, Inglewood, Northwest Pasadena, and Southeast Pomona) reported using the agency's demographic statistical data, but even these individuals generally identified SCAG as an entity with little impact on daily economic development activities. Only one neighborhood's respondent (Southeast Pomona) had actively participated in SCAG meetings to develop a regional development/transportation strategy, while another respondent (from Inglewood) said that his area had made efforts to educate the community about the wide impact of SCAG plans. While SCAG had developed a Regional Advisory Council with nongovernmental representatives and hosted conferences and other activities for the general citizenry, our community leadership interviews suggested that much remained to be done in terms of connecting with the low-income public.

Finally, the Community Development Bank was well-known, partly because some of the CBOs surveyed had staff or leaders who had participated in various advisory committees that helped set up the bank. As noted earlier, some were concerned about whether sufficient funds would be directed toward their neighborhoods for local entrepreneurs and community organizations. In general, suspicion was higher among those who had not been involved in the planning for the bank, suggesting the perhaps obvious point that public outreach and involvement can help improve CBO and neighborhood receptivity to key regional strategies.

The Regional Disconnect

As the 1990s dawned, Los Angeles leaders began to recognize the need for a regional approach to revitalize and restructure the Southern California economy. While some of the resulting initiatives were relatively traditional in concept, such as the MTA's attempt to prime the regional pump with spending on transportation infrastructure, others, including SCAG's Regional Comprehensive Plan, the New Economy Project, and the second phase of RLA, were innovative in their emphasis on new industrial clusters and business networks. Indeed, while several of the other initiatives forewent the language of clusters, they also effectively targeted certain sectors: CALSTART, for example, focused on the potential for one particular industry, electric cars and other advanced transportation vehicles, while the Alameda Corridor Project was premised on Southern California's prominence as a center of international trade.

While this industry cluster approach built on the newest business theories and the experience of successful areas like the Silicon Valley (see chapter 6), the linkage between these strategies and economic development in poorer communities was weak. This was perhaps unsurprising—after all, we began this chapter by reviewing how development strategies have often "urban renewed" the poor out of their homes, while chapter 2 suggested how the poor have been "emerging clustered" out of their industrial jobs. Nevertheless, the failure of the seven key initiatives unveiled in Los Angeles County in the early 1990s to clearly connect with the needs of lower-income residents was worrisome in light of both Los Angeles's high poverty and the unsettled political climate provoked by the 1992 civil unrest.

Why did these various initiatives suffer from less than adequate attention to the issue of incorporating poorer communities into regional strategies? First, the traditional paradigm that has governed regional development has emphasized growth in the aggregate, with the need to connect all residents to economic opportunity often put aside in the interests of the "larger" economy. Second, the business leaders concerned about regional recovery did not reflect the composition and concerns of an increasingly diverse population. For example, our analysis of the boards of directors of the forty largest firms in Los Angeles County indicated that less than 5 percent of their members were African-American, Latino, or Asian-Pacific. Furthermore, the area's business leadership had few ties to community organizations: totaling all other board and organizational club memberships of this group of directors revealed that 61 percent were with other corporations, business policy groups, or professional associations; 22 percent were with foundations, educational institutions, hospitals, and arts groups; and only 2 percent were with youth or community organizations.[71]

It is hardly surprising, therefore, that efforts to link regional strategies to community development in lower-income and minority neighborhoods were an afterthought. Indeed, in our own interviews with several top business leaders and regional decision makers in Los Angeles, most drew a blank when asked whom they might nominate to a blue-ribbon commission to deal with the issue of poverty in Los Angeles County. The disconnect was further demonstrated by interviews with leaders in ten low-income neighborhoods in Los Angeles: our respondents were quite knowledgeable about regional trends but were often unaware or felt left out of key regional initiatives.

Given the potential in low-income communities—knowledgeable leaders and pockets of energetic working poor—we began to believe that the region could gain by better incorporating low-income communities into the development and implementation of regional efforts. However, to develop and sustain such a community- or equity-based regionalism, community leaders needed to believe that "thinking and linking" to the region was essential to pursuing their own dreams of successful neighborhood development. At the same time, regional leaders needed to recognize that any initiative that did not target poverty was inadequate for the area's future. To make this argument, we needed to stretch beyond Los Angeles and examine the experience in the nation as a whole. This is the focus of the next three chapters.

4

Community Builders and Concentrated Poverty

Making the Regional Connection

For almost half a century, politicians, policy practitioners, and others have debated what to do about urban poverty. The discussion has often centered on the relative merits of place- versus people-oriented approaches, with some arguing that we should address the neighborhoods where poverty is concentrated and others favoring programs that focus on the poor as individuals. This is an unfortunate way of characterizing policy. One view suggests that something is wrong with the community and the other that something is wrong with the person. Indeed, urban poverty is often driven by forces beyond the control of individuals or neighborhoods, including the overall degree of inequality, the extent of economic growth, and institutional barriers to the desegregation of poor people and minorities.

Those with the biggest stake in this debate—the people who live and work in high-poverty neighborhoods—are understandably frustrated by the apparent unwillingness of the larger society to focus adequate attention and resources on persistent urban poverty. Not surprisingly, community leaders and activists in these neighborhoods have concluded that if social and economic conditions are to improve, residents will have to rely primarily on themselves.

Partly as a result, a dynamic movement of grassroots community developers, now often termed "community builders," has emerged in low-income neighborhoods across the country during the past two decades. Composed of a diverse set of organizations and institutions, such as community development corporations (CDCs), churches, neighborhood associations, and social service agencies, this movement rejects the view of urban ghettoes and barrios as "tangles of pathology." It instead stresses the assets, or social capital, found within any neighborhood, and utilizes the techniques of community organizing and community-based development to create affordable housing, spur job development, initiate youth programs, and coordinate the myriad of activities necessary to revitalize both place and people.

This community development sector has grown in both numbers and sophistication during the past few decades. It has helped to rebuild troubled neighborhoods that some observers concluded had reached, in David Rusk's (1995) words, the "point of no return." And while government policy and business concern about urban poverty waxes and wanes, community developers and organizers are in it for the long haul.

But the stamina of community developers should not blind us to the fact that they cannot realistically achieve their goals without making links with institutions and resources outside poor neighborhoods. To the extent that these community builders have been successful, it has often been by forging alliances and partnerships with political and business forces that can provide the economic resources necessary to strengthen community institutions. For example, community groups have utilized the federal Community Reinvestment Act to generate loans from reluctant lenders and they have drawn on federal Community Development Block Grants and private foundation monies to fund the key components of the community-building approach. In coalition with their counterparts around the country, they have used whatever leverage they could to get federal, state, and local government, national and local business firms, and national and local foundations to invest in their activities, most recently under the National Community Development Initiative launched in 1991 (Walker and Weinheimer, 1998).

Yet, with some notable exceptions, the community builders have done little to link their efforts to the burgeoning regional efforts across the country. In our view, this would be a natural marriage: both the new regionalist and community-building perspectives are predicated on the importance of social capital and social networks. If we are right that the economic game is indeed shifting to the regional level, it is absolutely necessary that community builders operate at that level as well. If not, they risk becoming, in Jeremy Nowak's (1997) sobering words, "managers of decline."

In this chapter, we discuss the reasons that those primarily focused on community development issues should also learn to "think and link" to the region. We begin by exploring the forces that have contributed to the concentrated poverty that has spawned community development efforts. We then explore the place-based and people-based strategies community developers and others have taken and suggest how the growing community-building framework has attempted to couple the two in a new approach to neighborhood revitalization. We close by arguing that those community builders who have been able to form "strategic alliances" with regional actors have been more successful at reaching their goals of individual and community empowerment.

Space and Inequality

The Growing Spatial Gap

While the rich have always tried to insulate themselves from the poor, the last several decades have seen growing gaps between central city and suburb, and an increasing concentration of poverty within the central city itself. In the 85 largest metropolitan areas, for example, central-city per capita income as a percentage of suburban per capita income fell from 105 percent in 1960 to 84 percent in 1989 (Ledebur and Barnes, 1992: 2). In 1959, central-city poverty was 50 percent higher than in the suburbs; over the next twenty years, poverty rates fell due to overall prosperity and the expansion of social welfare programs, but they fell faster in the suburbs than in the central city. As a result, central-city poverty was twice that of the suburbs in 1970s and since then the gap has continued to widen. By 1996, central-city poverty was 19.6 percent while suburban poverty stood at 9.4 percent.[1]

These city-suburban gaps were created partly by outmigration of the better off and partly by the downward mobility of those remaining (Hill and Wolman, 1997; Madden, 1996). During the 1980s, America's suburban population grew at 16.1 percent, triple the rate for central cities; in the Northeast and Midwest, central-city populations actually declined. Those feeding the "exodus to the suburbs" were more likely to be middle-class two-parent households, while the single-parent, female-headed households that often fall below the poverty line tended to stay behind in central cities (Kasarda et al., 1997). Meanwhile, manufacturing employment continued to decline in central cities as routine back-office service functions and retail jobs have followed the population out to the suburbs.[2] Given inadequate public transportation, many central-city residents had a hard time getting to these jobs. Moreover, as we noted in chapter 2, isolation in the inner city has meant limited social networks for the poor and thus a relative lack of information about suburban job opportunities (Blank, 1997; Jargowsky, 1996).

This suburbanization of population and employment produced sprawl as well as inequality.[3] Many Americans no longer commute from suburban homes to central-city workplaces. Instead, they live *and* work in the suburbs—although given the low-density and auto-dependent patterns of development, they may commute long distances (or for a long time) between suburban homes and suburban workplaces. Between 1970 and 1990, for example, the Chicago area population increased only 4 percent, but the land in the region used for housing and commercial development increased 35 percent, with more than 450 square miles (an area twice the size of Chicago itself) converted from agricultural to urban uses (Katz, 1997). During the 1980s and into the 1990s, the city of Chicago experienced a net loss of jobs, while its suburbs (particularly outer suburbs) gained jobs—a trend some have termed "job sprawl" (Immergluck and Wiles, 1998).

In some sense, the suburbanization of America has been a "natural" evolution, a result of millions of separate decisions by individual consumers seeking a single-family home, improved public schools, and a better life for their families. Yet, as historian Kenneth Jackson argues in *Crabgrass Frontier* (1985), these consumer choices were shaped (in fact, subsidized) by federal government policies that both pushed people out of cities and pulled them into suburbs. These included highway-building policies that opened up the hinterlands to speculation and development; housing policies that offered government-insured mortgages to whites in suburbia (but not in cities); and bulldozer urban renewal policies that scattered the residents of working-class neighborhoods to blue-collar suburbs in order to make way for downtown business development.[4]

Partly because these policies encouraged moving further and further to outlying suburbs, economic segregation now exists not just between central cities and suburbs but among suburbs themselves. So-called inner-ring suburbs—those older suburbs right on the edge of the central city—now have many of the same problems as the cities they border.[5] In his study of the Minneapolis/St. Paul metropolitan area, for example, Myron Orfield (1997: 30) found that, between 1979 and 1989, median household income went down 4.7 percent in the inner-ring suburbs of the Twin Cities, while it went up 8.4 percent in the outer-lying eastern suburbs. Similarly, the eastern suburbs saw their property values increase 75 percent between 1980 and 1994 while property values went up only 2.5 percent in the inner-ring suburbs and declined 8.3 percent in the central cities.

The general result has been an increasing concentration of the poor within metropolitan areas. The spatial concentration of poverty increased in 25 of the 30 largest metropolitan areas over the 1970s (Massey and Eggers, 1993). Over the next decade, the process of class segregation continued to worsen in most metropolitan areas (Abramson, Tobin, and Vandergoot,

1995; Coulton et al., 1996; Jargowsky, 1996). In his recent book *Poverty and Place,* Paul Jargowsky (1997) found that high-poverty areas grew in almost every possible way between 1970 and 1990: in the number of census tracts, in total population, as a percentage of the overall population, in the percentage of poor persons in them, and in geographical extent.

Concentrated Poverty and Urban Neighborhoods

The factors driving poverty are often global or national in scale: increased vulnerability to international trade can constrain wages; economic expansion or recession has a direct impact on employment; and national decisions regarding welfare eligibility can bring children and their parents above or below the poverty line. But while these factors may explain changes in poverty, they do not explain the concentration of poverty; after all, the poor could be scattered randomly within metropolitan areas.

To be sure, most of Americas's 40 million poor people do not live in neighborhoods characterized by concentrated poverty. In 1990, only 17.9 percent (3.7 million individuals) of all poor people living in metropolitan areas (20.9 million individuals) lived in extreme-poverty census tracts (in which the poverty rate exceeds 40 percent). However, this is a sharp increase from the 12.4 percent of all poor who lived in such tracts in 1970. And the degree of concentration is much higher for minorities: 33.5 percent of the black poor and 22.1 percent of the Latino poor lived in such tracts, while only 6.3 percent of all white poor did (Jargowsky, 1997: 41).[6]

The higher degree of poverty concentration among minorities stems from two factors: they are more likely to be poor *and* they are more likely to be segregated. In most major American cities, more than 70 percent of the population (and more than 80 percent in many cities) would have to move to achieve full integration, a level of segregation that has hardly changed since the 1960s.[7] Sixty-two percent of African-Americans live in blocks that are 60 percent or more black, and 30 percent in neighborhoods that are 90 percent or more black. Forty percent of Latinos live in blocks that are 60 percent or more Latino. At least two out of three white Americans live in essentially all-white neighborhoods. While this racial pattern contributes to poverty concentration, the problem is not reducible to money: higher income and well-educated blacks are just as residentially isolated from whites as blacks with low incomes and low levels of education.[8]

In any case, although whites were nearly 60 percent of the poor in 1990, they were only around 20 percent of those living in areas of concentrated poverty. In contrast, African-Americans composed over half of the population of extreme-poverty census tracts in metropolitan areas in 1990, though they were only 12.6 percent of the population of metropolitan areas. Latinos were 10 percent of the metro population but nearly 25 percent of those living in extreme-poverty tracts (Jargowsky, 1997: 63). Concentrated poverty, in short, often has a face of color.

The Consequences of Concentrated Poverty

The geographic concentration of poor people magnifies the problems they face. Certain challenges—infant mortality, adolescent pregnancy, victimization by or participation in crime—are more likely when poor individuals reside in a predominantly poor neighborhood than when they are distributed more randomly throughout the metropolitan region.[9] Concentrated poverty even has negative effects on health (see Fossett and Perloff, 1995; Polednak, 1997; and Gortmaker and Wise, 1997). The social conditions in high-poverty areas, including high crime rates, reduce resident access by dissuading health care providers from locating there. Meanwhile, health risks are more severe, including higher rates of exposure to frequent drug use and sexually transmitted diseases (including AIDS), injuries from firearms, lead paint poisoning, and environmental hazards.[10]

The economic effects of poverty concentration most clearly manifest themselves in the realms of job access and wealth creation.[11] The suburbanization of employment has brought a widening "spatial mismatch" between the residential location of the poor and the emerging job opportunities.[12] The generally poorer quality of schools in poor neighborhoods limits individual educational advancement, worsening the problem of "skill mismatch" as well. The concentration of poverty in urban areas also affects the poor in terms of networks and role models, feeding into a downward spiral of economic isolation (Pastor and Adams, 1996; O'Regan, 1993; Hughes, 1995).

On the wealth side, home ownership rates are obviously low among the poor but they are especially low for those living in areas of high poverty. For example, research suggests that bank and insurance redlining has restricted the opportunity to own a home even for those residents of concentrated poverty neighborhoods who can afford it.[13] Moreover, even when poor people do own their homes, they rarely appreciate in value. And since the major way most U.S. households accumulate wealth is through home ownership, it becomes difficult to sustain or develop savings (Oliver and Shapiro, 1995; Odland and Balzer, 1979). In turn, the resulting lack of collateral affects the ability to approach financial institutions for business loans, and thereby limits the formation of new small businesses.

The growing geographic segregation of the poor thus increases income inequality directly by affecting access to jobs, education, networks, and health. Geographic differences between poor and rich also increase social distance, making it easier to enact class legislation whose negative consequences are borne by the poor and the central cities they inhabit (Paget, 1998; Weir, 1995; and Stanfield, 1997). The color of poverty in most urban areas lends another degree of separation, reducing the sense of commonality that could sustain a more sensitive approach.

The Emergence of Community Development

People, Place, and Policy

How then do we address the "geography of opportunity" for the urban poor?[14] Traditionally, community developers and policy makers have focused on two approaches, often termed the "people" and "place" orientations.[15]

The so-called people-oriented approach to addressing urban poverty focuses on helping the urban poor escape the contagion effects of extreme-poverty neighborhoods. While some people-based approaches stress job training that can increase "mobility" in the labor market, some strategies are even more literally about moving people around. Housing mobility programs, such as Chicago's Gatreaux program and the federal Moving to Opportunity program, give the poor vouchers so they can rent apartments in the suburbs where there are better job prospects for the parents and schools for the children (Briggs, 1997; Rosenbaum, 1995). Education programs, such as Boston's Metco program, give poor inner-city children opportunities to attend schools in middle-income suburbs. Finally, there are "reverse commuting" programs, such as Chicago's Suburban Jobs Link program and the federal Bridges to Work initiative, that focus on transportation access to jobs outside the inner city.[16]

While people-oriented strategies focus on deconcentrating the poor, place-oriented strategies focus on bringing better housing and job opportunities to troubled areas. Many federal programs fall under this rubric, including public housing, Model Cities, Urban Development Action Grants, Community Development Block Grants, revenue sharing, the Community Reinvestment Act (the federal antiredlining law), enterprise zones, and now empowerment zones (Halpern, 1995). Big-city mayors and downtown business leaders have often supported these approaches, in part because funds could also be used to revitalize declining central business districts and/or attract private business and jobs to inner cities.

Another set of actors pushing for a place-based approach has been the growing number of nonprofit community development corporations

(CDCs). This bias toward place is not surprising: most CDCs work in specific geographic neighborhoods or clusters of adjacent neighborhoods and typically have neighborhood stakeholders—residents, clergy, merchants, and others—on their boards.[17] With political survival tied to the local community or neighborhood, CDCs naturally focus on serving local constituents.

However, CDCs and other community-based organizations (CBOs) have often struggled with politicians and business over the meaning of improving place, especially since physical improvements in housing, infrastructure, and neighborhood business run the risk of displacing the poor via "gentrification." Partly as a result, CDCs have attempted to go beyond a "bricks-and-mortar" approach to housing and neighborhood development. Most recently, they have broadened their perspective to include "comprehensive" community development and have begun to form the core base for a new "community-building" movement (Walker and Weinheimer, 1998; Gitell and Vidal, 1998; Kingsley, McNeely, and Gibson, 1997; Kretzman and McKnight, 1993).

CDCs, Urban Development, and Housing

The first generation of CDCs grew out of the political turmoil and policy efforts of the 1960s, particularly as community activists formed organizations to gain "community control" over federal and local efforts to "revitalize" their neighborhoods. By 1970, there were about one hundred CDCs in the country; a decade later, the number had grown tenfold. By the early 1990s, more than 2,200 nonprofit CDCs were engaged in a wide variety of housing and economic improvement activities in cities across the country.[18]

This rapid expansion was fostered by private philanthropies, especially the Ford Foundation. The federal government also provided support, initiating a pilot program to support CDCs (Title VII of the Community Services Act of 1972) and paying for some CDC operating costs through several other federal programs such as the Neighborhood Self-Help Development program and the Neighborhood Development Demonstration program of the U.S. Department of Housing and Urban Development (HUD), and the Department of Labor's Comprehensive Employment and Training Act (CETA) program.

While many CDCs initially focused on the delivery of social services, the pressing need for shelter in poor communities, a history of housing struggles, and the availability of funds from HUD's housing programs led to increasing attention to housing production. In San Francisco's Mission district, for example, community activists who fought the city's plan to tear down low-income apartments and promote upscale development formed the Mission Housing Development Corporation in 1971. This CDC has since developed over 1,300 units of low-income housing while continuing to serve as an advocate on neighborhood issues. In Boston's racially mixed Jamaica Plain neighborhood, a plan by state and city officials to build a highway through the community led organizers to form Urban Edge. By the early 1990s, the group had developed over six hundred housing units; started a company to manage the apartments; begun sponsoring youth programs, block clubs, and crime watch groups; and helped form a neighborhood coalition to recruit a YMCA, a bank, and other businesses into the area. In New York, the country's oldest CDC, the Bedford Stuyvesant Restoration Corporation, has restored 4,000 housing units and sponsored various retail developments.

Indeed, about 90 percent of the nation's CDCs are involved in housing development (National Congress for Community Economic Development, 1995). One study estimated that between 1960 and 1990, nonprofit groups had built or rehabilitated 736,000 housing units with federal funds.[19] More than half of these were completed since the 1980s, accounting for about 13 percent of all the federally subsidized housing provided during this period. In some cities, however, CDCs play a much larger role, accounting for 50 percent or more of new and rehabilitated housing (National Congress for Community Economic Development, 1995). In many American cities, nonprofit developers have moved from the margins to the mainstream and are now the backbone of the low-income housing delivery system (Yin, 1998; Metzger, 1998).

The importance of recent CDC housing activities is a reflection of both their maturation and the shifting balance of federal incentives.[20] During the 1960s and 1970s, federal housing programs (Section 236, 221d3, and especially Section 8, new construction and rehabilitation) provided almost 100 percent of the financing and insurance needed to develop low-income housing, making this market relatively simple, risk-free, and profitable. Since many for-profit developers took advantage of these housing programs, the early CDCs had only a small slice of this growing federally assisted housing pie. When Washington turned off the low-income housing spigot in the 1980s, most for-profit housing developers left the field. In many cities, nonprofits were "the only organizations willing and able to assemble the multiple sources of funding necessary to produce low-income housing" (Keyes et al.,1996).

The general scale of CDC housing activities is small: while about 45 percent of CDCs have produced at least one hundred units of housing since they started, CDCs average only about thirty housing units a year. Nonetheless, a growing number of CDCs have developed the sophistication to sponsor large-scale residential developments with several hundred units involving a complex mix of funding sources (Walker and Weinheimer, 1998). Moreover, CDC-sponsored housing developments are generally better-designed, and provide more resident services, than housing owned by private landlords and many public housing agencies (Bratt, 1989; Vidal, 1992; Walker, 1993). In a few cities, where CDCs are sophisticated and have the strong backing of local government, CDCs have made significant strides in combating social and economic deterioration in troubled neighborhoods.[21] Indeed, the presence of well-run CDC-sponsored housing in a neighborhood can help catalyze other positive changes, such as a reduction in crime and increase in property values (Goetz, Lam, and Heitlinger, 1996). In light of the adverse social, political, and financial conditions under which they have had to operate, especially the necessity of working with a crazy quilt of subsidies from public and private sources, the CDC track record on the housing front is remarkable.

Beyond Shelter: CDCs, Neighborhood Development, and Advocacy

Of course, healthy neighborhoods need job-creating businesses and retail services as well as housing. As a result, about one-quarter of the nation's CDCs are involved in some kind of economic development activity, acting as catalysts to bring new business enterprises into their neighborhoods or actually becoming entrepreneurs themselves.

As catalysts, CDCs often help organize associations of neighborhood merchants and sometimes encourage supermarket or drugstore chains to open new facilities in existing neighborhood commercial districts.[22] CDCs also administer loan funds for facade improvements by local merchants and work with local governments to plant trees or expand parking facilities. Some CDCs have used the federal Community Reinvestment Act to persuade lenders to expand small business and microenterprise loans to entrepreneurs in their communities. A growing number of "community reinvestment agreements" include such measures as small-business loan funds jointly administered by CDCs and lenders and equity pools and technical assistance programs for small neighborhood businesses.

In their role as community entrepreneurs, some CDCs have tackled major commercial projects, developing inner-city shopping malls and persuading supermarket chains to become anchor tenants. In Boston, Urban Edge induced Fleet Bank to become the anchor tenant in a shopping mall that included a drugstore and other retail businesses; this was the first bank branch in the Egleston Square neighborhood in over twenty years. Other CDCs have created industrial parks to attract new businesses to old neighborhoods. Again in Boston, the Jamaica Plain Neighborhood Development Corporation transformed a vacant brewery into an office and industrial complex housing a wide variety of businesses. In Los Angeles, the East Los Angeles Community Union (TELACU) turned a shuttered tire factory into a commercial outlet and created an active industrial park.[23]

Direct employment training is also a prominent CDC activity (29 percent of all CDCs have such employment development programs; see National Congress for Community Economic Development, 1995). Under a variety of past federal programs, such as Model Cities, the Comprehensive Employment and Training Act (CETA), and the Job Training Partnership Act (JPTA) program, community organizations have set up job training programs to help low-income individuals "market" themselves to potential employers. They complement these efforts with child care programs, literacy classes, school-to-work partnerships, youth counseling, and other activities that contribute indirectly to workforce preparation.

Finally, 66 percent of CDCs are engaged in "advocacy and community building" (National Congress for Community Economic Development, 1995). For example, CDCs and other community groups often negotiate with powerful private and public institutions to guarantee that local residents and adjacent communities will receive a share of the jobs and business created by high-impact development projects such as sports complexes, convention centers, new subway lines, or the expansion of university or medical complexes. CDCs and other community-based organizations served as the voices and bargaining agents to make sure that inner-city residents and neighborhoods received at least some of the benefits of projects such as the new White Sox Stadium in Chicago, the Century Freeway in Los Angeles, and the Artery Project in Boston.

CDC staff and board members often also advocate for broader policy changes, conducting research on social problems, educating the public about issues, and lobbying government officials. This advocacy role is crucial: altering a relevant federal, state, or local rule can have far more impact on creating jobs or eradicating poverty than the arduous day-to-day efforts of developing a retail mall. In Boston, Pittsburgh, and elsewhere, CDCs have attacked banks' redlining practices by participating in research, protests, and negotiations through the federal Community Reinvestment Act (Dreier, 1991; Squires, 1992). In Chicago, Boston, San Diego, and Cleveland, CDCs forged broad coalitions to pressure their city governments to expand municipal resources targeted for low-income housing.[24] In San Antonio, Pittsburgh, and other cities, CDCs and other community organizations have pushed local and state governments, as well as major employers, to set up job-training and hiring programs targeted to low-income neighborhoods and people (Harrison and Weiss, 1998). In Detroit and, to a lesser extent, in Los Angeles, CDCs played a key role in shaping the city's application for a federal empowerment zone designation.[25]

Community Builders and Concentrated Poverty

Toward Community Building

CDCs and other community developers walk a tightrope between people and place. They seek to help lift low-income people out of poverty, and they know that the best way to do this is to help them get decent-paying jobs. But does it really matter if the jobs are located *within* the neighborhood? Why not simply help people learn about good jobs outside their community, and then help them develop the skills and transportation access necessary to obtain those jobs? While such a people-oriented approach has appeal and could be cheaper than the incentive approach to attracting business, CDCs necessarily worry that successful families will flee the neighborhood, further concentrating poverty and its ill effects. Their goal is to help create healthy neighborhoods where residents have sufficient incomes to raise a family and want to stay in order to enjoy access to jobs, retail services, and decent, affordable housing.

Partly to pursue this difficult balance, many CDCs have become deeply involved in what are now termed "comprehensive community initiatives."[26] Also known as "community building," these efforts reject "a programmatic approach to poverty, in favor of efforts that catalyze personal relationships and social networks to improve community life" (Walsh, 1997: v). Indeed, the community builders go beyond the old place versus people debate. While they are geographically rooted in certain communities, they recognize that the real way to attract business and residents to a place is through revitalizing the intangible asset of community fabric and community relationships; while they are targeted toward poor people, they work specifically to reverse the negative effects of concentrated poverty that impede development in specific areas even as they expand networks connecting the poor with available resources.

In some sense, this new community-building movement returns to the original focus on community-based organizing and empowerment that characterized the early CDC movement.[27] And it is beginning to make a difference. In places as diverse as Baltimore, Savannah, and the Bronx, community builders are contributing to an improvement in various indicators of poverty, health, and other measures (Walsh, 1997). The community-building movement has also grown beyond its roots in CDCs to include churches, grassroots organizers, and labor unions.[28] Even the Department of Housing and Urban Development has launched a "Community Builders Fellowship" program that aims to revitalize urban areas by placing innovative professionals into community service agencies for two to four years to pursue comprehensive development strategies.[29]

Sailing against the Wind

This welcome shift to community building, however, cannot fully confront the challenges facing CDCs in low-income neighborhoods. Many of the trends that deeply impact these communities—the decline of manufacturing, the proliferation of low-wage service sector jobs, widening income disparities, the suburbanization of jobs and middle-class residents, the persistence of racial discrimination by lenders, employers, and others—are outside the control of CDCs. And while the community development movement has made remarkable progress, particularly in terms of housing, their efforts have made only a tiny dent in the overall housing problem and, more generally, in reversing the decline of the urban neighborhoods they seek to improve.

On a national scale, for example, CDCs have not produced sufficient housing to significantly improve the housing crisis facing the poor. In no single year in the past two decades has the CDC sector added more than 40,000 housing units; this pales in comparison with HUD's own conservative estimate of 5.3 million families with "worst case" housing needs.[30] Of course, this is less an indictment of the CDC movement, which must rely heavily on government subsidies to provide housing affordable to low-income families, than it is of the paucity of public funds targeted for affordable housing. Moreover, Nowak (1997: 5) argues that affordable housing efforts, which are often focused on the inner city since suburban "snob zoning" practices can preclude development of low-income house siting in many jurisdictions, may "reinforce the segregation of the poor by building housing in the worst employment markets."[31]

On the employment side, CDC housing activities have generated some construction jobs as well as jobs managing and maintaining housing (which may or may not go to inner-city residents). This, however, is not a major job generator, and one survey estimated that all CDC development activities have generated only about 68,000 permanent jobs, a number equivalent to one week of normal job creation in the U.S. economy during 1997.[32]

Of course, CDCs also create employment opportunities for local residents by attracting and sponsoring government-funded social services. But these programs do not, on their own, contribute substantially to strengthening neighborhood economies.[33] Meanwhile, CDC-sponsored economic development generally involves retail enterprises, such as supermarkets and pharmacies, which are essential for neighborhood business districts but tend to offer low-wage jobs.

As a result, some observers are quite skeptical about whether the new community-building effort will be successful at tackling the problems of concentrated poverty. David Rusk (1995), for example, examined the impact of CDCs in eleven cities. He looked at one neighborhood in each city in which CDCs had been engaged in community-building efforts for at least two decades. He found that in each case, the economic circumstances of these neighborhoods had declined between 1970 and 1990, as gauged by median household income, poverty rate, and other indicators, measured in both absolute terms and in terms of its relationship to the fortunes of the larger metro areas. These neighborhoods grew poorer not because poor families moved in, but because many middle-class families moved out.[34]

Rusk and others acknowledge that the CDCs' efforts might have helped make these neighborhoods better than they might otherwise have been. One could also argue that the CDCs lacked the resources to have more than a marginal impact: the largest and most successful CDCs generally have too few staff, too few subsidies, and too little access to credit to seriously address the myriad problems facing these neighborhoods. But Rusk contends that even if the CDCs and other community builders had dramatically more resources and significantly improved their numbers and their organizational skills, they would still be fighting a heroic but ultimately futile uphill battle against the larger forces undermining these areas.

Indeed, Nowak (1997: 4) insists that these organizations, on their own, "cannot reverse the downward spiral." He argues that even under the best circumstances, place-oriented community development approaches are inherently limited. "Just take a drive through the most blighted sections of Philadelphia, Baltimore, or Detroit, and it becomes clear that massive development intervention is required to restore the ordinary mechanisms of the marketplace and make the area a place in which anyone with choice will want to remain or locate." As a result, Nowak (1997: 4) asserts, "Even the best community-based development efforts function as managers of decline as much as catalysts of significant renewal."

Making the Regional Connection

In short, Nowak, Rusk, Hughes, and other analysts see a "disconnect" between the efforts of the community-building movement and the realities of regional economies and labor markets. They argue that while community builders are adding a handful of housing units and jobs in low income neighborhoods, the major economic and social forces in metropolitan areas, especially the suburban location of employment and population growth, are tilting in the other direction.

As a result, community builders need to widen their horizons and focus on the powerful economic and demographic forces that have "destabilized the cities and neighborhoods in which community institutions operate" (Katz, 1997: 32). They need, in other words, to link their neighborhood development strategies to a broader regional agenda, helping inner-city residents connect to metropolitan labor markets and forging political coalitions so that community-based organizations have a "seat at the table" of regional decision making.

A number of successful efforts by community builders to link inner-city residents to good jobs and to policy making within metropolitan regions give us reason for cautious optimism. As we detail in chapter 7, a growing number of CDCs, including Nowak's own Delaware Valley Community Reinvestment Fund (DVCRF), are enjoying success in employment training and placement by taking account of dynamics in their various regional labor markets.[35] Some CDCs, such as the New Community Corporation in Newark, the Center for Employment Training in San Jose, Project QUEST in San Antonio, and Chicanos por La Causa in Phoenix, have linked their job-training programs to regional employers as well as to business enterprises sponsored by the CDC itself.[36] Other CDCs, including WIRE-Net in Cleveland, the Chicago Jobs Council, COPS/Metro Alliance in San Antonio, and the Pittsburgh Partnership for Neighborhood Development, have taken the lead in establishing networks (or "business alliances") with specific employers and community colleges, that connect "neighborhood residents with mainstream institutions that can provide them with quality training and, eventually, lasting jobs" and thus build "bridges between inner city residents and the world of work" (Harrison, 1995: viii).

In a variety of cities, including Chicago, Boston, and St. Louis, community-based organizations are forging coalitions with their counterparts in inner-ring suburbs to address issues of neighborhood decline and employment conditions.[37] In a number of metropolitan areas, CDCs and other community-building organizations have also begun to encourage regional mobility by creating affordable housing outside of traditional low-income neighborhoods, affording inner-city residents an out from high-poverty areas. For example, the Metropolitan Boston Housing Partnership (MBHP) began in the 1980s as a consortium of Boston CDCs to develop low-income housing in inner city neighborhoods, but now works in the larger Boston metropolitan area. Like the Leadership Council for Metropolitan Open Communities in Chicago (which ran the Gautreaux program), MBHP administers about 3,000 Section 8 certificates and vouchers in 34 cities in the Boston area. It also runs HUD's Moving to Opportunity program in the Boston area. It provides housing counseling, search assistance, and landlord outreach. In the San Francisco area, the BRIDGE Housing Corporation, a regional nonprofit founded in 1983, develops mixed-income housing (more than 6,000 units by 1994) in suburban communities.[38]

In general, new networks and partnerships, particularly at the regional level, have lent strength to community builders. For example, in Cleveland, Chicago, San Francisco, Baltimore, Providence, Pittsburgh, New York, Minneapolis, and other cities, corporate leaders, government officials, foundations, and CDCs have formed public-private-community partnerships to raise operating funds for CDCs, offer financing for housing projects, streamline approvals, and expand the capacity of nonprofits to undertake large-scale development. Joan Walsh (1997) notes the positive effect of regional partnerships between community builders and government agencies, specific employers, educational institutions, and other groups in her discussion of the Atlanta Project, the Sandtown-Winchester "Community Building in Partnership" project in Baltimore, and the Urban Strategies Council in Oakland.

A key ingredient in the creation of these public-private-community partnerships, and in the numerical growth and improved capacity of the community development sector, has been the support of nonprofit intermediary institutions such as the Local Initiatives Support Corporation (LISC), the Enterprise Foundation, the Neighborhood Reinvestment Corporation, and many others.[39] To pursue community development with a regional focus, community builders will also need the sort of technical assistance intermediaries have provided for the construction of affordable housing. Training could focus on developing community capacities to identify business clusters, create new employment-training opportunities, and evaluate broad regional policies, especially the intersections of land use and economic development.[40]

Some may worry that yet another round of institutional capacity building, this time about regional opportunities, simply postpones the urgent need for immediate and localized action. Others may fret that a focus on the region will dilute the ability of neighborhood groups to coalesce and meet their own goals. But with the economic action moving to the regional level, community builders will have to follow. "Thinking and linking" to the region, as well as forming new metropolitan alliances to push for helpful policies, may be one way to reverse the concentrated urban poverty that has shipwrecked so many individual and community dreams.

Bonding and Bridging

Community development is a complex process. Neighborhoods plagued by poverty and scarred by neglect do not recover effortlessly, and the concentration of poverty in particular areas tends to make things worse. Traditional community development models have often focused on place—on resurrecting the physical locales where poor people live. Such approaches have been counterposed to the people-oriented strategies that target skill acquisition and mobility.[41] An emerging wave of community builders has offered a unique synthesis: one that starts with the neighborhood but stresses the need to develop the social attachments, networks, and leadership that can make it healthy. Community builders have, in short, retained the emphasis on place but shifted the focus to the people that make the place.

This new community-building movement has great appeal. It seeks to strengthen the social bonds of poor communities and it conjures images of the sort of community spirit and voluntarism valued by most Americans. Yet many of the forces affecting poor communities cannot be addressed by even the most generous dollops of self-reliance, self-help, and community organizing. As Walsh (1997: vi) notes in her review of model community development efforts,

> Community builders know inner city neighborhoods cannot
> rebuild themselves alone, when race and class discrimination and
> decades of disinvestment have done so much to fray the social
> fabric of urban communities. Thus these initiatives seek to build
> relationships between the poor and the powerful, to develop a
> sense of mutual obligation and reciprocity, a new social contract
> that keeps the urban poor from simply being the discards of a
> volatile, changing economy.

In short, the best of those in the community-building movement have learned that they need to focus simultaneously on two sorts of social capital: "bonding," or within-neighborhood relationships that constitute a community; and "bridging," or outside connections to private business, local government, and other key actors that help to leverage resources and policy.

In our view, the most likely arena for such bridging, given both the shift toward regional economies and the likely ability of CDCs and others to act more effectively at the subnational level, is the metropolitan region in which community builders work. In taking up this regional challenge, which inevitably means both forming alliances with and pressuring business and government for new approaches and decisions, leading CDCs and community organizers can return the community development movement back to its original roots in advocacy and action.

Forming a metropolitan community is itself complex. Community developers and regional leaders must see a clear set of reasons for coming together. In this chapter, we have suggested the rationale for community-based organizations: neighborhoods and their CDCs are affected by outside forces and seem to do better when they connect with others to secure both resources and influence over the key policy variables that set the terms of urban life. But regional leaders must also understand that the success of a region is diminished when its economy and society are scarred by poverty and despair. Suburbanites must recognize, as former HUD secretary Henry Cisneros has stressed, that "political borders do not seal off the problem of concentrated poverty" (Cisneros, 1995:15). We turn to this side of the argument in chapter 5.

5

Only as Strong as the Team

Poverty, Equity, and Regional Growth

Traditional arguments for helping the central city and its residents have relied on a combination of noblesse oblige and raw political power. Cities, it was rightly suggested, had experienced the exodus of middle-class residents and been weakened by the resulting suburbanization of employment and taxes. The guilty parties, suburbanites and business, should therefore transfer resources back to the central city, perhaps through federal taxes, transfers, and other policies. While some of the political will to do so would come from suburban residents—perhaps because they suddenly recognized the social consequences of their individually rational decisions—big city mayors could help matters along by using their weight in key national contests to direct policy and dollars toward central cities.

In recent years, noblesse oblige has given way to a politics of resentment and separation. Urban dwellers and their leaders may blame suburbanites for "abandoning" the city but suburban residents and their leaders point to urban problems of crime, economic distress, and fiscal trauma as a rationale for suburbs to claim a separate fate. Meanwhile, the suburbanization of the electorate has diminished the importance of the urban vote in Congress and statehouses, leading to tightened purse strings when it comes to subsidies to cities and their residents.[1]

Partly as a response, some big-city mayors and urban advocates have stressed the common fate of suburbanites and inner-city dwellers (see, for example, Peirce, 1993; Rusk, 1995; and especially Cisneros, 1995). Myron Orfield (1997), for example, has argued that problems once confined to central cities, such as crime, gangs, and unemployment, are increasingly evident in suburban settings of trimmed lawns and tract houses. While suburban communities may try to erect higher drawbridges of freeways and community gates, eventually urban problems leak out, first to inner-ring suburbs and later beyond. Having a "good" suburb in a "bad" region is no defense. Thus, we all have an interest in dealing now with such problems where they are most severe, that is, in the inner city.

Another variant of this argument offers a more "win-win" logic. This view suggests that those cities and suburbs that can cohere around a single metropolitan or regional agenda do better economically and socially than those that remain balkanized. When there are weak economic links or disgruntled partners, regional social capital is diminished and economic growth slows. In short, the region is only as strong as the team: the whole will not do well if individual members are left out. Therefore, central-city poverty is everyone's concern.

But are the fates of central city and suburban residents really linked? In this chapter, we begin with a brief discussion of the disappearing distinction between city and suburb, then review a series of studies that attempt to demonstrate that more equitable regions fare better in terms of their economic fates. Much of this research is beset by methodological problems, especially the challenges presented by the simultaneous relationship between metropolitan income growth and poverty alleviation. That is, while lowering poverty might build trust and promote growth, faster growth will also tighten labor markets and allow some residents to work their way out of poverty. We attempt to correct for these methodological problems in our own econometric study of the relationship between growth and poverty reduction in seventy-four regions in the United States. While our study also has its limits, we find that, even controlling for the fact that growth itself probably lowers poverty and inequality, improvements in various equity measures are likely to improve regional performance and therefore benefit city dwellers and suburbanites alike.

Growth and Poverty in America's Regions

Our Common Fate

There are several reasons that poverty, especially central-city poverty, should be of common concern to a region's urban and suburban residents. The first is quite simply that the distinction between city and suburb is disappearing. In Los Angeles, for example, problems that once were confined to the inner city are spilling over into surrounding communities. The 1990 poverty rates in the industrial cities of Bell, Bell Gardens, and Huntington Park were a full eight percentage points above those of the City of Los Angeles, while poverty rates in El Monte, Rosemead, and several other San

Gabriel Valley cities were about the same as in Los Angeles. Traditionally middle-class Glendale is a bellwether of the change: poverty there in 1990 was only four percentage points below the level in the City of Los Angeles and the gap has been narrowing since. And while poverty remains a prominent feature of areas like South Central, East Los Angeles, and mid-City, the within-city suburbs of the San Fernando Valley are not immune: by 1995, the poverty rate in that area had risen above national levels, with pockets in Pacoima and elsewhere exhibiting problems that rival those of the so-called inner city.[2]

The ethnic changes in Los Angeles County have also helped to erase a key aspect of the city-suburb distinction: the concentration of minority populations in the inner city. As noted in chapter 2, over half the cities that comprise Los Angeles County are "majority-minority." Meanwhile, the city's traditional "internal" suburb, the San Fernando Valley, has seen the Anglo population fall from 92 percent of residents in 1960 to 57 percent in 1990. These trends, paralleled in some other urban areas (see Frey and Geverdt, 1998), indicate that the historical avenue of Anglo escape to ethnically isolated suburbs is becoming less and less of an option. Moreover, the suburban poverty rates cited above suggest that the ability of individuals of any ethnicity to insulate themselves from the overall societal problems of economic restructuring, falling incomes, and crime is steadily diminishing.

Suburban residents and policy makers often think otherwise, believing that they can avoid the problems of their central-city neighbors. The divergence of interest is partly fiscal: Janet Rothenberg Pack (1998) has found that cities with a significant degree of concentrated poverty tend to spend more on both poverty-related services (such as health, hospitals, and public welfare) and non-poverty-related services, such as police, fire, courts, and general administrative functions. Suburbs often seek to avoid these costs, and therefore enjoy lower taxes and higher quality services, by zoning out affordable housing and otherwise excluding poor residents (see Summers, 1997; Chernick and Reschovsky, 1997). As a result, "the suburbs are likely to remain attractive when compared with the declining city neighborhoods"; because of this, "the benefits of cooperation [between city and suburb] . . . may not be readily apparent" (Voith, 1992:24). But, just like having the nicest house in an increasingly distressed neighborhood provides only a relative shield against declining property values, residing in the best gated community within a fragmented and increasingly impoverished region only hides the signs of potential and actual collapse.

As a result, reducing inner-city poverty should be an objective not only for those in the central city itself but also for politicians and policy makers who represent areas ringing the central city. Savitch et al. (1993: 347) note that "the blight of the inner city casts a long shadow. Companies will not grow or thrive in, or move to, a declining environment." Businesses often see central-city deterioration as a signal of gaps in labor force skills, infrastructural investments, and protection of property, and may decide to locate manufacturing, service, and retail activities in another region rather than in an outlying suburb. After all, the growing permeability of city and suburb suggests to investors and residents alike that the inner city may be showing the region its suboptimal future. By contrast, making the central city work offers a light at the end of everyone's tunnel.

The Research: Empirical Findings and Methodological Issues

The growing recognition of the common fate of cities and suburbs has led many researchers to explore empirically the relationship between suburban and central-city incomes.[3] Voith (1992: 30), for example, conducted a study of twenty-eight metropolitan areas in the Northeast and North Central parts of the United States, concluding that "it is uncommon to find suburbs that are experiencing robust growth while the central city is in severe decline."

In a study done for the League of Cities, Ledebur and Barnes (1993) examined seventy-eight metropolitan areas in the United States and found that those regions with the widest gap between central-city and suburban incomes in 1980 had the most sluggish job growth during the following decade.[4] Furthermore, the twenty-five fastest growing suburbs (identified by change in median household income) all had central cities that also experienced income growth.[5] Barnes and Ledebur argue that this correlation indicates economic interdependence between central-city and suburban incomes. The authors also argue that the revitalization of the inner city has large multiplier impacts: when the incomes of central-city residents in their sample increased, the incomes of people living in that city's suburbs increased by an even larger amount.[6]

Focusing on fifty-nine metropolitan areas, Savitch et al. (1993) reach the similar conclusion that wider city-suburb disparities increase the likelihood of regional stagnation. Moreover, they argue that the links between city and suburban incomes have become closer over time.[7] Their finding: "Neither suburbs nor central cities are self-sufficient" (Savitch et al., 1993: 341). The case, it would seem, is complete. Equity and growth go hand in hand; city and suburban prospects are linked.[8]

While the central message of this body of work is encouraging—greater equality and concern about the central city will lead to growing economic benefits for the entire region—much of the research suffers from methodological problems. For example, the link between central-city and suburban incomes offered by Savitch et al. (1993) is established by simple correlations and bivariate regressions. The correlation of city and suburban incomes cannot be taken as evidence that central-city prosperity necessarily generates wealth for suburban residents; some exogenous (outside) variable, such as the level of federal spending, fast-growing business clusters in newly emerging industries, and so on, could be the factor triggering growth in both the central city and the surrounding suburbs of a region.[9]

Even if it is not an exogenous factor causing both city and suburban incomes to rise, we can hardly be certain which income increase is causing the other. A "multiplier effect" derived from a bivariate regression of changes in suburban income on changes in the income of a suburb's associated central city assumes a particular cause-and-effect relationship. Yet one can easily imagine a booming suburban economy dragging the central city out of its doldrums, perhaps because the resulting demand for professional services favors firms disproportionately located in the central cities (for reasons of agglomeration economies) or because inner-city residents can fill entry-level service jobs in suburban areas via reverse commuting. In this case, it is suburban growth driving central-city prosperity and not the other way around.

The problem of causation has not gone unrecognized. Ledebur and Barnes (1992), for example, acknowledge that the positive relationship they find between central-city/suburb income disparity and employment growth does not comprise evidence for causation in one direction or the other. Voith (1998) seeks to address the weakness in the correlational analysis of city and suburban incomes via a neatly developed simultaneous model and two-stage least squares estimation technique.[10] Similar problems of possible simultaneity are evident in our own research focus: while alleviating central city poverty may help the regional economy grow, regional growth itself can improve the economic prospects of inner-city residents simply by tightening labor markets and thereby allowing the less skilled to enter new and better jobs.

To sum, most of the oft-cited research suffers from several different problems.[11] First, conducting simple correlations cannot account for exogenous factors; this suggests the need for a multiple regression analysis that can determine the impact of alleviating central-city poverty on metropolitan income *after* controlling for other variables that might also affect regional growth. Second, even a properly constructed variable list retains the potential for simultaneity. This suggests that we should specify, however parsimoniously, both the poverty-to-growth and growth-to-poverty relationships and then estimate each via two-stage least squares. Such an approach will allow us to see whether improving equity can, as previous researchers have contended, improve economic performance even controlling for the fact that growth itself will have a positive effect on equity.

Regional Growth and Poverty Revisited

Much of the previous empirical work has focused on the relationship between city and suburban incomes or the relationship between the ratio of these measures and the regional performance on income or employment. We take a different approach—one that reflects our general concern with poverty and low-income communities—and instead focus on the statistical relationship between metropolitan income growth and various measures of poverty, equity, and residential segregation.

Throughout the analysis, our perspective is that growth and these other measures are mutually causative and simultaneously determined. For example, we look to see whether lowering central-city poverty tends to help income growth in the overall region *after* controlling for the fact that higher income growth will reduce central-city poverty. While the underlying causal mechanisms in this poverty-growth effect are not tested directly in our analysis below, our view builds (as noted in chapter 1) on Robert Putnam's (1993) notion that regions succeed based on "social capital"—that is, dense networks of trusting relationships between various economic, social, and political agents. Such social capital is eroded by high inequality and deep poverty; in our case, when the central city and its poor are left out of the economic equation, the consensus necessary to consolidate a regional strategy is more difficult to obtain.[12]

Given this sort of focus on the politics of building social capital, we also investigate the effects of geographically concentrated poverty and city-suburb differentials in poverty levels. Our notion here is that significant residential segregation and large subregional differences might weaken the sort of common bonds (or social capital) that drive regional policy makers to pay attention to issues of both poverty and growth.[13] We also specifically test the relationship between growth and a measure of metro-level income distribution; unfortunately, this reduces the sample size, so while the results are quite conducive to our hypotheses, we tend to focus on the other measures.

Regression Design and Results

We begin our analysis by looking at the residential segregation of the poor and the difference between central-city and suburban poverty levels. The sample to be tested is drawn from Ledebur and Barnes's (1992) compilation of the eighty-five largest metropolitan statistical areas, or MSAs, that have an identifiable central city.[14] Several MSAs had to be dropped either because data was unavailable or because changes in the definition of MSA boundaries between 1980 and 1990 were too severe to make comparisons feasible.[15] The seventy-four MSAs and central cities included in the study are listed in table 5.1. Most data were taken from U.S. census material on population and employment with additional sources detailed in appendix B. We also draw data on metropolitan inequality from "The State of the Nation's Cities" (SNC), a database compiled by Norman J. Glickman, Michael Lahr, and Elvin Wyly.[16]

Below we look at four sets of regressions. Each takes the same basic form: the first regression in each set examines per capita growth in the MSA as a function of our poverty or equity measures (as well as other factors), while the second regression tests for the effect of growth itself (and other factors) on poverty or equity measures. We present here the most parsimonious specifications of our regressions; as we note later, the basic results do not change when we introduce other potentially relevant variables. The first pair of regressions is specified as follows (the signs in parentheses before each variable indicate the expected direction of impact on the dependent variable):

> (1a) *GROWTH REGRESSION:*
>> *MSA Growth, 1980s* (per capita income growth in the MSA between 1979 and 1989) as a function of:
>> (–) *MSA Unemployment, 1980* (the MSA unemployment rate in 1980);
>> (–) *Manufacturing Concentration, 1977* (a measure of the concentration of industry in the central city vs. the suburb in 1977);
>> (–) *% Central City, 1980* (the percent of MSA residents in the central city in 1980);
>> (?) *South, West, East* (a set of U.S. regional dummy variables); and
>> (–) *Ratio of Dissimilarity, 1990/1980* (the ratio of the 1990 to 1980 dissimilarity index, where the base dissimilarity index measures the degree of residential segregation of the poor as described further below).

which is estimated simultaneously with:

(1b) *DISSIMILARITY REGRESSION:*

 Ratio of Dissimilarity, 1990/1980 (ratio of the 1990 to 1980 dissimilarity index) as a function of:

 (–) *Dissimilarity of Poor, 1980* (the dissimilarity index for the MSA in 1980);

 (+) *Minorities, City/Suburb, 1980* (the presence of African-Americans and Latinos in the central city relative to the presence of such minorities in suburbs, measured by the ratio of the percent of said residents in each area in 1980);

 (?) *South, West, East* (the same set of U.S. regional dummy variables); and

 (–) *MSA Growth, 1980s* (per capita income growth in the MSA).

Note that both sides of this regression exercise are "dynamic," that is, we are considering both the change in income and the change in the geographic concentration of the poor. The two regressions are linked by the presence of *MSA Growth, 1980s* and *Ratio of Dissimilarity, 1990/1980;* these are the "endogenous" or simultaneously determined variables.

The *Ratio of Dissimilarity, 1990/1980,* for example, captures the changes in the dissimilarity index. The index tells us the percentage of poor residents that would need to move from one neighborhood (defined as a census tract) to another in order to attain an even distribution of the poor. A dissimilarity index of 100 would indicate total segregation of the poor (that is, 100 percent of poor residents would be required to move in order to redistribute the poor equally across space), while a dissimilarity index of 0 denotes a completely even allocation of poor residents.[17] The unit of analysis is the metropolitan region, with our underlying hypothesis being that a rising concentration of the poor makes city-suburb solidarity difficult and therefore impedes the sort of political and policy consensus that supports faster growth; as a result, we expect a negative sign on this variable. Going to the other side of the relationship (1b), we expect a negative sign on *MSA Growth, 1980s,* since faster growth should reduce the geographic concentration of the poor, either by reducing poverty in the central city or by creating the economic wherewithal for poorer individuals to move.

The other variables in (1a) and (1b) offer a rough approximation of some simple determinants of growth and the change in geographic concentration (i.e., they are among the other exogenous variables usually left out in simple correlation analysis). On the growth side, for example, we introduced two state (or beginning of period) variables. The first is *MSA Unemployment, 1980,* with the negative sign suggesting that higher levels of initial unemployment indicate an MSA that is in trouble and therefore likely

Table 5.1

MSAs and Central Cities in the Regression Sample

MSA name	Central City
Akron, OH	Akron
Allentown-Bethlehem, PA-NJ	Allentown
Anaheim-Santa Ana, CA	Anaheim
Atlanta, GA	Atlanta
Austin, TX	Austin
Baltimore, MD	Baltimore
Boston-Lawrence-Salem-Lowell-Brockton, MA	Boston
Birmingham, AL	Birmingham
Buffalo, NY	Buffalo
Chicago, IL	Chicago
Charlotte-Gastonia-Rock Hill, NC-SC	Charlotte
Cincinnati, OH-KY-IN	Cincinnati
Cleveland, OH	Cleveland
Columbus, OH	Columbus
Dallas, TX	Dallas
Dayton-Springfield, OH	Dayton
Denver, CO	Denver
Detroit, MI	Detroit
El Paso, TX	El Paso
Fort Lauderdale-Hollywood-Pompano Beach, FL	Fort Lauderdale
Fresno, CA	Fresno
Gary-Hammond, IN	Gary
Grand Rapids, MI	Grand Rapids
Greensboro–Winston-Salem–High Point, NC	Greensboro
Greenville-Spartanburg, SC	Greenville
Harrisburg-Lebanon-Carlisle, PA	Harrisburg
Hartford-New Britain-Middletown-Bristol, CT	Hartford
Houston, TX	Houston
Indianapolis, IN	Indianapolis
Jacksonville, FL	Jacksonville
Kansas City, MO-KS	Kansas City, MO
Knoxville, TN	Knoxville

Table 5.1   (Continued)

MSAs and Central Cities in the Regression Sample

MSA Name	Central City
Los Angeles-Long Beach, CA	Los Angeles
Louisville, KY-IN	Louisville
Memphis, TN-AR-MS	Memphis
Miami-Hialeah, FL	Miami
Middlesex-Somerset-Hunterdon, NJ	New Brunswick
Milwaukee, WI	Milwaukee
Minneapolis-St. Paul, MN-WI	Minneapolis
Nashville, TN	Nashville-Davidson
Newark, NJ	Newark
New Haven-Waterbury-Meriden, CT	New Haven
New Orleans, LA	New Orleans
New York, NY	New York
Oklahoma City, OK	Oklahoma City
Omaha, NE-IA	Omaha
Orlando, FL	Orlando
Oxnard-Ventura, CA	Oxnard
Philadelphia, PA-NJ	Philadelphia
Phoenix, AZ	Phoenix
Portland, OR	Portland
Providence-Pawtucket-Woonsocket, RI	Providence
Pittsburgh, PA	Pittsburgh
Rochester, NY	Rochester
Richmond-Petersburg, VA	Richmond
Riverside-San Bernardino, CA	Riverside
Sacramento, CA	Sacramento
Salt Lake City-Ogden, UT	Salt Lake City
San Antonio, TX	San Antonio
San Diego, CA	San Diego
San Jose, CA	San Jose
Scranton–Wilkes-Barre, PA	Scranton
Seattle, WA	Seattle
Springfield, MA	Springfield

Table 5.1   (Continued)

MSAs and Central Cities in the Regression Sample

MSA Name	Central City
St. Louis, MO-IL	St. Louis, MO
Syracuse, NY	Syracuse
Tacoma, WA	Tacoma
Tampa-St. Petersburg, FL	Tampa
Toledo, OH	Toledo
Tucson, AZ	Tucson
Tulsa, OK	Tulsa
Washington, DC-MD-VA	Washington, DC
West Palm Beach-Boca Raton-Delray Beach, FL	West Palm Beach
Wilmington, NY	Wilmington

to grow slower. The second is *Manufacturing Concentration, 1977,* which measures the relative concentration of manufacturing activity in the central city by comparing the ratio of city to suburb manufacturing employment to the ratio of the city to suburb labor force. We expect a negative sign: since suburban manufacturing has tended to spring up later in the U.S. industrial cycle, those regions with a central-city bias in their manufacturing employment are likely to have "older" and probably less competitive industries.[18]

Following the suggestions of Hill, Wolman, and Ford (1994:13), we have also included a variable for the relative size of the central city as well as dummy variables for different U.S. regions. We expect that regions with relatively large central cities may grow slower, primarily because they may reflect older industrial configurations (see above). We have no particular predictions with regard to the sign for the regional dummies but discuss below the hypotheses others might hold, especially regarding the ability of central cities in sunbelt areas to annex land. Before moving to the results, we should acknowledge that this reduced specification is more of a statistical snapshot or sophisticated partial correlation analysis than it is a full-fledged explanation of growth.[19] However, while a complete growth model might be useful for regional planning or other such purposes, our primary task here is to create a simple set of regression specifications that consistently illustrates the growth-poverty nexus as we move across our various measures of equity.

As for the regression accounting for changes in the geographic deconcentration of the poor, we assume that *MSA Growth, 1980s* has a negative sign—that is, that faster growth spurs residential deconcentration—for the reasons previously mentioned. As with the first regression, we introduce two state (or beginning of period) variables. First, we assume that the initial *Dissimilarity of Poor, 1980* has a negative effect: when an area is already very dissimilar, it is harder for the dissimilarity index to rise (or, better put, the sort of increases measured by our dependent variable will be smaller). Further, we expect that the variable *Minorities, City/Suburb, 1980* will have a positive sign: the larger the number of minorities in the city relative to the suburb, the more likely it is that residential segregation of the poor will grow over time. Note that we also introduce regional dummies here since different regions of the United States experienced different structural phenomenon in the 1980s that affected both growth and equality (see Hill, Wolman, and Ford, 1994).

The results from this first set of regressions are in the first two columns of table 5.2. As can be seen, the explanatory power, as measured by the adjusted R-squared, is relatively good considering the sparse specification of the model. In addition, the pattern of signs is as predicted. In the growth regression, initial unemployment and the percent in the central city are significant at the .10 level; the key endogenous variable, *Ratio of Dissimilarity, 1990/1980,* is significant at the .20 level. In the "equity" regression, the two initial measures of dissimilarity and racial separation are significant at the .20 and the .05 level; *MSA Growth, 1980* is "correctly" signed but has a t-statistic of –.676. This is weak evidence that the rising geographic concentration of the poor negatively affects regional growth and much weaker evidence that regional growth reduces the residential concentration of the poor.

To explore the growth-equity relationship further, we decided to shift the geographic variable of concern to the change in the relative poverty rate (that is, the poverty rate of the central city compared to that of the suburb) between 1980 and 1990. We measure this by calculating a ratio of two other ratios: the 1990 ratio of central-city poverty to suburban poverty and the 1980 ratio of central-city poverty to suburban poverty. Thus, if *both* central-city and suburban poverty doubled, the ratio would remain the same at 100; if central-city poverty rose at a faster rate than suburban poverty, our variable, called *Change in City/Suburb Poverty Ratio, 1980–90,* would be above 100.[20] Given the views presented earlier, we would expect such increases to be associated with a decline in growth, with the specification as follows:

Table 5.2

Regressions on Growth and Residential Dissimilarity and Relative Poverty

Dependent variable	MSA Growth 1980s	Ratio of Dissimilarity 1990/80	MSA Growth 1980s	Change in City/ Suburb Poverty Ratio 1990/80
Equation	(1a)	(1b)	(2a)	(2b)
Control Variables				
MSA Unempl., 1980	−2.330 (−1.843)*		−2.744 (−2.313)**	
Manu. Concen., 1977	−0.031 (−0.962)		−0.049 (−1.905)*	
% Central City, 1980	−0.200 (−1.730)*		−0.149 (−1.415) #	
Dissimilarity of Poor, 1980		-0.211 (−1.361) #		
Minorities, City/Suburb, 1980		0.005 (2.377)**		0.031 (4.799)***
City/Suburb Poverty Ratio, 1980				−0.079 (−2.574)**
Region				
South	−11.668 (−1.042)	−7.000 (−2.909)***	−2.084 (−0.344)	−4.290 (−0.599)
West	5.545 (0.819)	3.964 (1.301) #	−1.760 (−0.288)	−2.168 (−0.270)
East	21.336 (3.505)***	1.387 (0.364)	19.658 (3.428)***	−7.439 (−0.715)

Table 5.2 (Continued)

Regressions on Growth and Residential Dissimilarity and Relative Poverty

Dependent variable	MSA Growth 1980s	Ratio of Dissimilarity 1990/80	MSA Growth 1980s	Change in City/ Suburb Poverty Ratio 1990/80
Equation	(1a)	(1b)	(2a)	(2b)
Endogenous Variables				
Ratio of Dissimilarity, 1990/80	−1.526 (−1.457) #			
Change in City/Sub. Pov. Ratio, 1990/80			−0.317 (−1.699) *	
MSA Growth, 1980s		−0.076 (−0.676)		0.172 (−0.481)
Regression Statistics				
Adjusted R2	0.284	0.454	0.325	0.284
Number of obs.	74	74	74	74
F-value	5.127***	11.115***	6.020***	5.827***

*** significant at the .01 level;
** significant at the .05 level;
* significant at the .10 level;
# significant at the .20 level.

(2a) *GROWTH REGRESSION:*

    MSA Growth, 1980s as a function of:

    [(–) *MSA Unemployment, 1980;* (–) *Manufacturing Concentration, 1977;* (–) *% Central City, 1980;* (?) *South, West, East;* and (–) *Change in City/Suburb Poverty Ratio, 1980–90*]

which is estimated simultaneously with:

(2b) *RELATIVE POVERTY REGRESSION:*

    Change in City/Suburb Poverty Ratio, 1980–90 as a function of:

    [(–)*City/Suburb Poverty Ratio, 1980;* (+) *Minorities, City/Suburb, 1980;* (?) *South, West, East;* and (–) *MSA Growth, 1980s*]

MSA Growth, 1980s and *Change in City/Suburb Poverty Ratio, 1980–90* are now the endogenous variables in the system. Note that the initial or exogenous variables affecting *MSA Growth, 1980s* remain the same. The exogenous variables affecting *Change in City/Suburb Poverty Ratio, 1980–90* are nearly the same as those in our first poverty regression, with *City/Suburb Poverty Ratio, 1980* (the ratio of city to suburb poverty rates in 1980) taking the place of the state variable used in the specification for the change in the dissimilarity index. The pattern of expected signs follows the logic of the previous discussion.

The results, presented in the third and fourth columns of table 5.2, provide somewhat more support for our hypothesis that equity across space may have a positive impact on growth. All variables are signed as expected and significance levels are generally higher. Of particular importance is that *Change in City/Suburb Poverty Ratio, 1980–90* is negative and significant at the .10 level in the regression testing its impact on *MSA Growth, 1980s*. In the regression in which the *Change in City/Suburb Poverty Ratio, 1980–90* is the dependent variable, *MSA Growth, 1980s* is actually positive (that is, growth increases the ratio of poverty in the central city to poverty in the suburbs) but is not significant by any traditional standard. What the results suggest is that relative decreases in central-city poverty will likely improve overall MSA growth but growth itself will not necessarily trickle down to help the central city more than the suburbs. Those who have questioned whether growth helps make income distribution more equitable may find this result of particular interest.

Of course, the progrowth argument is not that faster growth will benefit the central city more than the suburbs but rather that "a rising tide will lift all boats," including those mired in inner-city poverty. In this view, the key issue is whether MSA growth helps reduce central-city poverty. For our hypothesis regarding the salutary effects of targeting the poor, the parallel issue is whether targeted efforts to alleviate central city poverty eventually trickle up to help the income profile of the region overall.

To look at this set of questions, the appropriate system can be written as follows:

(3a) *GROWTH REGRESSION:*
MSA Growth, 1980s as a function of:
[(–) *MSA Unemployment, 1980;* (–) *Manufacturing Concentration, 1977;* (–) *% Central City, 1980;* (?) *South, West, East;* and (–) *Change in City Poverty, 1980–90*]

which is estimated simultaneously with:

(3b) *POVERTY REGRESSION:*
Change in City Poverty, 1980–90 as a function of:
[(+) *City/Suburb Poverty Ratio, 1980;* (+) *Minorities, City/Suburb, 1980;* (?)*South, West, East;* and (–)*MSA Growth, 1980s*]

where *Change in City Poverty, 1980–90* is simply the change in central-city poverty rates between 1980 and 1990. Note that we are here assuming that *City/Suburb Poverty Ratio, 1980* will have a positive sign. While on the previous regression, the results on this variable were somewhat mechanically driven (the higher the initial ratio, the less would be the change), we are suggesting here that the relative concentration of poverty in the central city would tend to diminish the regional political will to undertake policy action and thereby lead to higher increases in central-city poverty.

The results of this specification are in the first and second columns of table 5.3. Note that explanatory power, as measured by the adjusted R-squared, is relatively high (especially in the growth regression) and all variables are signed as expected. In the growth regression, the relevant (non-dummy) variables are significant at at least the .20 level and *Change in City Poverty, 1980–90* has a negative and significant impact on *MSA Growth, 1980s* even after using the two-stage least squares method to control for the fact that growth itself has a statistically significant effect on reducing central-city poverty (see the results for the poverty regression in table 5.3).[21] While the sparse specification means that these results are only suggestive, they do indicate that both sides of the growth-versus-equity argument may have some validity: while growth is likely to trickle down to help the poor, a strategy targeted toward reducing inner-city poverty may also be able to help all the residents of a larger metropolitan area.

The final set of regressions is conducted using a measure of inequality itself. The two sides are:

(4a) *GROWTH REGRESSION:*

  MSA Growth, 1980s as a function of:

  [(–) *MSA Unemployment, 1980;* (–) *Manufacturing Concentration,*
  1977; (?) *South, West, East;* and (–)*Change in Inequality, 1980–90*]

which is estimated simultaneously with:

(4b) *INEQUALITY REGRESSION:*

  Change in Inequality, 1980–90 as a function of:

  [(–)*City/MSA Inequality Ratio, 1980;* (+) *Percent Minority in*
  MSA, 1980; (?) *South, West, East;* and (–) *MSA Growth, 1980s*]

The growth side of the picture is familiar, with our prediction now being that rising inequality will have a dragging effect on growth. We drop the control for the size of the central city relative to the MSA, mostly because the coefficient on that variable had a low t-value; as we will see, so did the initial unemployment variable, but this measure at least has an analytical (vs. control) reason for remaining in the regression.[22] On the inequality side, *Change in Inequality, 1980–90* is the difference between the 1990 ratio of the income of those in the top 10 percent of earners relative to those in the bottom 10 percent in the metro area and the 1980 measure of the same phenomenon. This measure is available for only forty-nine of the seventy-four cities in the larger regression sample, implying a reduction in degrees of freedom and problematizing direct comparisons between this and the other runs.

This inequality regression has two initial variables, aside from the regional dummies. The first is the initial ratio of inequality in the central city to inequality in the MSA, *City/MSA Inequality Ratio, 1980;* we expect a negative sign for reasons similar to those listed for *City/Suburb Poverty Ratio, 1980* in regression (2b). The second is *Percent Minority in MSA, 1980,* for which we expect a positive sign for reasons similar to those listed for *Minorities, City/Suburb, 1980* in the earlier regressions.[23]

The results, listed in the third and fourth columns of table 5.3, suggest that rising inequality can dampen growth and that growth can lessen inequality; the first result is significant while the second is not, again lending credence to those who worry that trickle-down often doesn't. As with the other regressions, overly broad conclusions are not warranted: not only is the specification sparse, but the sample size has been reduced considerably because of the scarcity of data on income inequality by metro region. Still, it is noteworthy that a measure of inequality indicates a negative impact on growth, an effect that squares even more directly with the social capital–based theses offered in our earlier discussion.

Table 5.3

Regressions on Growth and Change in Poverty and Inequality

Dependent variable	MSA Growth 1980s	Change in City Poverty 1980–90	MSA Growth 1980s	Change in Inequality 1980–90
Equation	(3a)	(3b)	(4a)	(4b)
Control Variables				
MSA Unempl., 1980	−1.310 (−1.303) #		−0.882 (−0.802)	
Manu. Concen., 1977	−0.044 (−2.359) **		−0.074 (−2.808) ***	
% Central City, 1980	−0.138 (−1.833) *			
Minorities, City/Suburb, 1980		0.002 (2.639) **		
City/Suburb Poverty Ratio, 1980		0.002 (0.416)		
Percent Minority MSA, 1980				0.025 (3.211) ***
City/MSA Inequality Ratio, 1980				−0.009 (−1.793) *
Region				
South	−3.080 (−0.650)	−0.512 (−0.530)	2.818 (0.589)	−0.173 (−0.630)
West	−1.941 (−0.436)	0.517 (0.478)	−1.890 (−0.398)	−0.323 (−1.137)
East	13.478 (2.357) **	−0.383 (−0.273)	21.853 (4.320) ***	0.132 (0.239)

Table 5.3   (Continued)

Regressions on Growth and Change in Poverty and Inequality

Dependent variable	MSA Growth 1980s	Change in City Poverty 1980-90	MSA Growth 1980s	Change in Inequality 1980-90
Equation	(3a)	(3b)	(4a)	(4b)
Endogenous Variables				
Change in City Poverty, 1980–90	−2.599 (−1.910) *			
Change in Inequality, 1980–90			−10.688 (−2.349) **	
MSA Growth, 1980s		−0.119 (−2.465) **		−0.014 (−0.756)
Regression Statistics				
Adjusted R2	0.512	0.386	0.521	0.284
Number of obs.	74	74	49	49
F-value	11.949 ***	8.656 ***	9.685 ***	4.169 ***

*** significant at the .01 level;
** significant at the .05 level;
* significant at the .10 level;
# significant at the .20 level.

How sensitive are the results above to various specifications? To explore this issue, we reran the full set of regressions several ways: without our measure of manufacturing concentration; with the manufacturing concentration variable and a measure of the educational level in the region as a proxy for growth potential;[24] with the basic set of variables but introducing different sorts of controls for the size of the MSA or the central city; substituting a measure of the population density of the MSA in place of the relative percent in the central city; introducing a measure of commuting time for each MSA; and using a different specification of the minority concentration in the central city.[25] None of these alternative specifications had any serious effect on the significance or sign of our key poverty and equity measures.[26]

We also explored the effect of a central city's "elasticity," or ability to expand its borders over time.[27] Rusk (1995) has argued that "elastic" cities are better able to capture economic and population growth and use the enhanced resources to tackle poverty and other equity issues. Another view, focused more directly on equity effects, is that the central city's ability to expand its own boundaries ties together the fates of the city and would-be suburbs and hence creates bridging social capital across the region (see, for example, our case study of Charlotte in chapter 6).

Since most elastic central cities are in the sunbelt areas of the South and the West—older eastern cities generally being bounded by existing development—the regional dummies might indirectly be capturing this elasticity effect. Looking over the pattern of signs and significance in tables 5.2 and 5.3, note that the results for the dummy variables do not seem to reflect this elasticity hypothesis: *East* generally has a positive and significant impact on growth (controlling for other factors), and only once does *South* or *West* have Rusk's expected impact on equity even at the .20 level.

We therefore decided to get more directly at the issue by coding the elasticity of each region's central city with a five-level measure offered in Rusk (1995).[28] We entered this elasticity variable in our full set of regressions along with the regional dummies; keeping them in place seemed appropriate since we originally entered the regional controls to account for other (non-elasticity) factors influencing growth and equity. In general, the elasticity measure was not at all significant, except in a regression with *Change in City/Suburb Poverty Ratio, 1980–1990* as a dependent variable; its presence there also diminished the significance of *South* and *West* in line with Rusk's argument. When we dropped the regional dummies and used just elasticity, the measure actually had a negative impact on growth; however, elasticity did have a positive impact on equity (that is, a negative impact on our inequality measures) although the effect was not significant for either *Change in City Poverty, 1980–1990* or *Change in Inequality, 1980–1990*.[29] Taken together, these results suggest that the capacity to expand city boundaries might play a limited role in proequity development, an insight we take up in our case study of Charlotte.

Parallels with International Findings on Growth and Equity

Interestingly, the result on equity and growth suggested here parallels a new finding in the realms of international and development economics.[30] Traditional approaches in these fields, much like the traditional approach of the corporate-center urban development model (see chapter 3), have long suggested that inequality can be "productive": it can help growth by distributing income to investors and is an inevitable part of kick-starting development.[31] However, a new wave of academic research is challenging the conventional wisdom regarding this equity-output trade-off.

Employing large multicountry datasets in complex multivariate regression exercises, researchers are finding that more egalitarian distributions of income may be better for macroeconomic stability and restructuring, as well as long-term growth. While the logic behind these international-level "proequality" findings remains an object of debate, the general lines of reasoning parallel those we have emphasized above: more equal distributions of income lead to less jockeying for government favors and hence more evenhanded growth-inducing policies (see, for example, Berg and Sachs, 1988); more equity leads to less political conflict over sharing the burden in times of adjustment, helping to speed recovery from external shocks (see Alesina and Drazen, 1991); a less skewed distribution of income generates the political basis for certain growth-enhancing policies, such as investment in basic health and education (see Birdsall and Sabot, 1994; Rodrik, 1994); and, finally, more even gains from growth lead to less resentment of the wealthy and therefore a more secure environment for investment (see Alesina and Perotti, 1993; Persson and Tabellini, 1994).

With cross-country econometric tests squaring with the presumptions of this new approach, many development practitioners, including officials in the World Bank and other international financial institutions, have begun to suggest that equity might not be simply an add-on to economic programming but rather a key ingredient of national success.[32] As a result, international institutions have begun to view poverty as a more central concern, partnering with local nonprofit groups and promoting community building, often under the rubric of constructing civil society.

What we are suggesting is that regional leaders and policy makers may also want to see equity and community empowerment as key to overall economic well-being. While the evidence still remains suggestive, the results here, and in the earlier literature on the United States and the emerging international comparisons, square with common sense. As anyone involved with group-building knows, stark inequalities and the resentment and frustration they engender can create barriers to cohesion—and cohesion and collaboration are key to winning. Neighbors, even across cities and suburbs, matter.

Growth and Poverty: Modeling the Relationship

While the econometric estimates of the previous section demonstrate that reductions in poverty and inequality can have a positive impact on growth, understanding the policy choices implied by this finding may be easiest if we "translate" the results into a simple analytical graph. To do so, figure 5.1 draws upon the slope coefficients obtained from regressions (3a) and (3b) (the first and second columns of table 5.3) to chart one view of the growth-poverty reduction relationship.[33]

The more steeply sloping line in the figure reflects the impact on growth from reductions in central-city poverty while the flatter line represents the impact of growth itself on the change in central-city poverty. The first thing to emphasize is that the system estimated by our regressions is, in fact, "stable" at the equilibrium point, E. To see why, consider what would occur if the economy was not at point E but rather to the left. At A, for example, a decadal growth rate of about 89 percent produces an increase in central-city poverty over the decade of around 3 percent. However, that increase in poverty is actually associated with a higher growth rate of around 105 percent (that is, the relatively low growth rate of 89 percent is generally produced by paying even less attention to alleviating central city poverty), and hence the economy moves to point B. At point B, faster growth yields even less of an increase in the poverty rate and the economy drifts to point C. Obviously, we will continue to zigzag until arriving at point E, where both relationships are simultaneously satisfied. A similar story can be told for returning to E from the other side of the equilibrium.[34]

Consider now changes in the equilibrium. Suppose a region decides to pursue a strictly growth-oriented policy, perhaps by bringing in new federal dollars, creating attractive infrastructure, or reducing regulatory burdens (each of which might affect our beginning-of-period variables such as initial unemployment or industrial concentration). For any given change in poverty, growth will rise: this implies that we can model this policy as a shift

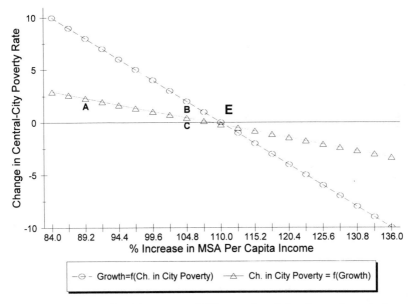

Figure 5.1. The relationship between MSA growth and the change in central-city poverty.

out in the growth function, a change shown in figure 5.2. The result, of course, is faster growth with a subsequent positive impact on inner-city poverty.

Alternatively, suppose a region decides to target its resources toward a focused antipoverty strategy, perhaps through an emphasis on community development in low-income areas, improved job-training programs, or a general improvement in labor legislation. This can be modeled as a shift downward in the change in central-city poverty function: at any given level of growth, there will be a reduction in poverty. The result, pictured in figure 5.3, is also faster growth and lower poverty, with more emphasis in this case on the poverty side and, as pictured, a slightly lower impact on overall income growth in the MSA than would be the case under a purely growth-focused strategy.

Another, and perhaps more politically viable, strategy is to improve the growth-poverty trade-off—that is, to redesign regional growth strategies to include the sort of measures (such as employment linkage requirements or special incentives for regional business clusters located in or around high-poverty tracts) that ensure that the fruits of growth, especially jobs and business opportunities, accrue to poorer central-city residents.[35] This attempt to get a bigger antipoverty bang for each growth-promoting buck is

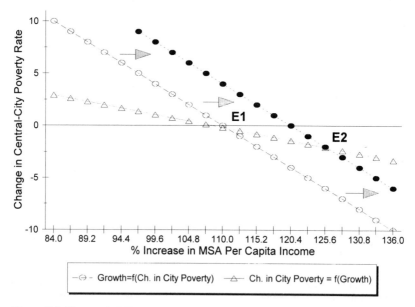

Figure 5.2. Change in MSA growth and central-city poverty for growth-oriented policy.

represented in figure 5.4 as a rotation downward of the poverty line (each increase in MSA income now has a larger impact on central-city poverty than under the previous policy regime). Note that the result is a sort of "virtuous circle": as we move between equilibrium E1 and equilibrium E2, faster growth has a more positive impact on poverty and the reduction of poverty builds regional trust and human capital and so brings faster growth.[36]

Of course, different cities or regions will place different emphases on the goals of growth and poverty reduction and these emphases also may change over time. In chapter 6, we detail three case studies of metropolitan regions that seem to have done relatively well at both encouraging growth and raising the prospects of the poor in the central city. As we will see, at least one of these cities seems largely to have ignored poverty per se and instead bet on a trickle-down strategy, while the other two implemented focused antipoverty efforts to varying degrees to ensure that growth would also reach the inner city. One region, the metropolitan area anchored by Charlotte, North Carolina, even instituted a set of political mechanisms to ensure that central city–suburban interests would be more consistent and hence more attention might be paid to inner-city poverty.[37]

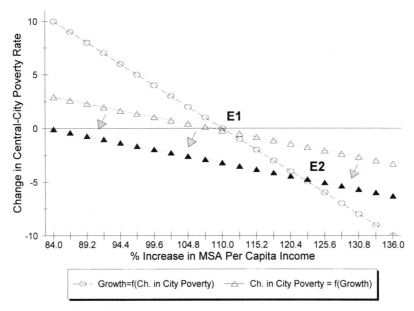

Figure 5.3. Change in MSA growth and central-city poverty for poverty-oriented policy.

The empirical results and formal modeling presented in this section suggest that both progrowth and proequity policies can yield useful results. While we have attempted to distinguish here between growth-oriented and poverty-oriented policies—if only to ensure that growth alone does not dominate the policy dialogue—clearly the best strategy is to combine the two. It is wrong to argue that the benefits of growth will never trickle down; a fast-growing economy can be in everyone's interest and tighter labor markets often help those on the bottom of the distributional hierarchy the most. Likewise, it is wrong to suggest that poverty advocates are concerned simply with redistribution: targeting central-city poverty can have benefits for the regional economy as a whole.

City and Suburb

It was once a key part of the American dream: the escape from the hustle-bustle of the city to a tranquil suburb where houses were larger, streets safer, and futures assured. In recent years, this vision of happy suburbia has been shaken, the victim of harried schedules, tangled traffic, and the increasing presence of "inner-city" problems, such as crime and poverty. Suburbanites have sometimes responded by trying to separate themselves even further, leading to the development of so-called exurbs at the periphery of the

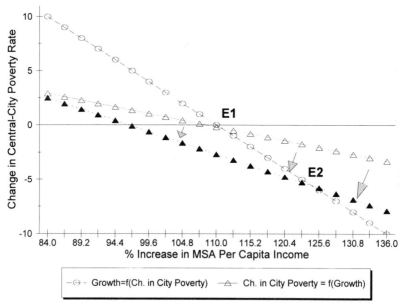

Figure 5.4. Improving the growth-poverty trade-off.

metropolitan area. But while such a strategy may preserve short-term individual gains, it fails to recognize that suburban fates are intricately bound with those in the central city. The economy is increasingly a regional matter and problems of poverty and joblessness, however concentrated they may be in certain geographic areas and ethnic communities, can constitute a drag on overall regional growth.

As usual, Southern California provides a dramatic example of the general relationship. Los Angeles is one of the largest counties in the United States; its very geography, often experienced as lonely driving time, has bred a certain insulation from others. The suburban ideal, perfected in Southern California to a developer's art form, has been a plot of land insulated from the hubbub of the city. The region's population has spread through the San Fernando and San Gabriel Valleys, gobbling up agricultural land, building new freeways, separating neighbor from neighbor with just a little more lawn and a slightly longer commute. Living apart has been the region's goal and its practice.

But L.A.'s drive to separate cannot overcome the essential interconnectedness of the region. The widening disparities and strained social capital of the 1980s provoked political tensions and civil unrest, raising investor fears and contributing to Southern California's slow growth in the early

1990s. The regional growth that affects all residents was constrained by an increasingly poorly trained labor force, itself the product of a suburbanization process that left both the inner city and inner-ring suburbs with weakened school districts and poorly performing students. Examining the wreckage wrought by neglect, in 1996 two L.A. business leaders concluded that "central to improving our city's business climate is a concerted attack on poverty."[38]

The evidence above suggests that such attention to the poor could actually benefit all the residents of a region. Tackling some of the methodological problems that have characterized earlier studies of city-suburb linkage, we found evidence that reductions in central-city poverty, or improvements in metro-level equity, will spur regional growth, even accounting for the fact that growth will itself diminish poverty and inequality. In short, focused efforts that create more opportunities for the poor can help expand the regional "pie," not just redivide it.

Of course, our regression analysis leaves open as many questions as it answers. First, the econometric work is more a statistical snapshot than a causal model; the simplicity of our approach means that the complex chains from equity to social capital to regional growth are largely unspecified. Second, as noted in our simple series of graphs, regions can achieve positive economic results by focusing either on growth-oriented or poverty-oriented policies. To see how to best mix growth and poverty reduction, and to see the actual ways in which such policies are determined and work, we need detailed case studies. Such case studies of "regions that work"—places where growth and equity measures have surpassed the national norm—are the subject of the next chapter.

6

Regions That Work

Growth, Equity, and Policy in
High-Performing Metropolitan Areas

American politics and policy making are fundamentally pragmatic. The hopeful message of the last few chapters—that low-income communities do better when their residents are connected to the region and that metropolitan economies grow faster when the poor are included—will remain just a message unless we can point to specific circumstances and policies under which regions have been able to achieve the dual goals of income and distributional improvement.

As it turns out, the late 1990s brought an emerging set of experiments and initiatives that do blend growth and equity in creative ways; we take these up in chapter 7. Here, we cast a retrospective view, examining three U.S. regions that exhibited superior performance in terms of both economic growth and poverty reduction during the 1980s (a period for which we had complete comparative data): the greater Boston area, the San Jose metropolitan area, and the metropolitan region anchored by Charlotte, North Carolina.

The choice of these areas may be surprising, particularly given the usual emphasis of the new regionalists and Smart Growth advocates on places like Minneapolis–St. Paul or Portland, Oregon, locations in which the machinery of regional government seems firmly in place. However, our three study areas were in the top ten of seventy-four major metropolitan regions when ranked by an index that took into account growth, poverty decline, and residential integration of the poor, and were among the top four when we added a measure of metropolitan equity to the mix.

Each region offers a range of demographic mixes and development patterns, and each appears to have chosen a different route to success in pushing growth and dampening poverty. San Jose essentially adopted a

variant of a trickle-down approach: its business leaders exhibited an exceptional level of regional consciousness, but business and government did little specifically to help the poor. Instead, rapid growth helped to increase
wages and dampen increases in poverty. Charlotte seems to have had in
place the elements necessary for a "trickle-up" strategy: city and suburb had
intersecting and common interests, partly because of a unique set of jurisdictional structures, and partly because regional elites retained a deep concern
for the fate of the central-city as the anchor of a dynamic regional economy.
Boston took a mixed approach: while much of the reduction in central-city
poverty was probably due to higher growth and tightening labor markets,
local policy makers took advantage of the macroeconomic situation to
enact policies that redistributed (or "trickled around") some of the benefits
of growth to poorer areas in the city and the region.

We begin below by detailing how we selected our case studies. We then
discuss each case study individually, examining the main demographic and
economic trends that have characterized each region, highlighting important regional and community initiatives, and evaluating each city's success
on the antipoverty front in order to draw positive lessons for the future. We
conclude the chapter by stressing a common theme that characterizes all
our cases: the ability to develop regional consciousness and consensus
among key actors.

Choosing the Cases

An award-winning article by Wolman, Ford, and Hill (1994) entitled "Evaluating the Success of Urban Success Stories" offers a cautionary tale: many of
the cities regarded by urban planners and other experts as revitalization success stories have actually not been all that successful. To explore the opin-
ions of experts, Wolman, Ford, and Hill first devised an index of "urban distress" based on unemployment rates, poverty levels, household income, and
growth in output and population for 162 central cities.[1] They then took the
bottom (or worst-scoring) third of the sample and asked 159 "experts" (of
which seventy-six responded) which of these "distress stories" had experienced the strongest "economic turnaround or urban revitalization" during
1980s.[2] The answers were then compared to an objective index based on
income growth, poverty reduction, and other factors. By the latter measure,
many of the cities deemed revitalized by the experts had performed no better and often worse than cities that were not considered to have undergone
urban revitalization.[3]

Why the discrepancy? Many of the expert-identified successes seem
to have experienced improvement in their central business districts, an

increase in gentrified (that is, upper-middle-income) housing, and expansion in the population of "young single individuals and childless couples (yuppies)" (Wolman, Ford, and Hill, 1994: 844). But a proliferation of bookshops and cappuccino bars, while certainly pleasant, should not lead us to identify a place as successfully revitalized. Thus, we were worried about problems of relying on expert identification when so many of our colleagues pointed to Portland, Minneapolis–St. Paul, and Seattle as shining examples of regionalism. We were also concerned that the relative racial homogeneity of these model regions meant that they had faced a different set of challenges in forging common interests than those present in the starting point of our analysis: the ethnically diverse, often fragmented, locale of Southern California.

We therefore decided to take a more quantitative approach. Drawing on the set of seventy-four metropolitan areas used in the regression analysis of chapter 5 (see the list in table 5.1), we arrayed the metropolitan statistical areas (MSAs) according to their growth in regional per capita income and their reduction in central-city poverty over the 1980s.[4] The general pattern, shown in figure 6.1, is in keeping with the regression estimates of chapter 5: faster growth and poverty reduction go together.

To analyze further and select "best cases," we divided the sample into four groups: (1) regions in which both growth and poverty reduction exceeded the sample medians; (2) regions in which growth was above the median but poverty reduction was below it; (3) regions in which growth was below the median but poverty reduction exceeded it; and (4) areas in which both growth and poverty reduction were below the median. The resulting twenty-seven relatively high performing regions (found in the lower right-hand quadrant of figure 6.1) are listed in table 6.1. It is interesting to note that the often-mentioned regional success stories (Portland, Seattle, and Minneapolis–St. Paul) are not among them. Neither is Los Angeles: it achieved growth that was slightly below-median and an increase in poverty that was slightly above-median during the 1980s, making it among the best in the category of "worst" performers (a group that included expected problem cases like Gary and Detroit).

The "above-median" performers, taken from the best performers quadrant of figure 6.1, are looked at more carefully in figure 6.2. Given that there are fewer observations to clutter the display, we list identifier codes adjacent to the marker of performance (with the codes taken from table 6.1). As with the larger figure, "southeast" is preferable as this indicates both higher growth and sharper reductions in poverty. But how do we weigh growth versus poverty when grading performance—that is, which of the

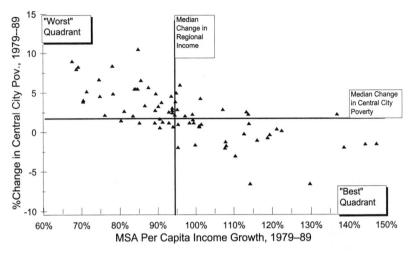

Figure 6.1. Income growth and the change in central-city poverty in seventy-four metro areas.

MSAs in, say, the Boston-Newark (BO-NW) cluster or the Oxnard-Jacksonville (OX-JC) cluster should be considered superior? Moreover, shouldn't we also rank regions by measures like the degree of residential segregation of the poor or the difference between central-city and suburban poverty, particularly since we have suggested that such differential poverty experience by geographic location may diminish the regional will to confront community development issues?

To get at these questions, we took the "best" performers from table 6.1 and figure 6.2 and created a series of scatterplots looking at the relationship between growth and the residential segregation of the poor (figure 6.3), the ratio of city to suburban poverty (figure 6.4), and a measure of metropolitan income inequality (figure 6.5).[5] Noting that southeast remains the best direction in all the graphs, the careful reader will observe that a series of regions, including Atlanta (AT), Boston (BO), Charlotte (CR), and San Jose (SJ), seem to have ended up with consistently favorable outcomes across the range of variables.[6] Since our field research on these cases was to occur in spring/summer 1996—just as Atlanta officials would be busy with preparation for the 1996 Olympic Games—we decided to focus on Boston, Charlotte, and San Jose.

To double-check our selection, we devised a "growing together" index that ranked all seventy-four regions by giving equal weight to three different criteria: the rapidity of growth, the size of poverty reduction, and the residential segregation of the poor. The three selected regions were in the top

Table 6.1

Economic Growth, Change in Central-City Poverty,
and Residential Dissimilarity in Regions with
Above-Median Growth and Above-Median Performance
in Reducing Poverty

MSA Region (in alphabetical order)	Code	Growth of Per Capita Income, 1979–89	Change in Central-City Poverty, 1980–90	Residential Dissimilarity of Poor, 1990
Allentown-Bethlehem, PA-NJ	AL	99.5	1.2	34.5
Atlanta, GA	AT	112.7	−0.2	39.6
Austin, TX	AU	97.2	2.1	37.6
Baltimore, MD	BL	116.1	−1.0	46.0
Boston-Lawrence-Salem, MA	BO	144.4	−1.5	37.4
Charlotte-Gastonia, NC	CR	99.9	−1.6	31.9
Greensboro–Winston-Salem, NC	GB	107.9	−1.2	29.3
Greenville-Spartanburg, SC	GN	95.3	−1.9	30.3
Indianapolis, IN	IN	95.4	1.0	39.9
Jacksonville, FL	JC	110.4	−3.0	32.5
Memphis, TN-AR-MS	ME	98.4	1.2	42.9
Middlesex-Somerset, NJ	NB	147.4	−1.5	36.4
Nashville, TN	NV	100.9	0.8	33.4
New Haven-Waterbury, CT	NH	138.6	−1.9	46.0
New York, NY	NY	118.8	−0.7	43.0
Newark, NJ	NW	129.7	−6.5	48.2
Orlando, FL	OR	107.7	−2.0	27.2
Oxnard-Ventura, CA	OX	122.4	0.2	30.9
Philadelphia, PA-NJ	PH	119.4	−0.3	47.9

Table 6.1   (Continued)

Economic Growth, Change in Central City Poverty, and Residential Dissimilarity in Regions With Above-Median Growth and Above-Median Performance in Reducing Poverty

MSA Region (in alphabetical order)	Code	Growth of Per Capita Income, 1979–89	Change in Central City Poverty, 1980–90	Residential Dissimilarity of Poor, 1990
Richmond-Petersburg, VA	RI	99.3	1.6	44.0
Sacramento, CA	SC	94.5	2.2	31.0
San Diego, CA	SD	101.5	1.0	31.9
San Jose, CA	SJ	114.0	1.1	31.3
Tampa-St. Petersburg, FL	TA	100.9	0.7	31.0
Washington, DC-MD-VA	DC	108.0	−1.7	38.1
West Palm Beach-Boca Raton, FL	PB	121.2	0.4	34.4
Wilmington, NY	WL	114.2	−6.5	34.6

ten, giving us additional confidence in our selection.[7] We then tried a ranking that gave equal weight to the aforementioned factors, as well as to our measure of metropolitan inequality in 1990. With the sample reduced to forty-nine regions due to missing observations on distributional equity, Boston, Charlotte, and San Jose occupied three of the top four positions.

Selecting these three regions appealed on other grounds. They offered a range of population demographics (see figure 6.6): San Jose has a significant population of Latinos and Asians; the Charlotte region is largely biracial (black-white); and while Boston itself has a significant minority population, the larger Boston region is predominantly white. The three regions also hail from distinct geographical macroregions of the United States (the Northeast, the South, and the West) and exhibit three different development patterns. Boston is a stereotypical eastern metropolitan area with a dense central city supporting a large suburban area. The Charlotte area is anchored by a relatively modern southern city that has sought aggressively to both position

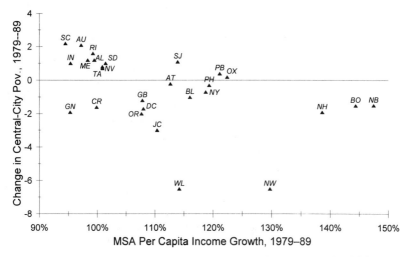

Figure 6.2. Income growth and the change in central-city poverty in "high performing" regions.

itself as a center of regional distribution and business and build a national presence in banking. San Jose, in the heart of Silicon Valley, is a technology-driven area with a large, diffuse central city, a sizable immigrant population, and extensive suburbanization of employment and manufacturing.

In our discussion, we make much of the fact that Charlotte, in particu-lar, was able to annex adjoining suburbs, arguing that this helped build a countywide commitment to the central and inner city. Of course, another explanation for the reduction of central-city poverty in Charlotte is simply that annexing higher-income areas into the central city boundaries may have "artificially" lowered the recorded city poverty rate. This implies that our choice of Charlotte as a "best performer" could be problematic: poverty was not really reduced but diluted (although we should note that this boundary issue does not affect improvements in metrowide measures of residential segregation or inequality). San Jose was also what Rusk (1995) terms an "elas-tic" city, leading to potential worries about that choice as well.[8]

While we could not conduct such an analysis for all the cities in our sample, we decided to "remap" Charlotte and San Jose, calculating 1990 poverty rates just for the tracts that constituted each city in 1980.[9] As it turns out, the improvement in our poverty reduction variable falls by 1.4 percent-age points in the case of Charlotte and .5 percent in the case of San Jose. These figures would still land both regions safely in the "best" quadrant and our three selected cases are now in the top eleven and top five of our respec-tive rankings rather than in the top ten and top four. Of course, given that

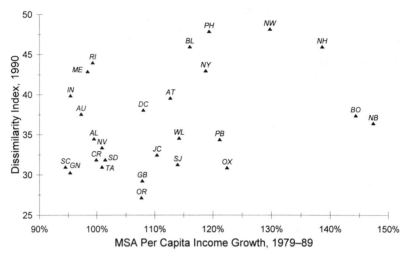

Figure 6.3. Income growth and the 1990 residential dissimilarity/segregation of the poor.

the vast majority of elastic cities are annexing higher-income areas, a full accounting would likely shift other MSAs down the scale; for this reason, we are confident that our city choice and the analysis that follows are not significantly distorted by the various boundary shifts between 1980 and 1990.

With the metropolitan areas selected, we did background research, then conducted a series of team visits to the three areas to interview regional and community leaders.[10] We begin with San Jose, an area that seems to have stressed growth; then turn to Charlotte, which focused on tying together the fates of the central city and its suburbs; and close with an examination of Boston, a region that used a creative mix of policies to ensure that the benefits of growth would reach the area's poorer residents.

San Jose: Regional Consensus and Growth

Demographic Context

The San Jose MSA (Santa Clara County) is anchored by the City of San Jose. Despite an early history as a relatively small agricultural center, San Jose is now the third largest city in California and the eleventh largest in the country. Population growth has been dramatic: while the MSA population tripled from 642,315 in 1960 to nearly 1.5 million residents in 1990, the central city's population nearly quadrupled over the same time period (from 204,196 to 782,248), partly as a result of aggressive annexation.[11] San Jose is a relatively wealthy central city, with the mean household income (in constant 1990 dollars) having increased from $46,776 in 1980 to $54,400 in 1995. In 1990,

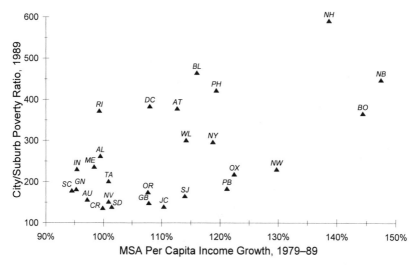

Figure 6.4. Income growth and the ratio of central-city to suburban poverty in 1989.

the city's poverty rate was 9.3 percent, higher than the 5.6 percent rate in the rest of Santa Clara County, but still favorable by national standards and much better than the state level of 12.5 percent in the same year.

Like much of the rest of California, the San Jose MSA has experienced a dramatic increase in its minority populations. Between 1980 and 1990, Santa Clara County's Asian population increased by 160 percent while the Latino population rose by 40 percent (well above the 15 percent growth rate for the county as a whole). By 1990, over 42 percent of the MSA population was minority, with the bulk of that population of Latino or Asian origin. While residential segregation remains a problem, the percent of Santa Clara County African-Americans and Latinos who reside in the central city is roughly similar to the percent of county Anglos residing in the central city; as in Los Angeles, San Jose's minority residents have increasingly moved into the surrounding suburbs.[12]

Economy and Workforce in the San Jose MSA

Part of the reason for San Jose's relatively strong growth in income is the high-tech base of Silicon Valley. The valley boasts the largest population of engineers, scientists, and high-tech business executives in the country; serving this sector are an array of law firms, banks, real estate agencies, and other high-end services (Saxenian, 1996: 41). The dynamism of the high-tech industry has helped lower unemployment and bring the region's wages to the top of the national scale.

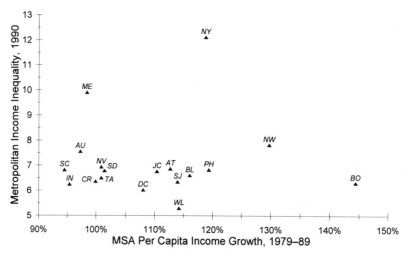

Figure 6.5. Income growth and metropolitan inequality in "high performing" regions.

While Silicon Valley has created broad growth in job opportunities, differential outcomes in occupation and income are evident. Anglos, for example, comprised 62 percent of the labor force in Santa Clara County in 1990 but were 76 percent of the executives and managers and nearly as high a percentage of those in professional specialties. The presence of Asian employees was highest in the areas of technician and machine operator, comprising about 25 percent of those in these fields although they were only 16 percent of the total labor force. Latinos were 18 percent of the labor force but were 36 percent of machine operators and nearly as large a proportion of those in the service category.[13] This occupational hierarchy by ethnicity is reflected in income differentials between Anglos and Latinos: while both groups are better off than the national average, the distance between them is more pronounced in San Jose than in the United States as a whole.[14]

As in Los Angeles (see chapter 2), the high- and low-wage jobs of Silicon Valley are complementary. Engineers design circuits and chips while lower-income workers labor directly on the assembly end of electronics, sometimes under sweatshop conditions (Hossfeld, 1990), and clean the offices where computer-aided design occurs.[15] Even the rapid expansion of the service sector is linked to high-wage employment: young professionals "overworking" in the software and design firms that populate the region have come to rely on immigrant and other workers in the food and child care industries. In short, one of America's most dynamic industrial areas

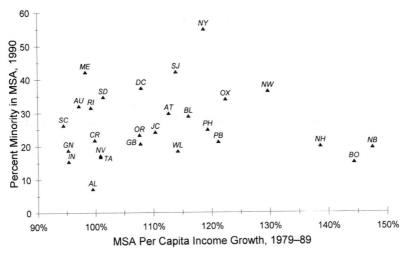

Figure 6.6. Income growth and the percent minority in MSA, 1990.

has two faces that are economically linked but differentiated by income and often by color.[16]

Growth and Poverty in San Jose

The San Jose MSA experienced the second fastest growth in per capita income of our three regions and ranked twelfth on this variable in the overall seventy-four-MSA sample. Unlike Boston and Charlotte, central-city poverty in San Jose actually rose during the 1980s. However, the region's performance on this front was superior relative to the dismal national record: San Jose's central-city poverty rate rose by slightly over 1 percent between 1979 and 1989 while the median increase for our sixty-two-region sample was 2.6 percent.

What accounted for the high rate of growth through the 1980s? One obvious answer lies in Silicon Valley's general strength in high technology as well as its ability to secure defense contracts, at least during that decade. But these factors are themselves rooted in other variables, such as the research and training capabilities embodied in local institutions of higher education and the links of business to these institutions.[17] Stanford, UC Berkeley, and other regional institutions traditionally have been a training ground for engineers and a source of new technological innovations. Equally important have been the California State University campuses and a superb set of local community colleges.[18]

Of course, many areas have rich educational resources and seem to make much less of them. Another key variable was what Annalee Saxenian terms Silicon Valley's "flexible industrial system." The region's high-tech firms have long been characterized by a high rate of turnover among the technical professionals, including a constant breaking away of key engineers to start new companies. Technological capabilities and know-how were therefore diffused throughout the region and not simply confined to one vertically organized firm (Saxenian, 1996: 37). The constant mobility has also blurred lines between firms and had an impact within companies, as shown by the replacement of traditional corporate systems of hierarchy with notions and practices of teamwork.

The valley, in short, is rich in the sort of social capital that leads to business success. This, in turn, has helped produce a heightened regional consciousness among business actors eager to preserve the social ecology that allows their firms to prosper. For example, the Santa Clara Valley Manufacturing Group (now called the Silicon Valley Manufacturing Group) was founded in 1977 by David Packard of the Hewlett-Packard Corporation and thirty-two other charter members representing electronics companies, banks, and other key employers. The organization has historically taken up social infrastructure issues like traffic congestion and the lack of affordable housing in the valley. It has helped organize broad collaborative efforts such as the Housing Action Coalition, a housing advocacy group that includes a broad array of interests, including environmentalists and labor unions, and has even lobbied for increased taxes in order to both expand the local highway system and support light rail development. Throughout its history, the Manufacturing Group has maintained a cooperative relationship with the public sector, crafting the basis for informal business-government collaboration in other areas.[19]

The most recent outgrowth of this sort of consciousness—regional in scope, led by business, and involving the public sector—is Joint Venture: Silicon Valley Network (JV: SVN).[20] This group was formed in 1992, partly because of the hard hits the valley took in the wake of defense downsizing. Joint Venture quickly became and remains a key actor in the region's destiny. Explicitly focused on developing a collaborative regional strategy, building social capital, and forming new strategic alliances, it has helped to coordinate public policies, "sell" the region to others, and induce businesses to work on broad issues such as education. Interestingly, even the group's geographic scope has reflected a new approach: rather than being limited to the political jurisdiction of Santa Clara County, it stretches over parts of three other counties with its coverage defined in terms of the industrial clusters said to comprise the competitive base of Silicon Valley.

Of course, "collaboration" is not entirely inclusive. The founders of the main businesses in the valley were a homogeneous group of young, white men largely from the Midwest (Saxenian, 1996: 30) and much remains unchanged: as of late 1998, no African-Americans or Latinos headed one of the top 150 Silicon Valley companies and only 8 percent of these firms had a person of Asian descent in the chair or CEO position.[21] Likewise, public policy has often reflected an imbalance by race. While the City of San Jose (through its Redevelopment Agency) has plowed millions of dollars worth of subsidies into showcasing its downtown as a corporate headquarters for the Silicon Valley, officials acknowledge that there has been insufficient attention to creating jobs and business opportunities in areas like the Mexican-American barrio of East San Jose.[22] Meanwhile, most of the manufacturing in the valley remains in the northern part of the city and county, yielding a spatial mismatch for low-skill workers in south and east San Jose.[23]

Lessons: Growth and Regionalism in San Jose

The San Jose/Santa Clara County experience suggests the potential positive impact on growth when business exhibits leadership in the arena of social infrastructure and economic restructuring. The City of San Jose (like Charlotte) also played an active role through its attempt to position the city as the center of the region, calling itself the "Capital of the Silicon Valley." Its strategy included a highly focused program to promote downtown redevelopment,[24] a remarkable effort since most of the manufacturing and business growth in the earliest days of the valley was in the northern and suburban part of the MSA.[25]

But these efforts to remake the region and its center city were not matched by any coherent strategy to tackle poverty. Indeed, many of the leaders we interviewed were surprised by the relative performance of San Jose on poverty and were hard-pressed to name any public policy that might have contributed to this result. San Jose's poverty performance—a modest increase that was nonetheless better than the national pattern of the 1980s—was instead probably due to the positive impact of a tight job market on lower-income residents.[26] One is left to wonder how much more could have been achieved had San Jose and the other cities in Santa Clara County entertained a more focused strategy.

Why was so little done on the poverty front? One answer lies in the lack of organized activities or interest groups working on behalf of lower-income individuals. Although unionization in the region is above the national average and San Jose has recently become home to one of the most dynamic central labor councils in the country, union presence is less significant in the most dynamic sectors of the economy.[27] Silicon Valley entrepreneurs are often individualistic and resist collective bargaining arrangements. Moreover, the management model "of shifting and horizontally linked confederations of work teams" (Saxenian, 1996: 55) tends to provide an alternative "voice" to employees, making it more difficult to organize.[28] Officials in San Jose also suggest that the relatively high pay of many workers has reduced the need for unions. The labor movement has tried to focus on organizing possibilities at the lower end of the service sector, especially with its Justice for Janitors campaign.[29] More recently, labor and community forces came together in late 1998 to put in place a living wage ordinance designed to raise the wages of low-wage workers in firms subcontracting with the City of San Jose.

Despite this recent labor-sponsored activity, there seems to have been a relatively modest amount of political organizing and grassroots development at the community level. In some sense, this is surprising. Minority communities have made political gains and there are an increasing number of Latinos and others in elected and appointed positions, including the 1998 victory of a Latino for the mayor's seat. San Jose also boasts what many believe is the most innovative and effective job-training program in the country, the Center for Employment Training (CET), and enjoys the presence of the Non-Profit Development Center, an often-praised organization that trains nonprofit leaders and helps build working and funding relationships between nonprofits and the government and corporate sectors.[30] Still, many community development corporations (CDCs) in the San Jose area seem less sophisticated operationally than those in other large cities, and city officials, when asked to identify their strategies for poorer neighborhoods in the early 1990s, pointed to programs like Project Crackdown, a police-community effort to rid neighborhoods of gangs and drugs. This hardly seems like the holistic development strategy many in the community-building field are now embracing.[31]

There are at least three central lessons to be learned from San Jose's experience. The first is that regions with significant amounts of "horizontal social capital," that is, networks among major economic and political players, are able to grow rapidly. The Silicon Valley boom of the 1980s was built in part on an existing set of relationships among firms and individuals; in this period, regional consciousness was high but "informal." It was only when job growth, which had held steady at around 7 percent annually through much of the 1980s, stopped in the early 1990s due to high-tech restructuring and defense spending cutbacks, that a more formal mechanism like Joint Venture was formed. The rapidity of the organization's coming together and its success in helping to restore growth quickly to the valley certainly indicates the effectiveness of the strategies its leaders adopted to develop, popularize, and implement new initiatives.[32] However, it also reflects the fertile ground of social capital developed through years of interactions.

Our second lesson is that growth matters. A robust economy will improve poverty—or moderate its increase—even in the absence of a conscious strategy to link poorer communities to the regional poles of success. This suggests that those concerned about poverty need to be cognizant of the policies and programs that will promote economic expansion: growth is the sine qua non for successful redistribution.[33]

The third lesson is just now emerging: antipoverty policies must go beyond a simple focus on growth per se. Given the relatively low levels of unionization and community organizing in this region, public officials and business leaders have seldom felt pressed to deal with poverty. Instead, attention has focused on transportation infrastructure and other initiatives necessary to keep the San Jose economy humming. But exploding housing costs, increases in child poverty, and rising inequality in the valley have led even some in the business sector to worry about the sustainability of a purely growth-oriented strategy.[34]

To secure a better future, San Jose will need to strengthen its much-vaunted social capital *vertically* as well as horizontally. Ties among businesses are not enough; community, labor, and other groups need to have a voice in the regional destiny as well.[35] Joint Venture and other business groups have begun to make steps in the right direction: during 1997–98, Joint Venture launched a multisector and multiracial visioning process that has led to a new strategic focus on environment and equity as well as economy. Meanwhile, the local labor movement has itself embraced regionalism; in 1995, it formed its own research think tank, Working Partnerships USA, to address growing inequality within Silicon Valley through well-researched strategic public interventions in the labor market (Benner 1998).[36] Whether the region can make the transition to a fully collaborative approach—one in which specific policies begin to better spread prosperity and opportunity across the usual gaps of class and ethnicity—remains to be seen.

Charlotte: Building the Region, Maintaining Community

Demographic Context

The Charlotte-Mecklenburg-Gastonia-Rock Hill MSA encompasses seven of the twelve counties that are considered part of the broader Charlotte metropolitan region. The City of Charlotte grew at a rate of 26 percent during the 1980s, exceeding the nearly 20 percent attained by the region; by 1990 the central city held 34 percent of the MSA's total population. Population growth has accelerated over the 1990s, with Charlotte's population rising by 15 percent over the first half of that decade.

Part of this central city population growth was due to a 1962 state annexation law mandating that any area within Mecklenburg County taking on the character of an urban locale automatically becomes a candidate for annexation by the county's biggest city, Charlotte.[37] As a result, twenty-seven unincorporated areas were annexed by Charlotte during the decade of the 1980s. This resulted in a direct population increase of 42,716—more than half of the population increase of the central city over this time period.[38] Still, over 42 percent of the MSA-level population increase of the 1980s was due to in-migration, indicating the attractiveness of the region.

Minorities totaled 21.8 percent of the 1990 MSA population, of which over 90 percent (19.9 percent of the MSA) were African-American. Within the city of Charlotte, African-Americans constituted 32 percent of the population, having increased in numbers by 28.8 percent over the 1980s. Since Latinos, Asians, Native Americans, and other ethnic groups made up only around 2 percent of the region's 1990 population, the ethnic dynamics of Charlotte politics have been largely black-white, a fact reflected in electoral strategies and political coalition building.[39]

Of the MSAs we review in this chapter, the Charlotte area posted the lowest increase in per capita income. Despite this modest performance as far as growth, the region managed to obtain the best central-city poverty reduction of our three comparative cases. In the MSA as a whole, the poverty rate declined by nearly 1 percent, going from 10.5 percent in 1980 to 9.6 percent by 1990, while in the central city (Charlotte) the poverty rate fell by 1.6 percent over the 1980s, ending the decade with a level of 10.8 percent. Charlotte may therefore offer some lessons about how to do well in terms of equity even in a context of only reasonably healthy growth.[40]

Economy and Workforce in the Charlotte MSA

Charlotte has long played a national role as a major textile power; by 1903, more than half the country's textile production was located within a one-hundred-mile radius of the city. The convergence of several railroad lines in the mid-1880s and the evolution of North Carolina's interstate highway system in the twentieth century paved the way for Charlotte to become a major distribution center. The establishment of a branch of the Federal Reserve in the 1920s marked the beginning of Charlotte's eventual evolution into a top banking center. Still, the workforce was largely industrial prior to the 1980s: in 1970, for example, over 40 percent of the nonagricultural labor force worked in a factory and some 62 percent of these workers were employed in a textile or related apparel facility (Stuart, 1995b: 5).

With global competition inducing contraction in the textile sector, finance, insurance, and other nonmanufacturing services emerged as the region's growth industries.[41] Mecklenburg County, the site of Charlotte, led the region, accounting for nearly 86 percent of the regional gain in non-manufacturing employment. By the end of the 1982–93 period, Mecklenburg County, with 35 percent of the regional population, had 49 percent of the total jobs, 25 percent of manufacturing employment, and almost 58 percent of the nonmanufacturing total (Stuart, 1995a: 7).

One of the key areas of expansion was banking. In 1988, NationsBank merged with First Republic Bank of Texas and, in 1996, acquired First Fidelity Bancorporation, making NationsBank the country's second-largest bank. By 1998, it had merged with California-based Bank of America to become the nation's largest bank. Growth on the part of the state's other major banks, Wachovia and First Union, has made Charlotte one of the fastest growing financial regions in the nation. Wholesale and retail trade have expanded, as Charlotte sought to market both the products of its diverse manufacturing sector (including textiles, food products, printing, publishing, and machinery) and products imported from abroad and from other regions of the United States. Construction of office space, housing, shopping malls, hotels, and restaurants has expanded rapidly to accompany the growing population and its service needs.

The Charlotte boom of the 1980s was not simply serendipity. The City of Charlotte consciously built up its role as a regional distribution center, making use of both the historical regional rail system and the major highways that provide convenient north-south trucking links.[42] It also has expanded the Charlotte/Douglas International Airport, converting this facility into the nation's twenty-fourth busiest airport. In addition, the city established the Charlotte Foreign Trade Zone, an "inland port" that provides customs and immigration services and helps attract foreign manufacturers. The region as a whole, but particularly the City of Charlotte, also has conducted an aggressive marketing campaign to attract new domestic business.

Partly as a result of these efforts, Charlotte's unemployment rate was extremely low by national standards, falling from 5 percent in 1979 to 3.2 percent in 1989.[43] Yet the impressive thing about Charlotte remains its superior performance on both poverty and income distribution (recall figures 6.2 and 6.5): the region was able to grow while leaving fewer of its residents behind.

Growth and Poverty in Charlotte

Of course, part of the reduction of poverty was due to the region's relatively rapid economic growth. But this cannot be a full account: other regions grew much faster but made less progress on poverty. Instead, several structural factors helped bridge the gap between city and suburb and provide more direct opportunity for the poor.

The first of these involved the city-suburb relationship itself. Both the annexation law governing Mecklenburg County and the related consolidation of schools into a countywide system (each of which occurred in the early 1960s) helped to solve classic collective action problems that have plagued many other regions. In most areas, for example, parents either can exercise their voice to improve a city school district or they and their progeny can exit to a suburb, leaving a declining school system in their wake. The resulting fall in educational attainment often creates a regionwide decline in workforce preparedness and hence lower incomes all around. Similarly, middle-class residents weary of high taxes to address poverty can defect from the central city, leaving concentrated poverty and fiscal crisis in their wake.

By contrast, Charlotte's annexation law and school arrangement constituted "ties that bind." They ensured that wealthier enclaves, which might find it in their immediate interest to separate jurisdictionally, would find it nearly impossible to do so. The law, for example, ruled out new freestanding municipal suburban areas surrounding Charlotte while school consolidation into a single Charlotte Mecklenburg County metropolitan system meant that parents seeking an alternative to public school would either have to choose expensive private schools or be forced to leave the county altogether.[44]

Equally significant was the decision of the Charlotte City Council in 1976 to declare that any additional public housing would be scattered-site. This policy reversed the earlier practice under which the city had concentrated low-income households in one of eight relatively dense projects.[45] As noted in chapter 4, deconcentration helps the poor, partly because it moves some public housing residents closer to suburbanized job opportunities, and partly because it means that the poor and their children then reside in communities with a broader mix of role models and social networks. Indeed, a Charlotte Housing Authority (CHA) report indicates that residents in scattered-site housing are over 20 percent more likely to be working than residents in the larger projects.[46] Such attempts to deconcentrate the poor can also help with evoking a sense of collective responsibility, partly because poverty becomes as close as one's neighbors.[47]

The late 1970s also brought a shift from an at-large council system to district, or neighborhood-based, representation in the City of Charlotte. With this change, Harvey Gantt was elected to the city council, and later served two terms as the first African-American mayor of Charlotte (1983–87). Partly as a result of the new neighborhood representation and Gantt's leadership, infrastructure spending began to be channeled to the historically neglected northern part of the city.

While Gantt's reign as mayor was eventually ended by a successful challenge from Republican Sue Myrick, the efforts to target inner city poverty had gained their own momentum. In 1989, Charlotte launched an effort called a "City Within a City," which still governs city policy making. Using census data, seventy-three different neighborhoods were classified as stable, threatened, or fragile. Each year, the city is committed to providing special attention to selected problem communities using a multidimensional approach that combines improved policing, enhanced human services, and special development strategies.[48]

In light of this policy and poverty reduction record, it is little wonder that urban expert Neil Peirce has suggested that "the totality of effort (in attacking poverty and promoting neighborhood development in Charlotte) is stunning. It is equaled in few cities around the nation. . . . The region has a long ways to go in fighting crime and poverty. But it is on the right track—something few other American cities can say" (Peirce et al., 1995).

Lessons: Building Ties That Bind

Peirce may have been overly optimistic. To some degree, the reduction of poverty levels in Charlotte resulted from an influx, partly through annexation, of a higher-income population. Moreover, while poor whites have been able to move into outlying areas and capitalize on new manufacturing employment growth, the residuals of racial discrimination seem to have inhibited the African-American poor from following suit. Many, particularly those in public housing, have languished even as growth swelled the economy around them.

Still, the record has been enough to impress outside observers and to suggest that perhaps something can be learned for policy in other cities. Certain factors were clearly important: annexation of suburbs helped to keep the social fabric continuous; scattered-site housing served to deconcentrate the poor; and enhanced neighborhood representation improved public sector responsiveness to community concerns. Yet the real question is why such policies were adopted, and the answer to this lies in part in the attitude of Charlotte's business leadership.

Charlotte's business class, often dominated by key leaders such as NationsBank Chairman Hugh McColl and First Union CEO Ed Crutchfield, has long sought to retain economic leadership in the region.[49] The Charlotte Chamber of Commerce, for example, considers its territory to be a thirteen-county area. The Carolinas Partnership, formed from what used to be the Greater Charlotte Economic Development Council, covers an even broader area. Charlotte's business class has played an important role in both organizations, partly out of recognition that the city's prosperity depends on its ability to continue to serve the financial and distributional needs of the entire region. The commitment of the business community to improving transportation infrastructure (such as a new outer-ring freeway) and enhancing other physical and social ties has helped facilitate the knitting together of a coherent regional economy.

But Charlotte's business leaders also have been important proponents of supporting the downtown and the central city. One reason is that several major business figures have lived in and adjacent to the downtown area for a number of years. This itself partly stems from Charlotte's annexation law: since freestanding suburbs are prevented from developing, outlying residential areas enjoy few of the amenities available in the center of the city and do not offer respite from city taxes or separate school systems.[50]

Yet business leaders' attachment to the city stems from more than residence. Business has been "progressive" by southern standards. As Stephen Smith (1997) notes, business leaders were proud of the busing plan that integrated the Charlotte schools in the 1970s. Business groups were helpful in electing the city's first African-American mayor, Harvey Gantt, and downtown and neighborhood interests have often been linked by policy as well as politics.[51] For example, bond measures to revitalize commercial areas in Charlotte have included funds for street improvements in low-income neighborhoods. One of the city's most recent consolidated plans mentions a "growing economic division of the 'haves' and 'have nots' in the community" and the "City Within a City" planning framework has attempted to address this by marshaling resources to eradicate the worst pockets of poverty. Even the Carolinas Partnership, one of the business-led regional groupings, has initiated a series of efforts to work with public housing residents in order to link them more closely to the economy.

Some of the elements of Charlotte's success are explicable but not easily reproducible. The sense of common destiny that drove public policy may have been facilitated by Charlotte's relatively small size.[52] The annexation law and the consolidated school system may have diminished the lure of suburban escape, but few municipalities in America's regions seem ready to give up such autonomy. What could be generalized is the need for business leadership and commitment to the central city and its inner-city neighborhoods. Charlotte's business and political leaders worked for the stability and vitality of the downtown, and were proud that usually explosive issues like school integration were resolved relatively calmly. Charlotte's business community, striving for regional leadership, recognized that more inclusive "win-win" outcomes tend to cement relationships and produce sustainable growth. Indeed, Charlotte's most prominent businessperson, Hugh McColl, continues to lead on these issues, arguing in a 1999 speech to developers that they should support emerging Smart Growth strategies (see chapter 7) and suggesting that everyone—"developers, business people, public officials, environmental advocates, ordinary citizens"—should be at the table when regional growth strategies are being discussed and determined.[53]

Boston: The Politics of Growth and Equity

Demographic Context

Boston is a city of nearly 600,000 residents in a five-county, 129-city metro area of around 3.2 million.[54] The metropolitan economy comprises about two-thirds of the state economy.[55] The City of Boston itself has less than 10 percent of the state's population, but provides about 16 percent of its employment, 24 percent of its production of goods and services, 21 percent of the total earned income, and 18 percent of state tax revenues.[56] It is the biggest city in, as well as the economic and cultural hub of, the New England region and its 13.2 million people.[57]

From 1950 to 1980, the City of Boston experienced a pattern typical of many older urban areas: the dramatic loss of about one-third of its population even as the surrounding suburbs grew. Then, during the 1980s, both Boston and its suburban area added population.[58] This latter pattern is especially unusual for Northeastern cities, particularly those like Boston that lack the ability to access additional land through annexation or other mechanisms.[59]

While minorities constituted only 15 percent of the metro population in 1990, they constitute about 41 percent of the population in the central city of Boston. African-Americans made up over 60 percent of Boston's minority population but, between 1980 and 1990, the city's Hispanic population increased from 6.4 percent to 10.7 percent, while Asians increased from 2.6 percent to 5.3 percent of total population.[60] Still, racial dynamics, as illustrated by the busing crises of the 1970s, have traditionally been black-white, and residential and schooling patterns are highly segregated.

The Boston area has the usual set of special-purpose regional institutions, including the Metropolitan Boston Transportation Authority (MBTA), which runs the public transportation system for seventy-eight cities and towns in eastern Massachusetts; the Massachusetts Water Resources Authority, a court-imposed agency to help clean up the polluted Boston harbor; the Metropolitan District Commission, a regional agency that oversees some parks, water treatment plants, and highways; and the Massachusetts Port Authority, which oversees Logan Airport, the ports, and the construction of the new harbor tunnels. The Metropolitan Area Planning Council, the region's planning agency, primarily issues reports on regional trends and has little legal authority.

As a result, general regional efforts to promote economic growth or to deal with social and economic problems have emerged mostly from a wide variety of ad hoc arrangements. One historically important leadership group was an organization called the Coordinating Committee, nicknamed "the Vault," that coalesced in the 1950s. The Vault helped engineer the City of Boston's makeover in the 1960s and 1970s through urban renewal, and by the 1980s was composed of thirty members representing the largest employers and some of the major business groups, such as the Greater Boston Chamber of Commerce and the Greater Boston Real Estate Board.[61] Many other forums for regional thinking and advocacy are provided by business organizations and trade associations, government-business partnerships, community-based coalitions, or some combination of these groupings (including the Central Artery Committee, the Greater Boston Chamber of Commerce, the Greater Boston Real Estate Board, the Private Industry Council, and the Metropolitan Boston Housing Partnership).[62] The state government (particularly under Governor Michael Dukakis from 1982 to 1990) has also played an important role in regional planning and economic development efforts.

Economy and Workforce in the Boston MSA

During the 1980s Massachusetts experienced what Case (1991) terms "unprecedented prosperity." From 1982 through 1988, Massachusetts had a 3.1 percent average annual growth in employment. In July 1987 the state's unemployment rate was 2.7 percent, the lowest in the country. This striking performance soon became known as the "Massachusetts Miracle."

Massachusetts's economic growth during the 1980s was based on the strength of a few key sectors: minicomputers and high technology, defense, finance and insurance (especially the growth of mutual funds), health care, higher education, business and professional services, and real estate. Rich in electronics and services, the Boston area shared, and in many ways led, the state's economic boom. The overall number of jobs in the metropolitan area grew from 859,654 in 1970 to 1.13 million in 1980, to 1.49 million in 1990, producing an increase in metropolitan income over the latter period that placed the Boston area second in our seventy-four-region sample.

The central city itself experienced sharp gains: while Boston's employment base had fallen from 466,200 in 1970 to 440,234 in 1980, it had climbed to 520,187 by 1990 (Torto and Wheaton, 1994). In fact, the City of Boston to some degree drove growth: while 85,000 Boston residents commute to jobs outside the central city, 391,000 suburbanites commute into Boston on a typical day.[63] This central role in the economy gave Boston leverage to secure better benefits for its residents, including low-income communities. Strikingly, per capita income grew by about the same rate in the central city, the metropolitan area, and the state over the 1980s, implying a relatively equal distribution of the gains.

Growth and Poverty in Boston

Boston was one of the few big cities in the country that saw a reduction in the poverty rate during the 1980s. Moreover, the poverty rate declined for all racial groups—whites, blacks, and Latinos. Osterman (1991) argues that much of this improvement, particularly in the 1980–88 period, was due to the tight labor market in Massachusetts. Much as in San Jose, falling unemployment led to increasing returns to work. In 1984, for example, average hourly earnings for production workers in Massachusetts were 7.5 percent below the nation as a whole; by 1987, Massachusetts's and national wage levels were about the same; and by the end of 1990, Massachusetts's wages were 4 percent above the national figure (Case and Shiller, 1994). The general rise in labor demand also helped the previously unemployed. While there were some public efforts to overcome existing mismatches in skills, the labor shortage led employers to hire and then train people whom they might otherwise not have hired. The ability of firms to incorporate new workers was enhanced by an earlier set of public investments in mass transit; where public transit was inadequate, labor-hungry employers found ways to overcome it, often by providing pick-up and shuttle services.[64]

Of course, not all boats were lifted by the rising tide. About three-quarters of those classified as poor in the city worked at least part of the time during the 1986 to 1989 period, suggesting that some active workers remained unable to access high-wage employment. The poverty rate for families headed by single parents, especially women, did not decline, and the economic boom also led to high housing costs, a phenomenon that meant that real wage increases did not always translate into improvements in economic well-being, especially for low- and moderate-income households.[65]

Still, the overall picture for Boston is one of success on both the growth and poverty reduction fronts. As noted, rapid growth gave employers incentives to overcome the usual barriers of skill, race, and geography. But policy makers also attempted to take advantage of the strong regional conditions by instituting new policies to ensure that lower-income residents would reap some of the benefits of the expansion.

Such public intervention was considered especially appropriate since it was government efforts that had helped prime the pump. The defense buildup of the early 1980s was especially important: from 1987 to 1989, Massachusetts received an average of $8.21 billion in prime defense contracts a year, a level that amounted to $1,405 per resident, almost three times the national average of $514 per capita.[66] Massachusetts garnered four times the national average in defense contracts for research, development, testing, and evaluation, reflecting the strength of the Boston area's higher education sector (particularly MIT) and the many spin-off firms tied to its educational institutions.

Federal funds were also available for the expansion of the region's public transit system, especially the MBTA subway and commuter rail system,[67] and for other infrastructure projects, such as the cleanup of the Boston Harbor. The modernization of Logan Airport by the Massachusetts Port Authority, and the depression of the Central Artery and construction of a four-lane tunnel under Boston Harbor have involved billions of dollars in new spending. Meanwhile, federal funds for medical research, hospital construction, and higher education accelerated Boston's growth in these key economic sectors.

In short, growth did not come from the market alone. Moreover, the improvement in Boston's poverty statistics did not flow simply from healthy labor demand: local policy strived to build formal and informal arrangements that could better link low-income residents to growth opportunities. The Boston Jobs Policy, initiated in 1984, required that developers hire Boston residents (50 percent), minorities (25 percent), and women (10 percent) in high-paying construction jobs. There were formal and informal set-asides for minority developers, architects, and others in the construction projects sponsored or subsidized by government agencies, including the MBTA public transportation construction. The Central Artery project, a major public works/infrastructure initiative, also had significant set-asides linked to community-based organizations and minority contractors. Given that minority firms have a higher probability of employing minority workers, all these efforts helped provide access to jobs for Boston's minority population.

But it is in the realm of community development, particularly housing, that the Boston experience stands out. Boston's boom in office construction and employment in the downtown core came in the context of an aging housing stock. Increased demand led to skyrocketing prices: between 1983 and the third quarter of 1987, the median price of existing homes in metropolitan Boston rose 121 percent, far above the national increase of 23 percent.[68] Landlords began converting apartments to expensive condominiums, while private developers rushed to add market-rate housing by building on vacant land and renovating existing buildings.

Even as the city became saddled with the nation's highest housing prices, Boston's African-American and Latino neighborhoods remained scarred with abandoned buildings and large swaths of vacant land, the result of decades of population loss, bank redlining, arson-for-profit, and slumlords milking properties.[69] In response, a strong and diverse housing constituency fought to put the issues of both affordable housing and community development on the city's political agenda. Tenant activists, homeless advocacy organizations, senior citizens and church groups, neighborhood associations, civil rights groups representing minority communities, labor unions with low-income memberships and/or involved in the construction trades, and community-based development organizations all mobilized to influence the public debate, the media, and the political agenda. During the 1983 races for mayor and city council, the city's housing crisis became the central issue. With support from the city's housing activists, city councilor Ray Flynn was elected mayor on a platform of "sharing the prosperity" of the city's downtown boom with its low-income and working-class neighborhoods.

During its ten-year regime, the Flynn administration carried out an ambitious and progressive agenda on housing. In 1984, for example, Boston initiated an office-housing linkage program, requiring downtown developers to contribute financially ($5/square foot) to a Neighborhood Housing Trust Fund for affordable housing. Between 1984 and 1992, this program generated over $50 million in funds. A separate "inclusionary housing" policy required developers of market-rate residential projects to set aside (without public subsidies) 10 percent of units for low- and moderate-income residents. The city also implemented a "parcel-to-parcel" linkage program, tying development rights for lucrative downtown sites to the development of commercial space in low-income areas.[70]

To carry out the housing agenda, the city turned to, and supported, its community-based nonprofit housing developers. City-owned property (buildings and vacant land), federal funds, linkage monies, and other support were targeted for Boston's strong network of over thirty-five CDCs and other nonprofit housing groups. City housing policies not only favored projects sponsored by community groups, but they specifically promoted resident-owned cooperatives, limited-equity home ownership, and mixed-income housing.[71] Between 1984 and 1992, Boston CDCs alone sponsored (through new construction and major renovation) more than 10,000 units of housing, about half of the city's new residential housing over the period. In addition, CDCs assumed ownership of thousands of occupied units (many in HUD-assisted developments) that required substantial rehabilitation.

The city also responded to community concerns about the lack of reinvestment in low-income neighborhoods by lending institutions. Boston passed a "linked deposit" policy that put city funds only in banks with a strong track record of investing in low-income areas and helped negotiate a $400 million community reinvestment agreement with the city's major banks, targeted for lending to low-income and minority neighborhoods. The municipal administration also enforced strong tenants' rights laws and provided financial assistance to local tenant groups to deal with slumlords and federal agencies, such as the Resolution Trust Corporation (RTC) and HUD. These efforts included pushing HUD to turn over its large inventory of distressed federally assisted projects to resident-controlled and community-based organizations.

These policies could not alter the underlying market forces driving housing prices upward, but the housing conditions for Boston's poor and working-class residents were better than they would have been in the absence of city support and CDC activism. The city's other programs—such as the Boston Jobs Policy and the Boston Compact (a collaborative agreement between the city, the school system, and the business community setting specific performance goals for students and providing jobs for graduates)—helped residents gain access to jobs even as the parcel-to-parcel linkage program brought some jobs to lower-income communities. Boston's ability to reduce poverty over the 1980s, in short, reflected a combination of a booming economy and activist policy.

Lessons: Politics, Partners, and Policy

Boston's progressive policy was partly a function of the boom itself. When the market is attractive, private firms are more willing to take on the added costs imposed by interventionist policies. But equally important was a high level of self-organization among community developers and business alike, as well as several key alliances between these two sectors.[72]

In interviews with Boston business and civic leaders, several informants emphasized that Boston was like a small town. Business leaders knew each other, and worked through policy groups and interlocking connections to corporate and civic boards. A long tradition of corporate giving, including support for Boston's cultural institutions, charities, and education also meant that business had occasionally met advocates of poorer communities across the philanthropic table, making it easier to consider other kinds of partnerships.

Community organizations have been as engaged and organized as business. Beginning in the 1970s, Boston experienced a wave of progressive activism as communities and organizers struggled over property taxes, utility rates, linkage, rent control, condominium conversions, urban renewal, bank redlining, and other issues. In the early 1980s, a change in the city's charter shifted the city council from nine at-large seats to a mix of four at-large and nine district seats, enhancing neighborhood control and helping to raise the power and profile of community-based movements. By the late 1980s, many of the city's CDCs had matured and were increasingly taking on complex endeavors like mixed-use projects, limited equity cooperatives and condominiums, revitalization of HUD-assisted developments, projects requiring multiple subsidies (including the low-income tax credit), and retail development.

The well-organized business and community sectors sometimes found common ground and formed productive alliances. For example, the Boston Housing Partnership (now called the Metropolitan Boston Housing Partnership) brought key business leaders, city and state government housing officials, and CDCs into an umbrella organization to promote CDC-sponsored affordable housing. The Boston Compact created a link between Boston's business leaders and its public schools to encourage young people to graduate from high school in exchange for the promise of a summer job, a permanent job upon graduation, and a scholarship to college.

Such collaboration did not preclude conflict over public policy. The private real estate industry did not support linkage, or rent control, or even the bias toward CDCs. Lenders were not happy with community attacks on redlining. While Massachusetts governor Michael Dukakis and Boston mayor Ray Flynn strongly supported progressive housing policies, they could not always marshal majorities in the city council or state legislature for their agendas. Moreover, the focus on housing led to a downplaying of questions regarding access to employment, a problem that policy makers were hoping the booming economy would solve on its own.

Nonetheless, the Boston experience was a relative success. The area experienced an economic expansion driven partly by federal spending and partly by the diverse private sector's ability to respond to a changing economy. While this had the usual positive impacts on poverty reduction, government officials were not content to let the market work its own magic. Instead, they implemented creative new policies aimed at ensuring that regional and community development would be linked. Such policies reflected the high level of political and technical capacity amassed by community organizations, especially CDCs. An equally organized business class and cadre of policy makers were forced to respond and sometimes did so in partnership with those in the community sector. The combination of a vibrant economy, extensive social capital among and between groups, and a willingness by government to intervene selectively were all hallmarks of the Boston experience.[73]

What Can Be Learned?

We began this chapter by using decennial census data to rank seventy-four major metropolitan areas in the United States along the dimensions of regional income growth, central city poverty reduction, residential deconcentration of the poor, and region income equality. Of all the areas considered, the Boston metropolitan area, the San Jose/Santa Clara complex, and the region anchored by Charlotte, North Carolina, turned out to be high performers in this growth-equity nexus. Of these, Boston was the fastest grower while Charlotte was the slowest. Despite the lower growth rate, Charlotte boasted the best performance in terms of poverty reduction, with Boston close behind. San Jose actually saw an increase in central-city poverty, albeit at a rate slower than that experienced by most of our sample of seventy-four regions.

Case studies show that each of these three areas took very different routes to their regional success, a diversity consistent with the model presented in chapter 5. San Jose largely focused on growth. While part of its rapid economic expansion was due to nimble electronics firms and a superior educational base, an equally important factor was the high level of regional consciousness and business-to-business social capital. But while organizations like the Santa Clara Valley Manufacturing Group and Joint Venture: Silicon Valley Network led the way to thinking regionally on issues of infrastructure and economic revitalization, the regional leaders so devoted to business collaboration were often as disconnected from the difficulties of the poor as were their counterparts in Los Angeles (see chapter 3). While wages continue to be high, temporary employment and its attendant insecurity has been rising, and income distribution has been worsening in Silicon Valley. Even business-dominated Joint Venture has begun to warn about the damage widening inequalities might do to the area's social capital and economic sustainability (Henton et al., 1998). Meanwhile, labor unions have taken the lead by organizing a successful campaign for a living wage ordinance—which, in keeping with the Silicon Valley's inflated costs, was set as the highest in the country ($9.50). The San Jose experience thus serves as a warning to both community developers and regional leaders about the limits of approaches that focus exclusively on growth.

Charlotte, by contrast, offers a striking example of how maintaining linkages between city and suburb can promote both regional consciousness and a deeper commitment to antipoverty efforts. The region's sense of collective destiny was created in part by annexation laws that continue to bring suburbs under the official jurisdiction of the central city.[74] A business leadership willing to maintain both corporate headquarters and residences in the downtown core also created an immediate interest in supporting a series of innovative antipoverty efforts. While some of the region's reduction in central-city poverty during the 1980s reflected the annexation of wealthier "would-be" suburbs, the commitment to a multidimensional approach to poverty reduction was unusual and had positive impacts on city and regional health.

Boston's path reflects yet another policy mix. Its economic boom in the 1980s was driven partly by defense spending, a factor that also explains the area's slowdown in the 1990s. Yet city, regional, and state leaders did not assume that growth would be enough to reduce the poverty experienced by their constituencies. Drawing on a dense network of political support, Boston implemented first-source hiring agreements, as well as linkage policies, to ensure that poorer communities would share in the housing and employment expansion of that decade. In this milieu of sustained growth and redistributionist policy, CDCs were able to expand dramatically to help tackle Boston's difficulties with housing and community development. Even business leaders got into the act: knowing that projects would be approved faster if they included some element of social equity, firms competed to find neighborhood partners and other mechanisms to address inequality. The

Boston experience suggests what political and community leaders can achieve if they are organized enough to implement an antipoverty policy when it is easiest: in the context of rapid growth.

Each case offers positive lessons for linking regional and community development. The San Jose experience suggests the importance of a regional culture of collaboration, the Boston experience suggests the advantages of having a highly organized community sector, and the Charlotte experience suggests the key role of business leadership. The next chapter draws on the lessons from these case studies and other successful initiatives throughout the country in order to offer a vision and specific policies for community-based regionalism.

7

Growing Together

Policies for Regional Prosperity and Equity

As we head into the twenty-first century, America's cities, suburbs and metropolitan regions confront both new challenges and new opportunities. Globalization has often led local and regional actors to reduce taxes, lower wage standards, and ease environmental regulations in order to lure new investment. In this escalating "race to the bottom," hard-won gains in the quality of life can be lost, undermining conditions for all who participate in the competition. Indeed, even those businesses that push for wage and tax breaks, pursuing what we might call a "low road" strategy, can soon find themselves faced instead with social, fiscal, and political turmoil.

But there is nothing inevitable about this downside of globalization. The internationalization of the economy, as we stressed in chapter 1, has also brought a new regional impulse, and much of the competitive advantage of regions is based on industrial clusters, social capital, and cross-sectoral ties. Business, labor, civic, and community leaders thus have a choice: they can come together across a metropolitan area to establish guidelines and promote a "high road" to economic development, or they can allow fragmentation and divisions to shipwreck both economic prosperity and social equity.

To pursue the high road, regional development should have three interrelated goals: (1) fostering economic growth, including a focus on job creation, improvements in productivity, and a healthy trade balance with other regions and nations; (2) encouraging environmental sustainability, including the efficient use of resources and improvements in public health and environmental conditions; and (3) strengthening the region's social fabric, including strategies to share prosperity, help residents gain access to high-skill, high-wage employment, and ensure that blue-collar or less-skilled jobs pay wages sufficient to bring individual workers out of poverty.

Combining these goals is not easy, even for those policy makers, politicians, and business, labor, and community leaders who recognize the importance of the regional economy. As we stressed in chapter 1, the new regionalism has many variants—what we call "efficiency regionalism," "environmental regionalism," and "equity regionalism." Efficiency-oriented regionalism, often supported by business, is primarily concerned with achieving low costs and a level playing field, partly by providing certain public services (sewage systems, water, public transportation, etc.) and certain regulations (air quality, building codes, etc.) on a regional scale. This approach faces the challenge of rigid government structures, but it at least enjoys the battering ram of corporate support. Environmentally oriented regionalism is primarily concerned with controlling regional growth, especially by preserving open space, reducing traffic congestion and pollution, and diminishing urban sprawl. This approach inevitably leads to conflicts over land use, but it at least enjoys powerful support in both the environmental movement and among middle-class homeowners concerned about the deteriorating quality of urban and suburban life.

Equity-oriented regionalism, the approach we seek to develop here, takes as its central mission the need to reduce inequalities between individuals, social groups, neighborhoods, and local jurisdictions within a metropolitan area. Of primary concern are the disparities in local tax bases, differential provision of public services, the location of affordable housing, access to mortgages and credit, the quality of public schools, and the availability of both high-wage and entry-level employment. Leaders of low-income communities, labor unions, and those public officials that represent poor and working-class areas are the key constituencies for this approach. Yet these sectors often lack political strength, making equity-oriented regionalism a challenging prospect.

However, as we have argued above, regional growth and community revitalization are two-way streets: Regional economic expansion is a precondition for tackling poverty, but addressing the problems of the poor, especially unemployment, underemployment, low wages, and racial discrimination, is key to promoting regional growth. The challenge is thus to build bridges between the advocates and constituencies of all three approaches, threading together the concerns of efficiency, the environment, and equity into a new vision of sustainable prosperity in America's metropolitan regions.

Of course, it is one thing to invoke the rhetoric of "we're all in the same boat." It is quite another to find specific ways to address the problems of regional growth and metropolitan inequality. In this chapter, we offer some broad recommendations based on the experiences of regions around the country that, in ways small and large, have devised policies and institutions devoted to the dual tasks of regional prosperity and community building.[1]

We classify the two major ingredients to success as *working together* and *growing together*. We begin the chapter with *working together*, discussing how to build new partnerships and collaborations within a region. We argue that regional leaders and institutions must build their capacity to "talk" (Storper, 1997), that is, to meet face-to-face and establish the trust among interest groups that is needed to build innovative alliances and partnerships. We then focus on *growing together*, that is, the creation of new policies and programs to link regional and community development. Here, we suggest how regional growth strategies, such as industry clustering and infrastructure repair, could be altered to deliver greater benefits to lower-income communities in metropolitan areas. We also indicate how low-income neighborhoods and community-based organizations can do their part in connecting to the dynamic sectors and institutions in their regional setting.

Of course, regions cannot go it alone. Existing rules and policies often pose obstacles to cooperation within metropolitan regions, and we suggest how the federal and state governments might nurture regional cooperation, especially by promoting links between regional initiatives and the poor. We then stress the importance of maintaining a buoyant economy: as William Julius Wilson (1996) has stressed, full employment is a necessary condition for a successful antipoverty strategy. We close by returning to Los Angeles to consider the possibilities for a new community-based regionalism in that metropolitan area.

Working Together

Our three case studies (see chapter 6) suggest that regional success in both expanding the economy and reducing poverty stems in part from the conviction of key stakeholders that the fate of the cities is linked with that of the suburbs, the fate of business with that of the workforce, and the fate of the middle class with that of the poor. This conviction requires a broad sense of civic identity and an understanding that the pursuit of prosperity and equity involves more than a quick fix. It requires communication, cooperation, and eventually collaboration among institutions representing the various key stakeholders. It requires thinking and acting like a region—that is, developing what Hamilton (1999) calls a regional "civic infrastructure."[2]

Thinking Regionally

Much has been written, mostly by scholars and planners, about why regional government may be better than the current system of fragmented and conflicting jurisdictions at tackling issues like economic development, environmental protection, and transportation. Yet only a handful of areas, particularly Minneapolis–St. Paul and Portland, have forged formal metropolitan or regionwide governance structures, partly because municipal jurisdictions tend to guard their powers jealously.[3]

Many metropolitan areas have adopted less dramatic changes in their governance structures, creating a variety of special districts and agencies to address particular problems (such as transportation, public education, water, parks, environmental cleanup, economic development, and other matters). Sometimes municipalities within a region can be induced to work together by external carrots and sticks, such as federal legislation like the Clean Air Act or the Transportation Equity Act-21 (the revised version of the Intermodal Surface Transportation Efficiency Act [ISTEA]). However, the agencies created are often single-purpose institutions, leading to a crazy quilt of governance bodies that is confusing to the careful observer, much less the average citizen, and constitutes only a limited basis for regional collaboration.[4]

Regional councils of government (COGs) could provide forums for public officials from across a region to forge a regional approach to a larger set of problems. But resistance from municipal jurisdictions has led to regional planning agencies or COGs typically having little authority.[5] Some COGs have nonetheless been able to build on their "power to convene." In the St. Louis region, for example, the local council of governments, the East-West Gateway Council, has worked in conjunction with business and civic groups to facilitate such diverse efforts as HUD's Bridges to Work program and a Regional Jobs Initiative (U.S. Department of Housing and Urban Development, 1998b; Parzen, 1997; NACO, 1997). In Florida, the Eastward Ho! effort spearheaded by a regional COG has linked together three counties all affected by disinvestment in their urban core areas and environmental degradation of the surrounding everglades.[6]

Still, the weakness of regional planning agencies and the balkanization of metropolitan-wide special districts has led some regional leaders to initiate new alliances and institutions.[7] Some of these are informal structures, as in Charlotte. Some are more organized but still nongovernmental entities, such as Joint Venture: Silicon Valley Network in San Jose (see chapter 6). One important effort, spearheaded by the San Francisco–based Irvine

Foundation, explicitly recognizes the absence of appropriate government structures and is attempting to nurture more than a dozen regional collaborations throughout California.[8] Other foundations have recognized the need for action and have formed a Funders Network on Sprawl, Smart Growth, and Livable Communities to encourage multisectoral regional efforts.[9] The exact form such collaborations will take is less important than the concept: local leaders must learn to think and act regionally.

Mapping the Region

The late architect and city planner Kevin Lynch used to ask students, community residents, and others to draw maps of their city and region. Inevitably, he found that people had very different visions of what their city and region looked like—and how the places where they lived, worked, and played fit into the larger picture. In short, people tended to live and work in relative isolation from the larger community, with this experiential segregation reflected in the "cognitive maps" that they drew for Lynch (see Lynch, 1960).

It is difficult to "think and act regionally" when the information we are provided fragments our world into geographic bits and pieces. Large daily newspapers and local television stations, for example, can engender or endanger a sense of belonging to a regional economy with common problems and perhaps common solutions. More often than not, however, these media outlets contribute to the fragmentation of the regional "map." Competing with suburban papers, large city newspapers often partition the paper into local editions based on advertising markets (where people shop), building revenues but exacerbating a sense of disconnection. In almost every major metropolitan area, the television news highlights sensational crimes and other "bad" news, telescoping and exaggerating the extent of crime in cities and metropolitan areas. This contributes to a "fortress" mentality among suburbanites and city dwellers alike, thickening the psychological walls between people and their communities.

A few media institutions have sought, however tentatively, to think regionally. In 1995, for example, the *Charlotte Observer* invited syndicated columnist and regional advocate Neal Peirce to study the Charlotte region by talking with leaders in a variety of sectors, examining economic and social trends, and making recommendations (see Peirce et al., 1995). The paper published Peirce's findings in a special edition and convened meetings to discuss it. Since then, the paper has sought to cover the Charlotte metropolitan region in ways that help readers and leaders see how they fit into the larger context.

Another way to unify the map is simply by providing a common set of data for the whole region. In today's information age, regional leaders need to collect and share knowledge about regional economic and social trends, including demographic changes, housing market trends, environmental quality, educational achievement, the condition of basic infrastructure, the quality of basic public services, the mix of regional occupations and industries, trends in income disparity, and whether the region is getting its fair share of federal and state dollars.

In many regions, it is not clear whose responsibility it is to gather, interpret, and disseminate this kind of information, particularly as the data necessary to draw the full regional picture necessarily comes from a wide variety of public and private sources. Like Lynch's cognitive maps, people with partial information will have only a partial understanding of the region and how they fit into it. Regional and community institutions thus need to collaborate and make sure that some organization—a planning agency, a business group, a local university—is responsible for producing a common base of economic and social data.

Some progress is being made on this front. Many regions, including Portland, Cleveland, the Twin Cities, Atlanta, and Chicago, have developed indicators, ranging from the economy to education, from government operations to open space, to evaluate their regions (see Garland and Galuszka, 1997).[10] Even the highly fragmented Los Angeles area now enjoys a very effective *State of the Region* report produced by the local council of governments (SCAG, 1999). Moreover, the National Association of Regional Councils has developed a project to create a National Regional Database and an annual state-of-the-regions report that will allow metropolitan leaders to compare their region's outcomes with those in the rest of the country.[11] In early 1999, Vice President Al Gore announced an initiative to make computer mapping technology more available to regions and communities for use in planning. Following up, HUD has requested special funding under a Regional Connections program to help regions gather and analyze information (as well as to engage in regional collaborations).[12]

Such indicator projects would benefit from the inclusion of measures of regional performance on poverty and equity; after all, what is not measured will not likely be targeted for improvement.[13] Occasionally, the impulse to expand the set of regional performance indicators may come from outside the usual regional organizations. In San Jose, California, for example, a labor-affiliated research center called Working Partnerships,

USA has developed its own analysis of the region's economy, complete with data showing widening income gaps in the Silicon Valley (Benner, 1998). Partly as a result, Joint Venture's seminal set of indicators has expanded to include various measures of wage inequality, educational disparity, and cross-sector regional collaboration (Joint Venture, 1999).[14]

Community and labor organizations should also be sure to secure direct access to regional data in order to formulate their own plans to improve their neighborhoods, collaborate with each other, and link their work to private sector, government, and other institutions. Researchers from the University of Wisconsin, Milwaukee, for example, have worked with neighborhood groups to collect data on local neighborhood labor and housing markets, allowing community organizations to play an important role in workforce development and other regional efforts.[15] In Los Angeles, RLA attempted to construct the contours of such a common database, a task that has been taken over by the Los Angeles Community Development Technologies Center, located at the Los Angeles Trade-Technical College.

Building Bridges

Even with a supportive media and access to information, it is difficult for regional leaders in different sectors to develop a common map if they do not engage in honest and respectful conversation. Business leaders often have a false or distorted sense that they know and understand their community because they read the local newspaper, employ "community outreach" staff, or serve on the boards of philanthropic endeavors. Yet this is no substitute for direct communication. Corporate leaders in Los Angeles, for example, were astounded by the outbreak of riots in 1992 and then supported the ultimately misguided top-down investment strategy initially favored by Rebuild LA.[16] One of the reasons for this misstep, as we noted in chapter 3, was that the civic and philanthropic activities of L.A.'s business leaders were focused on private hospitals, arts organizations, and similar organizations, and did not include as many direct ties with the community-based or youth organizations that could have given them a true "ear to the ground."

In some cities, business leaders have made a concerted effort to establish these connections with community issues. In Charlotte, business leaders maintained both corporate headquarters and residences in the downtown core, creating an immediate interest in supporting a series of innovative antipoverty efforts. In Boston, business leaders and community developers met face-to-face on a regular basis through the Boston Housing Partnership (now called the Metropolitan Boston Housing Partnership). Through this public-private-community partnership, leaders in the different sectors learned about each other's activities and developed relationships of trust (if not always agreement) that allowed for effective collaborations on issues of mutual interest.

To bring together capital and the community, business leaders—the CEOs, CFOs, and presidents of major firms—must actively seek out and offer to serve on the boards of community-based organizations and participate in community-building efforts. Major employers and business organizations should also diversify their boards of directors, not simply by adding minorities and women but also by recruiting leaders from community-based organizations.[17] To help matters along, councils of governments could expand regional advisory groups to include representatives of community-based organizations, providing a space for neighborhood leaders to learn about regional issues and interact directly with regional policy makers and business representatives.[18]

Another key bridge is to the federal and state legislative delegation that represents a region. Regional leaders typically monitor the political landscape with a form of tunnel vision: they may know how a particular piece of legislation affects their industry, their business, their city, or their neighborhood, but they often have a dimmer sense of how the myriad of federal and state actions—regulations as well as laws—affects the whole region in which they live and work. Legislators themselves frequently miss the regional picture, suffering from differences of party, ideology, and geography.

Yet there are many situations where such divisions are irrelevant to regions and communities. For example, the same Los Angeles business class that was divided over President Clinton's 1993 public works bill, many believing that it would contribute to expanding the deficit, united after the 1994 earthquake to push for a recovery plan that eventually poured far more public works dollars into the area than would have been delivered by the original Clinton plan (Dreier and Rothstein, 1994).

We shouldn't need a disaster to recognize the common good. Working with local universities, councils of governments and other regional institutions could regularly monitor federal and state policies, and then convene meetings with the area's congressional members, state assembly representatives, and staffs to discuss a shared legislative program. In the Chicago area, for example, inner-ring suburbs have organized as the First-Tier Consortium to lobby the Illinois legislature for a more equitable share of infrastructure spending, and thus redirect development from growing exurbs to already urbanized areas (Garland and Galuszka, 1997).

Thinking and Linking: Challenging CDCs

Residents and leaders of impoverished communities sensibly want to redirect capital and economic activity back into their neighborhoods. But as Jeremy Nowak (1997:7) has written, "effective community development requires an explicit emphasis on poverty alleviation, which in turn requires linking the possibilities of the inner city to the regional economy."

As executive director of the Delaware Valley Community Reinvestment Fund (DVCRF), Nowak has followed his own advice, helping to finance new growth-oriented businesses unable to secure capital from more traditional investment institutions and aiding in the development of the Philadelphia Jobs Initiative, a workforce program designed to help lower-income workers.[19] In the Chicago area, the Center for Neighborhood Technology (CNT), a twenty-year-old nonprofit whose vision of self-sufficient, healthy, empowered, and sustainable communities has traditionally had a neighborhood focus, has spent the last several years advocating for a regional approach (Bernstein, 1997). Starting in the mid-1990s, for example, CNT launched a Metropolitan Initiative across twelve U.S. regions to see which federal-level changes could better promote community-based regionalism (Vogel et al., 1997). CNT also brought this community voice to its participation in President Clinton's Council on Sustainable Development; along with the National Community-Building Network, it has sought to provide assistance for community organizations seeking to become involved in regional debates.

"Thinking and linking" to the region—building the capacity to understand the regional economy and be a player in its development—is a key challenge for community developers who may be accustomed to a focus on neighborhood concerns and wary of adding new tasks to an already overcrowded agenda. Fortunately, many Foundations, including the Ford and Annie E. Casey Foundations, have launched multiyear pilot programs designed to strengthen CBOs and allow them to function and advocate effectively in the emerging regional economic landscape.

It is a challenge to take up regional thinking—but it is one that cannot be bypassed by community organizers and community development corporations. Organizers will have to press where they must and build coalitions where they can. The EPA's Brownfield Economic Development Initiative, for example, has sought to restore old industrial sites to productive use by bringing together businesses, community residents, and local governments; the result is environmental cleanup, economic development, and a sense that collaboration can yield positive results.[20] Indeed, the process may be the goal: talking together leads to working together, and this can lead to growing together, partly because the resulting personal and institutional ties put everyone—rich and poor, city and suburb—on the same "map."

Growing Together: Linking Regional and Community Development

Regional conversations and connections are good starting points but concrete strategies are needed to ensure that regional prosperity occurs and is shared. There is no single path to linking regional and community development: no two metropolitan regions are exactly alike and formulas that may work in one place may not in another. Even so, there are a variety of broad strategies that policy makers and practitioners at the regional and community levels have demonstrated can work, each of which could be amended to fit specific circumstances. Below, we outline eight such approaches.

1. Growing Clusters That Promote High-Wage/High-Skill Jobs

While conventional economic development strategies focus on attracting business through reduced taxes and labor costs, newer approaches recognize that businesses tend to "cluster" in certain geographic locations (see Luria and Rogers, 1997; Scott, 1988; Storper, 1997). The reasons for such clustering are complex but the basic notion, introduced in chapter 1, is that there are advantages to being near other related firms, including substantial reductions in intrafirm transaction costs, a more innovative environment, and improved access to a skilled labor force. Of course, a city or region can become so overreliant on a single industry that it lacks the ability to adjust when the fortunes of a particular firm or industry decline; the pains of Detroit (automobiles) and Pittsburgh (steel) serve as clear warning signals. To avoid overdependence on a specific industry, a region works best when it promotes clusters of firms and industries.[21]

Why should those concerned about poverty support an industrial "cluster" strategy? In essence, the power of capital comes from its mobility. When firms can easily move, communities and labor lack bargaining power. By contrast, clustered industries are "sticky." The firms within them tend to value their local assets: they recognize that the health of the business climate depends on the general quality of life in the region, and are therefore more apt to respond positively to groups concerned about social and economic justice.

Not just any cluster will do. From the point of view of low-income communities, the goal is neither software boutiques nor low-wage furniture production. Regional clusters should be evaluated not simply based on growth potential but also on their willingness to locate in and/or employ residents of low-income communities, their ability to provide accessible entry-level employment, their collectively constituted or interfirm career ladders, and their capacity to connect with local small business. Right before it ceased operations, RLA in Los Angeles adopted such a multidimensional cluster strategy, helping to form trade associations for the emerging industries with the highest potential to provide employment and contracting opportunities for low-income communities and their residents.

The Center on Wisconsin Strategy (COWS), a labor-supported university-based think tank in Milwaukee, has taken a comparable approach. Stressing the need for targeting industrial clusters that take a "high road" of livable wages, COWS has served as lead technical advisor to the Wisconsin Regional Training Partnership, an effort involving forty metalworking firms employing around 60,000 workers in southeastern Wisconsin. These firms faced a classic collective action problem: worried that their own expenditures on training would be wasted when workers leave, each engaged in low spending on skill development, insuring that the overall industry wage level, skills, and productivity would decline. COWS brought together employers and unions in a consortium, persuading the industry as a whole to raise spending on retraining workers and positioning the cluster for improved competitiveness and higher wages (Dresser and Rogers, 1997: 13–15).

In Cleveland, three CDCs founded the Westside Industrial Retention and Expansion Network (WIRE-Net) to encourage the retention and growth of industrial firms that could provide cluster-based employment for residents of low-income communities (Indergaard, 1997).[22] In Newark, New Jersey, one of the nation's largest and best known CDCs, the New Community Corporation, has generated an incubator project to facilitate the growth of new small minority firm clusters, partly to build upon Newark's proximity to regional cultural institutions (Zdenek, 1998; Harrison and Weiss, 1998). And in Los Angeles, the aforementioned Community Development Technologies Center is training community development practitioners to scan the region, analyze industrial clusters, and position their CDCs to best take advantage of regional opportunities.

Minority-owned businesses, which usually disproportionately employ minority workers, should play an important role in any cluster strategy. Regional planning agencies could help provide the technical assistance and networking to assist minority firms with connecting to regional market niches. Municipalities could condition subsidies to larger, majority-owned businesses partly on their good-faith efforts to forge joint-venture partnerships with smaller, minority firms. To create an incentive for lending to such enterprises, a number of counties and cities have developed "linked deposit" policies that require that their cash balances be placed in banks that have a good record of lending to small entrepreneurs and promoting community development. To help this process along, the federal government could expand the Community Reinvestment Act (CRA) to include commercial loans, at least in terms of reporting requirements.[23]

2. Reducing Bidding Wars

Across the country, cities, counties, and states engage in bidding wars, lowering taxes and waiving regulations to attract business investment. Competition has been particularly sharp in California, where the 1978 passage of Proposition 13 has crippled the ability of local governments to use property taxes to finance public services (see Schrag, 1998). The result has been a fiscalization of land use: municipalities are more eager to generate sales tax from shopping centers, auto plazas, downtown development projects, and sports complexes than they are to lure large employers with higher-wage jobs (Fulton, 1997). In many cases, this situation pushes jobs further and further from the central city, a tendency one study has called "job sprawl" (Immergluck and Wiles, 1998). Such a scattering of employment can exacerbate the problems of traffic congestion and environmental pollution, and widen the mismatch between where poor people live and where jobs are located.

Developers have often promoted this competition between jurisdictions, pitting one city off against another in a search for larger subsidies and lower taxes. Yet in most cases, businesses decide where to locate (or expand) based on business networks, physical infrastructure, and/or markets; only after choosing a region with the right assets do they attempt to extract maximum benefits from particular localities. Municipal competitors who then auction off their tax base simply ensure that the lucky winner pockets less fiscal gain even as the overall benefits to the region are reduced. Surely there is a better approach.

One way to reduce bidding wars is to share the regional tax base. Under such a plan, municipalities agree to place a portion of the increment of new development revenues into a regionwide fund. Such regional tax sharing would reduce competition and provide a basis for fostering regional collaboration (Hamilton, 1999). The Minneapolis–St. Paul region has enacted a version of tax base sharing and the evidence suggests that it has made cooperation easier (Orfield, 1997). Similar results have come from regional tax strategies in Ohio, New Jersey, Pennsylvania, and elsewhere.[24]

Bidding wars can also involve competition over regulations. Rather than promote competition among muncipalities to lower regulatory standards, which in the long term undermines the health and safety of all parties, business would gain more by encouraging more uniformity of regulations across regions. In the Silicon Valley, for example, the business-led consortium Joint Venture: Silicon Valley Network worried that compliance with a range of differing municipal building codes was limiting firms' ability to develop real estate and set up industrial employment rapidly. But rather than playing one city off against another until codes were gutted, they persuaded twenty-seven cities across two counties to adopt a uniform building code and enter an ongoing process to agree on common interpretations of the code. The result has been a speedier construction process as firms do not have to weigh different codes against each other in their location decisions, enhancing the region's competitiveness and avoiding the "race to the bottom."

3. Infrastructure and Equity

Basic physical infrastructure, especially the roadways and transportation networks that move goods and workers, is critical to a healthy regional business climate. As a nation, the United States is far behind other advanced industrial nations in updating its infrastructure (Aschaer, 1993). But despite local fiscal constraints and reductions in federal spending, many regions do continue to receive tens of billions of dollars in federal (as well as state, local, and bond) funds for a wide variety of public projects. In Los Angeles, for example, both the expansion of the transportation system under MTA and the Alameda Corridor project are massive public works projects with significant economic impacts (see chapter 3).

Such projects can generate thousands of construction jobs, affect dozens of neighborhoods, and have substantial ripple effects throughout the regional economy. Yet the benefits to poorer communities, as we saw in chapter 3, are often less clear. Why not conduct Social/Economic Impact Reviews (SIRs), similar to environmental impact reports, that would assess large public works projects not only with regard to their contributions to economic growth, but also in terms of their impact on reducing poverty, fostering community development, and limiting urban sprawl?[25] Similar analyses, focused more on whether spending is disproportionately directed to the urban fringe, have led several regions, including Atlanta and Chicago, as well as the state of Maryland, to enact legislation refocusing public expenditures on existing urbanized areas.[26] The SIR exercise would, at the least, provide information to community groups who then could lobby and work with private sector actors to encourage a broader distribution of the benefits of development.

4. Workforce Development for a Regional Economy

One barrier to expanding employment among residents of low-income neighborhoods is the lack of job skills, and the usual remedy is job training. Yet this approach, often based on general education and preparation, tends to focus on individuals rather than the labor force as a whole. Moreover, it frequently fails to recognize that many poor adults actually work but receive inadequate incomes. A broader "workforce development" strategy would focus on elevating overall skill levels, including those of the currently employed, thereby helping regions to compete effectively *and* helping lower-income communities gain access to decent employment opportunities.

Such a workforce development approach must be as regional as the labor market itself. Private Industry Councils (PICs) are often fragmented by locales; where possible, they should be consolidated at the metropolitan level. Given the suburbanization of employment and the spatial mismatch often faced by the poor, such regionwide PICs should make special efforts to steer workers to where jobs actually exist.[27] The Milwaukee Jobs Initiative points in the right direction: funded largely by the Annie E. Casey Foundation, the initiative links central-city workers (through the Central City Workers Center) with jobs throughout the metro region, steering participants to suburban employment, creating new lines of regional collaboration, and stressing higher-wage jobs.[28]

Workforce development should also be tied into the general regional strategy of targeting competitive industrial clusters. The Center for Employment Training (CET) in San Jose, for example, brings in advisors from regional industries to help determine training curriculum and uses these contacts to develop networks that help with the placement of graduates within the regional labor market. Harrison and Weiss (1998) argue that such networks are critical: the job programs with the best records are those that develop "strategic alliances" with major employers—formal and informal connections that help CDCs understand which sectors of the economy are growing, what employers are looking for, and how to provide the best "job readiness" training.[29]

One key group of players in the workforce development area are the community colleges. Some community-based job developers, like Newark's New Community Corporation and Chicago's New Bethel Life, have developed community college ties with great success.[30] Moreover, CBO–community college relationships can lead to positive institutional changes in the colleges themselves: a 1996 report to the Ford Foundation indicates that one of Project QUEST's significant achievements was a change in job training in local community colleges, partly through multisector conversations held between local educators and local employers under the aegis of Project QUEST's occupational advisory committees (see also Campbell, 1994). Community colleges are also especially well-placed to take up the retraining of workers through evening classes and other flexible strategies (Cisneros, 1996). Such a retraining emphasis is particularly appropriate for the working poor, many of whom have the requisite "soft skills" (such as reliability, promptness, and the ability to work in groups) to secure employment but need to develop further the "hard skills" (technical capacities) that will allow them to move up a career ladder.

Positive examples abound, but the central point is simple: training people for work should be seen as part of an overall development strategy for the region. The mutual interest of the poor and businesses should be stressed, and collaboration and movement across the geographic spaces of the labor market should be encouraged.

5. Enhancing Labor Mobility: Housing and Transportation

Even with the right skills and networks, individuals from low-income neighborhoods often face difficulties in getting to places of employment reliably and quickly. Strategies for improving mobility should focus on two fronts: housing and transportation.

The first approach involves helping families move from high-poverty neighborhoods to communities where schools are better and employment prospects brighter. The federal Section 8 housing allowance program, begun in 1974, provides poor families with vouchers to help them pay the rent in private apartments.[31] But while there are currently more than one million households nationwide with Section 8 certificates, waiting lists are years long in most major urban areas.[32] Even if a family is lucky enough to get a certificate, families are not always aware of housing opportunities outside their own neighborhoods. Moreover, because housing agencies receive administrative funds based on placement within their jurisdiction, they have little incentive to encourage or help families identify rental housing opportunities elsewhere.[33]

The Section 8 voucher program could help foster wider economic opportunity if participants were able to search for and secure housing outside of the local jurisdiction that issued the certificate. Enhancing such "portability" could enable low-income people to move closer to suburban employment. To do this, the program should be operated on a regional, rather than city-by-city basis.[34] Indeed, deconcentration could become an explicit goal of such regionwide administrators. For the last several years, for example, the U.S. Department of Housing and Urban Development (HUD) has been operating a small pilot program, called "Moving to Opportunity" (MTO), that required that local housing authorities team up with community nonprofit organizations to help low-income families in public housing move to private apartments in a "low poverty" neighborhood (that is, to census tracts where the poverty rate was below 10 percent). While the results are still incomplete, preliminary indications are that the program has had a positive effect on the lives of those who have been able to move.[35]

Of course, there must also be available housing. Unfortunately, local "snob zoning" rules restrict the construction of multifamily housing in some suburban areas, thus limiting those communities to affluent residents who can afford to purchase homes on large lots. A few states, including Massachusetts and New Jersey, have tried to overcome restrictions through "inclusionary zoning" laws that give state housing agencies the authority to overturn local zoning decisions when communities restrict low-income housing. Similarly, Portland's regional government mandates that its constituent counties and cities, including suburbs, develop plans in which 50 percent of new housing is multifamily or attached units, most of which is more affordable than typical suburban housing (Richmond, 1997: 58; Abbot, 1997:29). Regional, state, and federal authorities could encourage such "fair share" housing—the construction of affordable housing outside high-poverty areas—by withholding funds from localities that are out of compliance with affordable housing requirements. At the very least, regions should assemble the housing elements of municipalities into a single document, creating a vehicle for cities already "overburdened" with low-income housing to recognize their common predicament and therefore jointly pressure other cities to accept more.

If workers can't move closer to the jobs, they could at least be afforded the means to get there. HUD, in partnership with Public/Private Ventures, has successfully promoted "reverse commuting" via its Bridges to Work programs in Baltimore, Chicago, Milwaukee, and Denver.[36] The recent reauthorization of ISTEA as TEA-21 included an allocation of approximately $750 million over five years for Access to Jobs and Reverse Commute programs. Eligible projects under the Access to Jobs program include the use of transit vouchers for welfare recipients and low-income individuals; those under the Reverse Commute program must specifically target transporting residents of urban and rural areas to suburban job centers but do not need to be income specific. Finally, while rail projects can generate construction jobs and transit-oriented development, making bus service more regular, affordable, and flexible is critical, especially in decentralized regions such as Los Angeles where buses are a primary means of mobility for many low-income residents (see chapter 3).

6. Making Work Pay

The benefits of living near, or having accessible transport to employment diminish if the resulting jobs still leave employees among the ranks of the working poor. One route to higher pay is through training, education, and connections, all of which we have stressed earlier. But regionalists must also insist on raising the standard for those on the bottom. Three approaches are necessary.

First, businesses, foundations, religious institutions, community organizations, unions, and the media should engage in a wide-ranging outreach campaign to expand participation in the federal government's Earned Income Tax Credit (EITC) program. This program, which was expanded in 1993, provides additional income to eligible participants who earn poverty-level wages through a refundable tax credit. Yet many workers do not avail themselves of this resource; Williams and Sander (1997), for example, report that fewer than half the eligible workers in the City of Los Angeles participate in the program. Increasing participation would lift thousands of households above poverty, pump millions of dollars in additional income into regional economies, and have especially important ripple effects on small businesses in low-income neighborhoods.[37]

Second, regions should consider "living wage" laws similar to those adopted by a growing number of local governments. Such laws generally require that firms involved in municipal contracts pay their workers above a set wage (Pollin and Luce, 1998); despite the fears of conservatives, such laws do not lead to job flight or the collapse of businesses, primarily because they target firms that are not especially mobile. And while labor economists rightly insist that the more efficient approach involves raising national standards, local living wage ordinances have several advantages. They can respond to the health of a region's economy, setting wage and benefit standards to reflect local conditions.[38] Moreover, they are easier to win than the national battle: living wage campaigns force local citizens to come face-to-face with their responsibility, via local subcontracting, for helping the working poor, and this tends to build the sort of sympathy needed to bridge the usual political divides.[39]

A third element of raising standards involves strengthening unions and other representative organizations. The long-term decline of union membership is partly due to the erosion of the large-scale heavy manufacturing sector where unions were traditionally strong (Mishel and Bernstein, 1995). However, the nation's outdated labor relations laws have also made it extremely difficult for even the most committed and talented organizers and workers to win union elections, partly because company lawyers can easily force delays on procedural grounds. As a result, certain organizing efforts, such as the Service Employees' Justice for Janitors campaign in Los Angeles, have relied on civil disobedience and so-called corporate campaigns to force companies to the table.

While we believe that the company-union playing field should be made more level by changing federal labor law, it is unlikely to occur in the near future. In the interim, public officials can help unionization campaigns among low-wage employees by supporting municipal development agreements that give unions a chance to use the "card-check" system for union representation or require that firms receiving subsidies indicate how they plan to maintain labor peace and nondisruption of their services. Unions themselves can work to influence policies at the regional level. The AFL-CIO seems to have gotten the message. It recently published a handbook on economic development that stresses the importance of regions and "metro unionism" (AFL-CIO Human Resources Development Institute, 1998), its local labor councils have helped the living wage movement, and labor is the driving force behind the model Milwaukee Jobs Initiative.

7. Regularizing the Informal Sector

Unions and other organizations can also help ameliorate conditions in the informal sector documented in chapter 2. In general, there are two configurations in which informal activities occur: one in which an individual, household, or collective engages in a small venture, and the other in which the worker is at a structural disadvantage vis-à-vis the employer. While we recommend a more understanding approach to the small storefront and mobile businesses (such as trucks and carts) that dot the landscape of low-income and immigrant communities, the latter arrangement generally involves sweatshop-style exploitation and should be actively discouraged.

To do so, vigorous enforcement of existing labor laws and health and safety codes is necessary. Recent highly publicized revelations of business transactions between major retailers and sweatshop contractors reveal the extent to which businesses have taken advantage of inadequate vigilance— and also suggests the degree to which simply documenting and publicizing negative labor conditions can allow religious, consumer, and other groups to pressure mainstream firms that contract with abusive employers.

On the entrepreneurial side, we should recognize that small-scale businesses and vendors contribute to their neighborhoods and our society. They provide critically needed services and goods to racially segregated and economically abandoned low-income communities and facilitate the circulation and creation of local capital. For these reasons, we encourage public and private sector support of entrepreneurial ventures by people of modest means through small loans and training programs.[40] We should consider street vending zones and a cessation to the harassment of street vendors by law enforcement personnel. With zoning flexibility and financial assistance, these small firms can minimize labor exploitation and maximize their ability to accumulate and invest capital in poorer communities.

8. Building the Neighborhood

Focusing on the region should not preclude the sort of place-based improvements that strengthen neighborhoods and their economies. Improving the physical and aesthetic quality of life for residents in low-income neighborhoods is essential for restoring community fabric. Also, many individuals helped by people-based strategies will want to stay in their original neighborhoods; place-based efforts, which build up neighborhood amenities and livability, can give them reasons to do so and thereby help local areas retain spending power and job networks.

But poorer neighborhoods cannot achieve such revitalization alone. Regional organizations, such as the COGs, could help by conducting regional "neighborhood business district" audits to identify and map all the major supermarkets, banks, pharmacies, and other retail services. This would aid in identifying which areas have a shortage of such facilities and which areas have their fair share (or more). Communities could then develop a neighborhood business district plan, working with government agencies, business groups, and others to attract needed investments.[41] Business involvement and investment will be essential. As Michael Porter (1995) has stressed, firms should be encouraged to take advantage of the opportunities for profit in low-income neighborhoods and see these communities as both assets and potential markets.

Government agencies could formally or informally condition subsidies on linkages to accompanying retail development in low-income areas. As noted in chapter 6, Boston had a parcel-to-parcel linkage policy that tied the development of prime downtown real estate sites with the revitalization of publicly owned sites in low-income areas. Equally important is credit availability for mortgage loans and neighborhood business expansion; redlining by banks could be combated by continuing the 1977 Community Reinvestment Act (CRA) and by the sort of municipal- and regional-level linked deposit strategies mentioned above.

Place-based strategies remain important, even for some forms of job development (see Dressner, Fleischer, and Sherwood, 1998). Community development corporations (CDCs) can and should continue their role as the linchpin of government and private efforts to rebuild inner-city areas. But it is only appropriate that community developers recognize Jeremy Nowak's admonition that "strong neighborhoods are destination places and incubators; they are healthy, not because they are self-contained or self-sufficient but because their residents are appropriately linked to non-neighborhood opportunities" (Nowak, 1997: 9).

In short, there is no need to abandon place-based strategies or the exciting new attempts at community building. Rather, the challenge is to creatively combine place- *and* people-based approaches, to stress both neighborhood livability *and* regional job connections. Community organizing will remain crucial, both to affect the local neighborhood and to influence the regional strategies that will set the terrain for community development.

Helping Build the Bridge: Changing Federal and State Policy

Even those people and institutions most committed to regional collaboration face an uphill battle: the rules are often stacked against them. For the most part, federal and state policies, programs, and regulations have promoted competition between states, between regions, and between jurisdictions within regions. Tax and spending policies have also fostered suburbanization, leading to an abandonment of central city concerns and the political fragmentation of many regions. New federal and state policies could help build the bridges now needed in America's regions.

Promoting Suburbanization: The Old Approach

Suburban voters frequently picture the central cities as heavy users of federal programs like welfare and housing subsidies. Yet federal policies have, more often than not, worked against the interests of the inner city. For example, the suburbanization of postwar America that hollowed out many of the nation's urban areas was driven by the federally sponsored interstate highway-building program, which opened up the hinterlands to speculation and development even as urban renewal policies destroyed working-class neighborhoods to make way for downtown business development.[42] Sprawl was further induced by federal subsidies to the expansion of water and sewer infrastructure in these outlying areas; in 1966, the federal government paid for 47 percent of sewer expenses while by 1980, the federal government was paying for 75 percent of sewer construction (Hamilton, 1999: 151–52).

Yet the most significant federal impulse toward suburbanization has involved tax policy and expenditures. For instance, the ability of corporations to get tax breaks for new capital investment but not for modernizing older facilities fostered the deconcentration of manufacturing. Meanwhile, the politically popular mortgage interest deduction encouraged consumers to buy bigger houses that were usually located outside of the inner city. The interest deduction remains a clear example of the imbalance of federal incentives: in 1997, foregone taxes on home mortgage payments, a benefit more likely to be taken by higher-income suburbanites, were about four and a half times HUD's direct spending on housing subsidies, a benefit more likely to be taken by the inner-city poor. The tax break is also highly regressive; in 1995, for example, the top 12 percent of taxpayers received 71 percent of the total mortgage interest benefits.[43]

Federal spending has also played a role. After World War II, the Pentagon located most of its new military bases and awarded most of its large contracts to firms outside central cities. This helped push private manufacturing and research-and-development firms into suburbs and once-rural areas, a form of government planning that had it been called what it was— "industrial policy"—would have been anathema to the Pentagon's biggest boosters (Markusen, Hall, Campbell, and Deitrich, 1991). Meanwhile, federal labor law encouraged fragmentation and competition by allowing states to enact anti-union "right-to-work" laws, thereby inducing private businesses to pit states against each other in a race to hamper unionization and lower wages.

State policies were also critical. In many states, legislation encouraged the creation of new suburbs, each with its own capacity to tax, zone, and establish school systems (Jackson, 1985). In California, Proposition 13's limits on raising property taxes also led to an increasing reliance by municipal governments on sales taxes; the resulting push for "big-box" retail tends to favor outlying suburban areas where land is abundant and consumer incomes are higher. Poorer areas, including older, more built-out, inner-ring suburbs, are often unable to assemble large parcels of vacant land and instead rely on "redevelopment" strategies. Wealthier suburbs have caught on to the strategy of declaring "blight" and passing on tax benefits, giving yet another push to the suburbanization of employment and fiscal resources (see Fulton, 1997; Schrag, 1998).

The central point is that the political, economic, and social landscape that we now take for granted was not simply a matter of market forces or consumer choices. Federal and state policies helped shape individual and corporate decision making. At least since the end of World War II, the incentives that promoted suburbanization and sprawl vastly outweighed those that encouraged people and firms to locate in cities. In the struggle between suburban sprawl and inner-city redevelopment, it was hardly a fair fight.

Promoting Regionalism: A New Approach

While federal policy has generally been biased toward fragmentation and suburbanization, certain measures have helped foster regional cooperation. For example, some federal grants have been contingent on regional coordination of services in specific areas, primarily health care (coordination to avoid a glut of hospital beds), transportation, and the environment (Hamilton, 1999: 141–75). In these cases, a single federal agency has promoted regional coherence for *its* particular programs. But this idea has never cut across all federal agencies—that is, the various federal departments have not themselves cooperated in order to encourage (or require) local governments within a metropolitan area to collaborate.

There have been a few examples of success. Federal regionalist efforts, which reached a peak in the 1970s, led to the creation of a variety of regional planning agencies and regional organizations of governments; although their authority is typically quite limited, in recent years, they have played a role in changing the political debate and putting regionalism on the public agenda. The Intermodal Surface Transportation Efficiency Act (ISTEA), passed in 1991 and reauthorized in 1997 as TEA-21, granted the "metropolitan planning organizations" created in an earlier era broad discretion to allocate federal transportation dollars in ways that best served the region; this created a concrete mechanism and incentive for intercity cooperation (Rusk, 1995: 120).

After more than five decades of encouraging suburbanization, it is time for Washington to be much more proactive in promoting regional cooperation. This does not mean that all regions should be forced to dress in the same federally mandated straitjacket. There is still plenty of room for local and regional innovation. At the same time, the federal government needs to shift gears and begin to work with states and metropolitan areas to regulate growth on the suburban fringes. It needs to encourage the pooling of fiscal and technical resources within metropolitan regions. And it needs to promote broader regional efforts to address poverty and inequality.

One obvious step would be to build on the regional approach taken in transportation policy through ISTEA, and require that planning, resource allocation, reporting, and evaluation for all federal domestic grant programs be undertaken on a metropolitan basis. For example, HUD should seek to consolidate the fragmented housing authorities into metrowide programs that could more easily facilitate housing mobility for the poor (Katz, 1998). Collaborative regions could also be given priority status for future federal funding like Community Development Block Grants (CDBG), job training funds, and other such programs; one hopeful sign is the 1998 announcement by Secretary Andrew Cuomo that HUD would allocate $100 million in special CDBG incentive funds for areas producing collaborative regional plans.[44]

Additionally, the federal government could help by providing more accessible and uniform information on the state of regions and sponsor research through the National Research Council, HUD, and other institutions on the evolving relationships between regions and communities. It could also reduce inter- and intrametropolitan competition by declaring the value of such tax abatements and private-benefit financing to be subject to federal taxation.[45] Finally, as a March 1998 report by the National Academy of Public Administration notes, the "bully pulpit" is critical: national leaders need to talk about the importance of combining regional and community agendas.

If some of these ideas seem small relative to the need, we should recall how important specific changes can be. For example, the Center for Neighborhood Technology in Chicago has worked together with the Natural Resources Defense Council in San Francisco and the Surface Transportation Policy Project in Washington to develop the concept of location-efficient mortgages (LEMs). Under the LEM scheme, individuals buying houses closer to public transit qualify for higher mortgages or lower down payments in recognition of the savings they are likely to generate by avoiding automobile use; in September 1998, Vice President Al Gore announced that Fannie Mae will develop a $100 million pilot program. At first glance, the impact may seem obscure and mostly environmental, but given where transit-rich areas are, the LEMs will favor home buyers in the inner city, spurring urban reinvestment, neighborhood business districts, and community building.

Both the development of the LEM and the authorization of TEA-21, the successor to ISTEA, speak to the power of having community-based policy organizations actively tracking regional initiatives. The Surface Transportation Policy Project (STPP), for example, is a public interest group tied to a network of grassroots groups interested in transportation policy. Its lobbying for ISTEA and TEA-21 were critical to their adoption—and STPP worked to make sure that the more recent TEA-21 included innovative elements such as the Job Access program, designed to ease the transition from welfare to work.

Action on the state level could help as well. Maryland's Smart Growth Initiative, for example, mandates that no state funds can be spent on new infrastructure outside of existing urbanized or already-served areas, forcing "ex-urbs" to bear the full costs of their development and thereby steering more real estate and commercial development to central cities and older suburbs.[46] In California, Speaker of the Assembly Antonio Villaraigosa announced in

September 1998 the formation of a blue-ribbon commission to reconsider state finances, particularly the impact of Proposition 13; changes in this arena would reduce the incentives for the fiscalization of land use that has fed new sprawl and limited the creation of higher-paying industrial jobs.[47]

While each level of government must be involved, the federal role in linking regional and community development is central: it alone has the power to right the bias in federal programs, dampen the perverse incentives of the current system, and offer rules that could foster the necessary new regional institutions. The clear political challenge is to find the common ground between the nation's central cities and suburbs that will enable and inspire them to construct an electoral and legislative majority that will adopt the measures outlined here.

When Work Reappears

In *When Work Disappears,* Wilson (1996) argues that in the past, many residents in inner-city neighborhoods worked, providing a regularity and order to family and community life. With the economic transformations of recent decades, particularly the slippage in traditional entry points into industrial employment, work largely disappeared in "ghetto" neighborhoods. This, in turn, eroded the social structures that used to proscribe certain behaviors and thereby prevent community breakdown. The community-building movement we have profiled directly tackles the consequences of these transformations, particularly the rips in the social fabric. Still, as many practitioners have observed, the best antipoverty program is a job. "Reappearing" work is crucial.

While a buoyant economy does not necessarily lift all boats, a drought is likely to affect poor and minority communities first.[48] In maintaining economic opportunity, we have stressed the need to connect to regional dynamics (see also Jargowsky, 1997). But regional thinking and action are not enough: states, metropolitan regions, and municipalities cannot, on their own, generate full employment.

Again, the role of the federal government is critical. Some have stressed the need for flexible federal spending, particularly on infrastructure and jobs programs (see Dreier and Rothstein, 1994; Wilson, 1996). Others worry about deficits and suggest that the budget-balancing efforts of the Clinton administration allowed for a more accommodating monetary policy and hence higher employment. Conservative leaders continue to press for business and personal tax cuts, although given the history of the 1980s, this hardly seems like a viable strategy for either the economy or the poor.

Whatever the approach, "tighter" labor markets help the poor directly and indirectly. In times of labor shortage, firms are willing to provide training and take chances on those with spotty employment records. Low unemployment also shifts the power balance between workers and firms, generally allowing community and labor organizations to leverage more from their business partners (as in Boston in the 1980s). Rapid job growth is not sufficient—targeted efforts to help the poor at federal, state, and regional levels are still needed—but the terrain for community-based regionalism will improve if the federal government maintains and acts on its stated commitment to high employment.

Returning to Los Angeles

We began this book as a way of responding to the political, social, and economic issues raised by the 1992 civil unrest in Los Angeles. Our initial objective was to find ways to bring the greater L.A. community closer together, not in the simplistic and sentimental "Brotherhood Week" symbolism, but by building an analysis and developing policies that would help people and institutions divided by race, income, geography, and ideology find common ground.

Politically, postriot Los Angeles has lurched in often conflicting directions. On the one hand, the election of Republican businessman Richard Riordan as mayor in 1993 and his subsequent reelection in 1997 has led Los Angeles to be counted among the ranks of big cities now headed by conservative mayors. But while Riordan promoted a more free-market approach to municipal policy, he was soon thwarted by a left-of-center city council that, for example, overrode his veto and successfully passed a living wage law in 1997.

Indeed, L.A.'s community and labor movements have gained significant ground, often by taking a broad regional approach. Living wage advocates have regrouped into a larger coalition (the Los Angeles Alliance for a New Economy, or LAANE) with an agenda that includes efforts to promote a living wage for the whole county, and a subsidy accountability campaign designed both to dampen jurisdictional "bidding for business" and establish safeguards to protect local wages and opportunities.[49] AGENDA, a CBO based in South Central, has initiated a regional Metro Alliance to pressure emerging regional employment centers, such as the new DreamWorks studio, to provide job training and other opportunities for residents in the inner city. Meanwhile, the Labor/Community Strategies Center has continued its struggle to enhance mobility for low-income workers, organizing bus riders, suing the Metropolitan Transit Authority (MTA) to improve service, and more recently joining with the MTA to monitor compliance.

As a result of the new resurgence of community advocates, a variety of regional economic development initiatives have begun playing by a new set of rules. The Southern California Association of Governments (SCAG) has begun to issue an annual state-of-the-region report, and "equity" issues play an important and growing role in their analysis of the region (SCAG, 1999). The Alameda Corridor Authority has set a national standard with regard to hiring local residents and creating small business opportunities—primarily because the Alameda Corridor Jobs Coalition (ACJC), a collection of CBOs, churches, and neighborhood groups, successfully lobbied the authority for a commitment to place local residents in training slots and allocate 30 percent of the total hours for new hires. The corridor project can now boast the largest local hiring plan of any public works project in the history of the United States.

Of course, even as the proponents of regionalism and community development have begun to find common language, the proponents of fragmentation have made headway as well. Residents of the more affluent and suburbanized San Fernando Valley section of Los Angeles have crusaded to establish a separate municipality and residents in a growing number of other Los Angeles neighborhoods have begun to echo the valley's call for secession. Some have called for the breakup of the nearly one-million-student Los Angeles Unified School District on the grounds that its unwieldy size and complexity have contributed to the district's low educational outcomes; this is the clear opposite of the single school district approach adopted so successfully in Charlotte.

Yet the overall direction may be positive. On a statewide level, business, environmentalists, and community activists in the late 1990s began voicing common concerns about the negative consequences of unregulated sprawl, the need to invest greater public resources in the state's outdated infrastructure, and the importance of linking these two concerns to a Smart Growth strategy that could also abate poverty and inequality.[50] Governor Gray Davis has appointed a task force on infrastructure that includes representatives of diverse constituencies, including environmental, labor, business, and community sectors. State Treasurer Phil Angelides has used his influential position to promote "smart investments" to curtail sprawl and reduce inner-city poverty (Angelides 1999). As noted, Speaker of the Assembly Antonio Villaraigosa created a commission to recommend ways to eliminate the fiscal competition between municipalities exacerbated by Proposition 13, and despite having been one of the fiercest opponents of the 1998 antibilingual ballot initiative, Villaraigosa appointed the author of that initiative to serve on the commission. Perhaps a new common ground can be found in Los Angeles, California, and the nation.

Meeting the Challenge

Two broad and seemingly disparate trends characterize both our economy and our society. On the one hand, we are more global: money rockets through world financial markets; goods and people cross borders in increasing numbers; and ideas, news, and perspectives flash through an uncontrolled and seemingly unlimited cyberspace. On the other hand, we are more local: new agglomerations of social interests increasingly come together under the rubric of "community"; people long for manageable urban areas and livable neighborhoods; and regional economies have deep roots and often very specific geographically rooted assets.

This book has argued that we can bridge this seeming contradiction between globalization and community. The new regionalists, after all, argue that internationalization has helped regions emerge as the key level of economic activity, partly because it is at this level that actors can constitute effective social capital (that is, the sense of a regional community) and a set of industrial clusters. The new community builders likewise stress social capital, noting that the first step to neighborhood development is often rebuilding the basic community fabric and recognizing that neighborhoods should be seen as part of a regional whole in a deeply globalized economy. Community and regional development can and should be linked.

Getting there will not be easy. Some regional analysts, like Myron Orfield (1998), have suggested a rough-and-ready political calculus of combining inner-city advocates and inner-ring suburban leadership, suggesting that these actors could be persuaded to impose regional taxes on wealthier, outlying suburbs and then redistribute resources in their own direction. Curtis Johnson, former chair of the Minneapolis–St. Paul Metropolitan Council, one of the few effective metropolitan governments in the country, worries that such "ganging up on the suburbs at the edge . . . is destructive to a sense of region."[51] Even within the circle of supposedly common central-city and inner-suburb interests, there are challenges to communication and collaboration: in light of historic patterns of segregation and mobility, bringing together city and suburban residents is not just face-to-face but also race-to-race (Powell, 1998; Delgado, 1999).

Despite the difficulties, we must act. Regional policy makers can no longer "ghettoize" community development and antipoverty efforts, pretending that poverty is simply a problem of the central cities. Regional business can no longer remain passive, insisting that redistributing opportunities will somehow shrink the overall pie even as they seek to leverage subsidies from fiscally starved local governments. Community builders cannot accept the usual politics of place and must instead stretch to the new frontiers and opportunities of regional politics and decision making.

The national concern about these issues is evident. Antisprawl measures and candidates did well in the 1998 elections, Vice President Al Gore made regional vitality and community livability an important component of his presidential campaign, and Smart Growth measures to contain suburbanization and encourage central city development have been gaining popularity.[52] Yet while controlling the forces of sprawl can create the conditions for community development, equity concerns could just as easily be left off the table. Ensuring that community-based regionalism takes hold requires both vision and political struggle; while federal policies could help, we will also need a "bottom-up" approach that builds consensus one neighbor and one region at a time.

The challenge is before us. We cannot go back and rewrite a past characterized by metropolitan sprawl, environmental indifference, and widening economic and racial disparities. But we can adopt a new approach that creatively links regional and community development. We can decide that we have had enough of the political, economic, and moral pain caused by the past decades of growing apart. We can commit ourselves to growing together.

Appendix A

Neighborhood Profiles

In chapter 3, we discuss our examination of ten neighborhoods in Los Angeles County. These areas represented various balances with regard to geographic location: five of the selected neighborhoods were from the City of Los Angeles (Boyle Heights, Pacoima, South Vermont, Westlake, and Watts) and five were from the rest of the county (Belvedere/East LA, Huntington Park, Inglewood, Northwest Pasadena, and Southeast Pomona). Moreover, Boyle Heights, South Vermont, Watts, and Belvedere are located in the traditional inner city; Pacoima and Southeast Pomona are situated in the San Fernando and San Gabriel Valleys, Huntington Park is located in the eastern part of the Alameda Corridor, Inglewood is in the West Los Angeles area, and Northwest Pasadena is in one of the county's oldest suburbs.

While all of the areas selected had a heavy representation of African-Americans and Latinos, the actual composition varied. South Vermont had the highest percentage of African-Americans; Watts, Inglewood, and Northwest Pasadena were traditional African-American areas heavily affected by recent Latino in-migration; Belvedere, Boyle Heights, and Huntington Park were the most Latino of the areas; and Westlake was the most immigrant (see table A.1).

These neighborhoods were generally much poorer than the city or county in which they are located. Certain areas, such as Watts, Westlake, and Boyle Heights, had poverty rates in excess of 30 percent; South Vermont and the other areas are not far behind (see table A.2). The populations of these areas were generally less educated than the city and county population as a whole and all of the selected areas experienced higher-than-average unemployment. The occupational mix was more complex, with some areas leaning toward manufacturing (such as machine operation) and others toward the lower end of the service sector. All areas, however, had a lower-than-average percent of residents in high-end executive or professional jobs (see table A.3).

There was a wide divergence by area with regard to "job density" (the number of jobs in each area divided by the number of residents of working age). Boyle Heights and Westlake were "jobs-rich," a pattern that squares with working poverty in those neighborhoods. Northwest Pasadena was above the county figure for job density, although this was mostly because some of its tracts stretched into the commuter magnet of downtown Pasadena. Most of the neighborhoods were "jobs-poor," implying that community developers needed either to generate more local employment or to link employable residents with other job centers in the region.

As demonstrated by a section of the questionnaire that focused on how local individuals acquired employment, linking of residents with outside employment was made difficult by the quality of local social networks in the labor market. While search mechanisms such as newspapers and the state Employment Development Department were mentioned, respondents noted that many residents used "word-of-mouth" to find work. Unfortunately, the relatively low-end employment of neighbors and friends often led to inadequate job opportunities and wages.

Finally, the importance of the region to the local economy was evident in our analysis of these neighborhoods' economic pasts and prospects. As noted in the text, many areas were hard-hit by the region's economic transformations detailed in chapter 2, particularly the loss of higher-wage manufacturing and the emergence of working poverty. Moreover, the more economically successful neighborhoods had been able to weather these changes in part by connecting to new regional opportunities. Huntington Park, Inglewood, and South Pomona, for example, had explicitly regional strategies that focused on bringing in employment and sales revenues from outside their immediate neighborhoods (either through regional services such as sports facilities in Inglewood, Pomona, and Huntington Park, retail sales as in Latino-oriented downtown shops in Huntington Park, or specific industrial employment such as ethnic food processing in both Pomona and Huntington Park).

In short, regional connections were crucial for better performance, implying that it might make sense from the view of antipoverty activists to link these neighborhoods and their residents more tightly to regional opportunities and initiatives. However, most of the Los Angeles regional initiatives reviewed in chapter 3 fell short on this front; suggestions for a new approach are the subject of chapter 7.

Table A.1

Demographics of Ten Selected Neighborhoods in Los Angeles County, 1990

	L.A. City Neighborhoods						L.A. County Neighborhoods					
Neighborhood	Boyle Heights	Pacoima	South Vermont	Westlake	Watts	Compared to: LA City	Belvedere	Hunt-ington Park	Ingle-wood	North-west Pasadena	South-east Pomona	Compared to: LA County
Total Population	102,607	98,347	95,580	118,757	32,145	3,485,398	62,986	56,065	109,602	47,268	45,664	8,863,164
Ethnic Breakdown												
Anglo	1.9%	13.1%	1.3%	8.7%	0.5%	37.3%	2.1%	5.4%	8.5%	15.7%	16.0%	40.8%
African-American	1.0%	10.5%	64.4%	3.1%	55.7%	13.0%	0.0%	0.8%	50.1%	34.1%	8.4%	10.5%
Latino	93.5%	71.1%	33.4%	77.3%	43.3%	39.9%	97.0%	91.9%	38.5%	45.4%	70.1%	37.8%
Asian-American	3.3%	4.6%	0.5%	10.2%	0.1%	9.2%	0.5%	1.4%	2.2%	4.0%	5.0%	10.2%
Other	0.4%	0.6%	0.5%	0.7%	0.4%	0.6%	0.4%	0.6%	0.6%	0.7%	0.6%	0.6%

Table A.1 (Continued)

Demographics of Ten Selected Neighborhoods in Los Angeles County, 1990

| | L.A. City Neighborhoods | | | | | | L.A. County Neighborhoods | | | | | |
Neighborhood	Boyle Heights	Pacoima	South Vermont	Westlake	Watts	Compared to: LA City	Belvedere	Hunt- ington Park	Ingle- wood	North- west Pasadena	South- east Pomona	Compared to: LA County
Percent Immigrant												
Arrived, 1980–90	26.3%	21.8%	15.1%	47.3	15.0%	21.6%	21.9%	30.8%	16.3%	19.3%	26.9%	17.2%
Arrived, 1970–89	18.7%	16.3%	16.3%	15.2%	8.5%	10.7%	17.6%	19.7%	9.3%	9.8%	12.0%	9.6%
Age Breakdown												
0–17	35.4%	34.4%	32.7%	27.1%	43.5%	24.8%	34.5%	34.5%	30.1%	30.1%	36.3%	26.2%
18–24	15.6%	14.2%	12.1%	19.3%	12.9%	13.2%	15.4%	16.1%	12.6%	13.1%	15.6%	12.3%
25–44	33.3%	36.3%	34.4%	39.4%	30.5%	40.8%	33.9%	36.2%	40.9%	39.1%	35.7%	40.2%
45–64	8.5%	9.2%	12.1%	7.5%	7.1%	11.3%	8.9%	7.6%	9.6%	8.4%	6.9%	11.6%
65+	7.2%	5.9%	8.7%	6.7%	6.0%	10.0%	7.4%	5.6%	6.8%	9.4%	5.5%	9.7%

Table A.2 (Continued)

Economic Characteristics of Ten Selected Neighborhoods in Los Angeles County, 1990

Neighborhood	L.A. City Neighborhoods						L.A. County Neighborhoods					
	Boyle Heights	Pacoima	South Vermont	Westlake	Watts	Compared to: LA City	Belvedere	Hunt- ington Park	Ingle- wood	North- west Pasadena	South- east Pomona	Compared to: LA County
% Poverty	30.9%	17.7%	28.3%	36.9%	50.7%	18.9%	24.4%	24.3%	16.5%	24.9%	28.4%	15.1%
Income Distribution												
0–$15,000	37.2%	18.2%	37.3%	46.7%	55.6%	24.3%	32.3%	31.6%	22.8%	33.0%	29.5%	20.3%
$15,000– $25,000	23.2%	15.4%	19.5%	23.3%	19.3%	16.7%	22.6%	21.0%	18.0%	20.5%	23.4%	15.2%
$25,000– $35,000	16.0%	15.7%	13.9%	14.3%	11.0%	14.5%	16.8.%	18.6%	17.4%	15.4%	16.1%	14.5%
$35,000– $50,000	12.8%	22.1%	13.7%	9.4%	8.5%	15.7%	16.0%	15.0%	18.6%	15.0%	16.5%	17.3%
$50,000– $75,000	8.2%	19.5%	11.1%	4.4%	4.2%	14.6%	9.4%	9.6%	15.2%	11.4%	11.2%	17.3%
$75,000 and up	2.5%	9.1%	4.6%	1.8%	1.3%	14.3%	2.9%	4.2%	8.0%	4.7%	3.3%	15.3%

Table A.2 (Continued)

Economic Characteristics of Ten Selected Neighborhoods in Los Angeles County, 1990

| | L.A. City Neighborhoods | | | | | | L.A. County Neighborhoods | | | | | |
Neighborhood	Boyle Heights	Pacoima	South Vermont	Westlake	Watts	Compared to: LA City	Belvedere	Huntington Park	Inglewood	North-west Pasadena	South-east Pomona	Compared to: LA County
Education												
Less than H.S.	73.6%	57.0%	44.4%	63.9%	63.2%	33.0%	71.6%	69.4%	34.0%	41.7%	58.9%	30.0%
H.S. only	12.7%	18.6%	23.6%	13.8%	22.5%	19.2%	14.6%	14.8%	19.8%	17.7%	19.2%	20.7%
Some College	9.8%	17.2%	25.5%	13.2%	11.9%	24.8%	10.6%	10.5%	31.2%	24.1%	17.5%	27.0%
College Degree	3.9%	7.2%	6.5%	9.1%	2.5%	23.0%	3.1%	5.3%	14.9%	16.6%	4.4%	22.3%
Labor Force Participation Rate												
Male	75.2%	79.2%	67.9%	76.7%	54.7%	76.6%	75.2%	80.8%	77.6%	74.5%	79.2%	77.1%
Female	47.4%	56.8%	51.7%	56.4%	32.8%	58.0%	46.7%	53.0%	62.7%	52.1%	48.0%	57.4%
Unemployment												
Male	13.3%	8.9%	16.0%	11.2%	22.9%	8.5%	10.5%	11.7%	9.6%	10.9%	11.3%	7.4%
Female	14.6%	9.6%	12.3%	11.7%	30.4%	8.2%	13.1%	14.6%	10.5%	11.0%	15.0%	7.3%

Table A.3

Occupation and Employment in Ten Selected Neighborhoods in Los Angeles County, 1990

| | L.A. City Neighborhoods | | | | | | L.A. County Neighborhoods | | | | | |
Neighborhood	Boyle Heights	Pacoima	South Vermont	Westlake	Watts	Compared to: LA City	Belvedere	Huntington Park	Inglewood	North-west Pasadena	South-east Pomona	Compared to: LA County
Occupational Mix												
Executive	4.1%	6.0%	7.0%	5.2%	4.3%	12.5%	4.1%	5.0%	9.7%	9.0%	4.8%	13.2%
Prof. Specialty	5.3%	5.5%	8.4%	5.1%	4.4%	14.7%	3.6%	4.1%	11.3%	11.5%	5.0%	14.4%
Tech. Support	1.4%	2.4%	2.1%	1.3%	1.2%	3.1%	2.2%	1.7%	3.4%	3.0%	2.5%	3.4%
Sales	6.6%	7.3%	6.2%	7.2%	6.2%	11.3%	8.2%	8.2%	8.6%	7.5%	6.1%	11.6%
Admin. Support	14.2%	15.5%	21.5%	11.4%	16.5%	16.8%	15.9%	13.7%	21.1%	16.3%	11.8%	17.4%
Private Service	1.3%	1.2%	1.4%	4.2%	0.8%	1.7%	1.1%	1.4%	1.0%	2.2%	0.7%	1.1%
Other Service	14.9%	12.3%	15.8%	19.4%	15.9%	12.2%	12.7%	10.5%	16.4%	20.3%	13.7%	11.2%
Farm, Mining, Fish	1.6%	2.8%	1.5%	1.5%	2.1%	1.4%	1.9%	1.1%	2.2%	4.2%	4.5%	1.2%
Precision Prod.	13.1%	16.8%	11.6%	11.8%	11.4%	10.3%	13.5%	15.0%	10.7%	9.5%	16.4%	11.0%
Machine Operation	24.0%	18.6%	12.9%	23.1%	22.0%	8.8%	22.7%	26.2%	6.7%	7.4%	19.3%	8.2%
Trans./Moving	5.0%	4.0%	6.0%	3.1%	7.0%	3.0%	5.6%	5.3%	4.5%	3.3%	5.0%	3.4%
Helpers/Cleaners	8.6%	7.5%	5.4%	6.6%	8.1%	4.0%	8.5%	7.7%	4.5%	5.7%	10.1%	4.0%

Table A.3   (Continued)

Occupation and Employment in Ten Selected Neighborhoods in Los Angeles County, 1990

| | L.A. City Neighborhoods | | | | | | L.A. County Neighborhoods | | | | | |
Neighborhood	Boyle Heights	Pacoima	South Vermont	Westlake	Watts	Compared to: LA City	Belvedere	Huntington Park	Inglewood	North-west Pasadena	South-east Pomona	Compared to: LA County
Employment Rate												
Male	65.2%	72.2%	57.1%	68.2%	42.2%	70.1%	67.3%	71.4%	70.1%	66.4%	70.3%	71.4%
Female	40.5%	51.4%	45.3%	49.8%	22.8%	53.3%	40.6%	45.3%	56.1%	46.4%	40.8%	53.2%
Total Residents Employed	37,443	41,949	34,179	53,750	6,069	1,670,488	23,523	22,649	50,059	19,340	17,247	4,203,792
Total Number of Jobs in Area	47,437	24,283	15,596	63,408	3,572	1,902,069	14,323	19,029	46,167	30,723	14,786	4,612,829
Jobs in Area / Working Age Pop	74.8%	39.0%	26.4%	77.3%	20.6%	80.5%	36.7%	53.5%	63.9%	102.4%	52.7%	78.0%

NOTE: The resident employment rates are calculated by dividing the number of employed area residents by the working age population (age 16–64).

Appendix B

Data Sources and Strategies for Chapters 5 and 6

The geographical unit used to measure a metropolitan area's economic and demographic phenomena in chapters 5 and 6 is the Metropolitan Statistical Area (MSA). MSAs, which are defined by the Office of Management and Budget, generally contain a primary central city and its surrounding suburbs (some MSAs have two significant central cities, such as Minneapolis–St. Paul). In some cases, such as Los Angeles and San Diego, the MSA shares its boundaries with the county. Other MSAs (Charlotte and Boston, for example) consist of several component counties. In 1980, Standard Metropolitan Statistical Area (SMSA) was the accepted nomenclature, but since 1990 the terminology has become somewhat more complicated. Freestanding metropolitan areas are now simply MSAs. In locales such as the Bay Area, where several large cities are in close proximity, individual metropolitan areas are called Primary Metropolitan Statistical Areas (PMSAs), which together form the more encompassing Consolidated Metropolitan Statistical Area (CMSA).

When comparing census data across time for metropolitan areas, researchers are bound to encounter minor obstacles. There are two primary data-gathering dilemmas: (1) a particular data series might not be readily available for the desired time period; and (2) the definitions of metropolitan areas are not necessarily consistent over the relevant interval. With regard to the first point, the use of New England County Metropolitan Areas (NEC-MAs) rather than MSAs in certain data series (such as Boston, Providence, and Springfield) presents a minor problem. For the metropolitan areas in New England, NECMA data was used whenever possible; these variables include 1980 and 1990 unemployment, 1980 and 1990 population, 1980 ethnicity percentages, 1977 manufacturing, 1980 education, and 1979 per capita income. However, certain variables were available only for MSAs: 1990 poverty, 1990 income, and 1990 ethnicity. While not a perfect match, NECMA and MSA series are nearly identical; data for MSAs and NECMAs differ only in their composite and "outside central-city" figures while central-city data is identical.

Between the 1980 and 1990 censuses, the Census Bureau redefined its definition of several metropolitan areas. Some MSAs absorbed surrounding areas, while others were split into two or more new MSAs. Thus, some care must be taken when comparing 1980 and 1990 census data. To account for these changes, data from CMSAs was used in 1990 for several cities in order to maximize comparability with 1980 MSAs. These metropolitan areas included Buffalo, Dallas, Denver, Pittsburgh, Portland, and Providence. Many other MSAs changed slightly between 1980 and 1990, as a small county or town was deleted. These alterations are generally minor.

The data used in the regressions of chapter 5 and in the figures and tables of chapter 6 are generally drawn from various U.S. Bureau of the Census publications. Population and ethnic percentages are from *1980 Census of Population: Poverty Areas in Large Cities,* table S-1, and *1990 Census of Population and Housing: Summary Population and Housing Characteristics,* table 2. Poverty data for 1980 (which actually comes from 1979) was taken from table B of *State and Metropolitan Area Data Book, 1986.* Poverty data for 1989, along with 1989 per capita income, was obtained from table 3 of *1990 Census of Population: Social and Economic Characteristics: Metropolitan Areas* (section 1 of 6). Per capita income for 1979, 1980 unemployment, 1980 labor force participation, and 1977 manufacturing employment are all from table B of the *State and Metropolitan Area Data Book, 1982;* 1990 unemployment data comes from the 1991 edition of the same publication. MSA density and commute time, used in alternative regression specifications, are taken from table B of the 1982 *State and Metropolitan Data Book,* table D of the 1991 *State and Metropolitan Area Data Book,* table 232 (chapter B, part 6) of *The 1980 Census of Population,* vol. 1, and table 2 (section 1) of the *1990 Census of Population: Social and Economic Characteristics: Metropolitan Areas.* The dissimilarity indexes are taken from Abramson, Tobin, and VanderGoot (1995), while the inequality measures are taken from Glickman, Lahr, and Wyly's "The State of the Nation's Cities" (SNC) database.

Notes

1. The New Regionalism and the New Community Building

1. For reviews of the causes of the unrest and the city's immediate responses, see Estrada and Sensiper (1993), Johnson et al. (1992a, 1992b), Ong et al. (1993), and Pastor (1993, 1995), as well as the articles in Baldassare (1994), especially Regalado (1994). Kotkin and Friedman (1993) are less convinced of the economic explanation of the unrest but devote much of their analysis to economic fixes, albeit along very different lines than some of the authors above.

2. See Pastor (1993, 1995).

3. For example, a Census Bureau study found that the percent of persons who had year-round full-time employment but still had annual earnings below the poverty level for a family of four rose from 14.6 percent in 1984 to 16.2 percent in 1994 (Ryscavage, 1996).

4. For more on the general forces driving suburbanization and sprawl, see Jackson (1985) and Mollenkopf (1983). For more on the specific impacts of federal policy, see National Academy of Public Administration (1998) and Katz (1998); for specifics on the impact of the mortgage deduction policy, see Dreier (forthcoming).

5. During the 1980s, for example, Los Angeles grew by 17.4 percent, while its suburbs grew by 29.5 percent. Baltimore lost 6.4 percent of its population while its suburbs grew by 16.5 percent.

6. According to a study by political scientists Swanstrom and Sauerzkopf (1993), the late 1940s represented the peak year of city electoral dominance. For example, in the 1948 presidential election, New York City had 50 percent of the total votes cast in New York state while Chicago had 46.5 percent of Illinois's turnout, Baltimore had 42.3 percent of Maryland's vote, Detroit had 31.8 percent of Michigan's, Los Angeles and San Francisco combined for 51.3 percent of the California vote, and Philadelphia and Pittsburgh had 30.7 percent of Pennsylvania's electorate. By 1992, New York City represented only 30.9 percent of the votes cast for president, with the share of statewide voters in Chicago (22.3 percent), Baltimore (13 percent), Detroit

194 • Notes to Chapter 1

(7.9 percent), Los Angeles and San Francisco (12.9 percent), and Philadelphia and Pittsburgh (16.1 percent) also showing dramatic declines.

7.   In 1990, about 40 percent of African-Americans and Latinos lived outside of
     central cities compared to 67 percent of Anglos and Asians; both groups had
     seen around a seven percentage point increase in suburbanization since 1970,
     but given the lower initial base for African-Americans and Latinos, this repre-
     sents a faster rate of increase. Despite the progress, African-Americans and
     Latinos comprised about 44 percent of those living in the seventy-four central
     cities in 1990 but were only 16 percent of the suburban population, a compo-
     sition that suggests why creating city-suburban linkages is also complicated by
     the dynamics of racial division. Data on the relative rates of suburbanization
     are taken from "The State of the Nation's Cities" (SNC, version 2.11A, Septem-
     ber 22, 1997), a database that includes information on seventy-four of the
     country's largest cities and metro areas, with most variables drawn from the
     1970, 1980, and 1990 censuses.

8.   Wood (1961), Aron (1969), and the Advisory Commission on Intergovernmen-
     tal Relations (1967, 1969).

9.   For a wide array of views of the new regionalism, see the special issue "Initia-
     tives for America's Regions" of *The Regionalist,* vol. 2, no. 4 (winter 1997). Hiss
     (1997) also uses the term "new regionalist" to refer to this emerging research
     and policy trend.

10. One important piece of evidence supporting this view is the increasing diver-
     gence of economic fortunes by economic region: growth rates between differ-
     ent metro areas have widened over the last 20 years. For evidence on regional
     income divergence, see Browne (1989); Phillips (1992); and Drennan, Tobier,
     and Lewis (1996). For more evidence on the emergence of the region as an
     economic unit, see DRI/McGraw-Hill (1998).

11. For examples of the argument that local and national economies are increas-
     ingly weak in the face of internationalized investment and trade, see Steinmo
     (1994) and Palley (1994).

12. Reich (1991) also stresses the importance of geographically based human and
     physical capital assets, arguing that the best way for the United States to com-
     pete internationally is to ensure that it is attractive to producers not in terms of
     wages but rather on the basis of skills and infrastructure. We are essentially
     applying this argument to the regional level.

13. See Friedman (1992) for a powerful analysis of networks and regions in Japan.
     Freidman emphasizes the importance of "sticky" businesses—firms that stay
     in an area because of network linkages to suppliers and customers. Michael
     Storper (1997) has labeled these relational assets as "untrade-able interdepen-
     dencies." For more on the connection between globalization and the rise of
     metropolitan economies, see Stegman and Turner (1996).

14. For early analyses of regions and the new flexible manufacturing, see Piore and
     Sabel (1984) and Sabel (1988).

15. She also makes a series of critical distinctions between the Boston electronics
     complex and Silicon Valley, arguing that the former involved vertically inte-
     grated firms that did not pursue horizontal business networks as successfully
     as their Silicon Valley counterparts. Horizontal networks, she suggests, allowed

the Silicon Valley region to develop a regional (rather than firm-specific) consciousness and to adjust more quickly to the rapid changes in the electronics industry in the late 1980s.

16. See Joint Venture: Silicon Valley Network (1995) and the review of the San Jose/ Santa Clara experience in chapter 6 of this volume.

17. For an early and classic formulation of this issue as applied to business firms, see Coase (1937).

18. Friedman (1992) stresses the importance of trust and collaborative relations at the regional level, arguing that the national level is too distant for the effective crafting of such cross-constituency partnerships. Richard Levine (quoted in Hiss, 1997:3) suggests that metro areas may be "the largest unit capable of addressing the many urban architectural, social, economic, political, natural resource, and environmental imbalances in the modern world, and, at the same time, the smallest scale at which such problems can be meaningfully resolved in an integrated and holistic fashion."

19. Putnam's most direct application of this social capital framework to regional analysis is in his 1993 analysis of northern Italy.

20. On spatial mismatch, see Fernandez (1997), Kain (1968), and Kasarda (1993).

21. See the results in Pastor and Adams (1996). Fernandez and Weinberg (1997) offer a general view and compelling evidence on the role of social networks in hiring; see also Oliver and Lichter (1996).

22. See Odland and Balzer (1979:87–93), and Oliver and Shapiro (1995). Part of this contagion effect is redlining; see chapter 4 and Squires (1992, 1999).

23. For more on the role of social capital in community development, see Gittell and Vidal (1998); for more on "community building," see Kingsley, McNeely, and Gibson (1997), Kretzmann and McKnight (1993), and Rabrenovic (1996).

24. The "efficiency" and "redistributive" arguments for regionalism are drawn from Summers (1997).

25. See Manuel Pastor, "L.A. Should Take a Cue from Silicon Valley," *Los Angeles Times*, February 16, 1997, D4.

26. One version of this is the New Urbanism movement. New Urbanists, such as architect Peter Calthorpe, stress the importance of sustaining and building "compact" neighborhoods in which it is possible to access jobs, shopping, and public spaces close to home (Fulton, 1996). For a New Urbanist perspective linked more closely with equity issues, see Cole, Kelly, and Corbett (1998).

27. See the discussion in Rothenberg Pack (1998).

28. This strategy is emphasized by Orfield (1997).

29. See Garland and Galuszka (1997). Gurwitt (1998) also notes how older inner-ring suburbs—those closest and most tied to the central city—have been finding that they share common problems and common goals with inner-city residents and are building political alliances with the central city.

30. This discussion draws on Nunn and Rosentraub (1997), Savitch and Vogel (1996), and Hollis (1997).

31. William Celis, "Michigan Votes for Revolution in Financing Its Public Schools," *New York Times*, March 17, 1994, A1; Clifford Krauss, "Clinton Aims to Redirect School Aid to the Poor From Wealthy Districts," *New York Times*, September 15, 1993, B7, B15; Jennifer Preston, "Wealthier School Districts Chafe at Whitman's

Spending Plan," *New York Times*, August 12, 1996; and George Judson, "Lawyers Look at Hartford Case as Model," *New York Times*, August 15, 1996, A17, B1.

32. For a discussion of voluntary and court-ordered regional housing mobility programs, see Atlas and Dreier (1997), Calavita, Grimes, and Mallach (1997), Dreier and Moberg (1996), Ehrenhalt (1993), Haar (1996), Keating (1994), Kirp, Dwyer, and Rosenthal (1996), Peterson and Williams (1994), Polikoff (1995), Roisman and Botein (1993), Rosenbaum (1995), and U.S. Department of Housing and Urban Development (1994a, 1994b, 1995, 1997).

33. The Coalition of Neighborhood Developers (CND) was actually formed in 1990 but it broadened considerably and was incorporated as a freestanding nonprofit organization after the civil unrest. For more on the history of CND, see Morales and Pastor (2000).

34. As noted, we focus our data and analysis on Los Angeles County. It is arguable that the actual economic region is in fact much larger and includes the surrounding four counties—Orange, Riverside, San Bernardino, and Ventura—that have been brought together under the regional umbrella of the Southern California Association of Governments. But for purposes of our research, eighty-eight cities, nine million people, and an economy nearly the size of Australia's seemed a useful starting point, partly because there is no effective governance unit for the larger region.

35. For another pioneering effort to define "community-based regionalism," see Bernstein (1997).

36. California's state economic strategy, for example, is explicitly based on a definition of economic regions and their industry clusters. See California Economic Strategy Panel (1996).

37. See Gore's discussion of sprawl and Smart Growth in a key speech delivered at the Brookings Institution, September 2, 1998, and his December 4, 1998, speech to the National League of Cities ("Gore Pledges Help for Urban Sprawl," *San Jose Mercury News*, December 5, 1998, 13A).

2. When Work Doesn't Pay

1. By its third year, the organization had been restructured with new leadership and more streamlined governance. It also had adopted more modest (and realistic) goals focused not so much on persuading corporations to come to South Central as on helping create business networks to ensure that existing businesses would stay. For a review of the shift in RLA strategy, based largely on cultivating business networks, see RLA (1995) and Wong (1996: 77). For more on the investment controversy, see Nancy Rivera Brooks and Henry Weinstein, "19 of 68 Firms Question Listings by Rebuild LA," *Los Angeles Times*, November 18, 1992, A1. We review RLA in more detail in chapter 3.

2. On why the empowerment zone application failed, see Ronald Brownstein, "L.A. Left Out of Urban Aid Program, U.S. Officials Say," *Los Angeles Times*, December 20, 1994, A1, and Rich Conell, "Delay, Lack of Focus Dogged L.A.'s Grant Bid," *Los Angeles Times*, December 25, 1994, A1. These analyses suggest that the problems lay in a degree of overconfidence, an absence of complementary commitments by the private sector, and a lack of specificity in the plans. Los Angeles did eventually receive an empowerment zone designation

in 1998, with the program slated to take effect in 1999 (see David Friedman, "Power in Name Only," *Los Angeles Times,* February 8, 1998, M1). For more on the development of the Community Development Bank, see Jean Meri, "Community Development Bank Takes Important Step," *Los Angeles Times,* May 26, 1996, B1.

3. The policy document, entitled *From the Ground Up: Neighbors Planning Neighborhoods,* represented an innovative attempt to determine common planning issues in distinct distressed areas of the city (Coalition of Neighborhood Developers, 1994). For analyses of why this effort did not live up to its initial ambitions, see Morales and Pastor (2000) and Leavitt (1997).

4. For a concise history of urban efforts since the Nixon administration, see Stegman (1996: 237–45).

5. See Bowles, Gordon, and Weisskopf (1983), Marglin and Schor (1991), and Bernstein and Adler (1994).

6. This describes the behavior of average hourly earnings for private nonagricultural, nonsupervisory or production workers as adjusted for inflation. Data from various issues of the *Economic Report of the President,* Washington, D.C.: U.S. Government Printing Office.

7. For more on the general history of Los Angeles, see Fogelson (1967), Erie (1992), and Fulton (1997).

8. Manufacturing employment plateaued in 1979 at approximately 900,000 employed and, after a slow decline, was nearly back at the 1979 level in 1988. What followed was a period of sharp contraction. By 1996, manufacturing accounted for 634,000 jobs, 266,000 less than at the 1979 peak.

9. Figures based on data provided by the Los Angeles Economic Development Corporation; original data from the Southern California Association of Governments (SCAG).

10. The term "deindustrialization" was popularized by Bluestone and Harrison (1982), who were among the first to notice and document the trend.

11. The term "reindustrialization" is associated with those studying the role of immigrant labor in Los Angeles; see, for example, López-Garza (1989 and forthcoming), Morales and Ong (1993), and Pastor (1993).

12. For an analysis of the emergence of the garment industry, see Wong (1996), Southern California Edison (1995), and Bonacich et al. (1994).

13. See the analysis in Ong et al. (1989). The combination of low- and high-wage labor is also stressed by Morales and Ong (1993: 61).

14. Grobar's (1996: 76) shift-share analysis of Southern California suggests that the area's industrial structure and the severity of the recession were connected: according to her, the majority of jobs lost in the recession came from "being in the wrong industry at the wrong time—that is, having a high concentration of employment in industries that lost jobs on a nation-wide basis."

15. In 1988, Los Angeles aerospace and high-tech employment stood at 274,200; however, by 1996, only 132,800 of these well-paying jobs remained. This decline accounts for over half of the job shrinkage in manufacturing over that time period. On job losses in Los Angeles County as a percentage of the state's, see Patrick Lee, "UCLA Forecast for State Is Surprisingly Rosy," *Los Angeles Times,* September 21, 1994, D1. Another estimate suggests that the county's

share of state job losses during 1991–94 was 71 percent; see Jeffrey L. Rabin, "State and L.A. County Have Begun a Comeback, Economist Says," *Los Angeles Times,* March 6, 1996, B3.

16. In this and the next paragraph, the 1990 demographics are from the U.S. Bureau of the Census Summary Tape File 1 on CD-ROM. The 1980 figures are from the Los Angeles County Department of Regional Planning Research Section. The 1970 figures are from *(Almost) 8 Million and Counting: A Demographic Overview of Latinos in California with a Focus on Los Angeles County,* Claremont, CA: The Tomás Rivera Center, 1991. The percentage of Latinos in the 1970 population is an estimate since the Census Bureau was inconsistent in distinguishing between Hispanics and non-Hispanics until the 1980 count. For more on the ethnic transformation of the Los Angeles area, see Waldinger and Bozorgmehr (1996) and Allen and Turner (1997).

17. The boundaries for the South Central area are drawn from the Los Angeles Regional Office of the U.S. Bureau of the Census Special Study on South Central Los Angeles prepared in the immediate aftermath of the April 1992 unrest. The Census Bureau study, in turn, drew upon the neighborhood definitions (or "minor statistical areas") devised by the Los Angeles County Department of Regional Planning and include unincorporated areas of the county, as well as areas of the city. The mid-1990s ethnic balance is projected from the previous trends from 1980 to 1990.

18. Ong and Lawrence (1995), for example, documented that African-Americans and Latinos were disproportionately affected by the shrinkage in aerospace jobs.

19. This 1990 data was drawn from that year's Public Use Microdata Sample (PUMS), available on CD-ROM from the U.S. Bureau of the Census. While more recent figures on the ethnic breakdown of poverty would be preferable analytically, the PUMS allows for extremely detailed analysis and breakdowns and is consistent (in terms of time frame and variable definition) with the Summary Tape File data used to map poverty and other measures by census tract. The general patterns described below are likely to have persisted through the 1990s, especially with regard to ethnic composition of the poverty population and the nature of working and jobless poverty in Los Angeles.

20. The cutoffs employed in the poverty figure follow the usual definitions of high and extreme poverty; most other cutoffs were derived after exploring the data to find natural breaks. As is typical of such geographic information system analysis, the data are for "whole" tracts (which sometimes cuts across jurisdictional lines). With the exception of the employment data, made available to us at the tract level by the Southern California Association of Governments, the data in this section is drawn from the Summary Tape Files for Los Angeles County.

21. The textile sector alone (excluding garment assembly) registered $1.5 billion in sales, and over half of these firms, which provide the raw materials and occupy the relatively high-tech and capital-intensive end of the fashion industrial chain, were located in poorer areas. Moreover, the sales and employment figures associated with the textile sector in these "neglected" census tracts were surpassed by those associated with relatively high-tech operations such as

biomedical technology and entertainment crafts; indeed, at the time of the RLA calculations, 25 percent of L.A.'s $4 billion biomed industry was located near poorer areas. Other important economic sectors with a large presence in the poorer tracts are furniture and toy manufacturing. As we note later, the presence of this wide range of enterprises led RLA to adopt an economic development strategy based on encouraging manufacturing networks among existing firms. Data taken from RLA (1997,1996, 1995); also see Wong (1996).

22.   On the job market tests, see Keeny and Wissoker (1994) and Kirschenman and Neckerman (1991); on the interviews with employers, see Kirschenman, Moss, and Tilly (1996) and Moss and Tilly (1993).

23.   The location tagged in PUMS is the Public Use Microdata Areas (PUMA). There are fifty-eight such PUMAs in Los Angeles County; these are large areas, averaging 150,000 in their population, but they are, in the L.A. case, generally geographically compact and square with a general sense of local labor markets and residential areas. In any case, they are the only locational level available in the PUMS; see Pastor and Adams (1996) for more details and further justification.

24.   Another cut at the same issues using a different database is available in Pastor and Marcelli (1998); there, we measure spatial mismatch with a variable capturing the local or PUMA-level rate of job growth and find a stronger spatial effect.

25.   In keeping with standard practice, we also use years of work experience squared, reflecting the notion that the wage-enhancing impact of experience diminishes over time.

26.   For example, we found that an additional year of education raised wages by 6.1 percent and an additional year of work raised wages by 2.5 percent, effects quite consistent with other research. Lack of English skills, recent immigration, and being African-American, Latino, or Asian-Pacific all lowered wages by varying amounts.

27.   Briggs (1997:215), however, questions whether networks are spatially constrained, suggesting that detailed ethnographic research on the social interactions of the poor "might disabuse us of the notion, inspired by myths of the neighborhood as urban village, that poor folks' immediate neighbors are always and everywhere at the center of their interpersonal exchanges, attitudes, aspirations, and decisions."

28.   Ong and Blumenberg (1998) find that geographic proximity to employment, as measured by local job density, matters for job access for AFDC recipients in Los Angeles. However, they do not control for any network effects.

29.   We also ran the regressions as two-stage least squares to control for the simultaneity of neighborhood effect and neighborhood choice (to see whether the effect of neighborhood poverty on wages was simply a statistical artifact resulting from the fact that low wages drove one to a poor neighborhood or whether there was actually an additional impact on wages, due to the lessened economic resources of area contacts, not reflected in that "choice"). We also ran ordinary least squares on only long time residents as another way to reduce simultaneity since this procedure eliminated recent movers. Results of both procedures were consistent with the more general results described in the text.

30.   PUMS is used mostly because the usual aggregations by tract or county

provided by the census offer no cross-referencing of work and poverty. Another reason is that such aggregations by tract or county often tend to obscure key variations by ethnicity in the poverty experience. Consider, for example, the ethnic breakdown of poverty using aggregated data. The Census Bureau does offer a breakdown of poverty rates by race and Hispanic/non-Hispanic; however, in its actual census questionnaire, the bureau first asks respondents their race (white, black, American Indian, Asian, and other), then their self-designation as Hispanic or non-Hispanic. Latinos in Los Angeles County obviously report themselves as Hispanic but in response to the race query, 43 percent report themselves as white while 55 percent report themselves as "other" (with the remainder scattered in the other racial categories). As a result, the "white" poverty rate reported by the census—if by white we mean the usual Southern California conception of non-Hispanic white or Anglo—is actually overstated.

31. The cutoff age of sixty-five at the time of the census (or sixty-four in the previous year) squares with the usual age breakdown used by the census when reporting poverty rates for the elderly.

32. Some might suggest that the percentage of working poor Latino households is artificially swollen by the inclusion in such household units, particularly in those headed by immigrants, of unrelated individuals who may work even though the head of household does not (for example, a boarder or friend who temporarily resides in the household immediately after entering the country or the city). The census removes such individuals from its own calculation of household poverty rates although it does include related family members; to be consistent with the standard practice, we also removed the unrelated individuals from the determination of whether any household member was working but included the related family members.

33. The figure is even higher for poor 1970s immigrant households, 40 percent of which are headed by individuals with full-time or significant employment.

34. The labor force work attachment of Latino immigrants also translates into limited use of social welfare. Using the Census Bureau's definition of public assistance (which includes income received as supplementary social security payments, Aid to Families with Dependent Children, and general assistance) we found that use of public assistance by immigrant households with a working-age householder declines significantly by recency of arrival for immigrant Latinos but rises for non-Hispanic whites and Asians. Moreover, directly comparing use of public assistance from the two largest groups of immigrant households headed by working-age individuals, Mexicans and Armenians, we found that the number of recent Armenian immigrant households on public assistance in Los Angeles County in 1990 was roughly equal to the number of recent Mexican immigrant households in the same category, although there were over twelve times as many Mexican immigrant households in the total population. This does not capture fully the fiscal impact of immigration in terms of schooling and health care, which the general public relies on as well, but the results suggest that much of the public perception linking immigrant Latinos and welfare is misleading. For more details, see Pastor (forthcoming); Bean, Van Hook, and Glick (1994) offer a similar analysis while Fix and Passel (1994) and Passel (1994) offer broader analyses of the fiscal impacts of recent immigration.

35. See, for example, Edin and Lein (1997); Harris (1993); Piven and Cloward (1993); Stack (1974); Jencks and Edin (1995); and Tienda and Stier (1991).

36. In Charleston (South Carolina), for example, ethnographic research revealed that single mothers "made and sold handicrafts, worked for cash at fishing docks heading shrimp and cleaned in houses of rich northern retirees," often hiding earnings in order to not risk losing their much-needed public benefits (Edin and Lein, 1997: 218).

37. Despite the seeming proliferation of informality in Los Angeles, few detailed studies exist pertaining to this sector in the county. Most investigations of the informal sector in the United States have focused on the east coast (Portes, Castells, and Benton, 1989; Sassen, 1989, 1991; and Stepick 1989). Only a few have touched on the west coast (Fernandez-Kelly and Garcia, 1989) or been comparative (Fernandez-Kelly and Sassen, 1992): Sirola (1991a, 1991b) has focused specifically on Los Angeles; the most recent studies on Los Angeles are those by López-Garza (forthcoming) and Marcelli, Pastor, and Joassart-Marcelli (1999).

38. Moreover, as Saskia Sassen (1994b: 2292) notes, the informal economy "does not include every transaction that happens to evade regulation. The concept excludes certain types of income-generated activities, such as teenage babysitting, that we almost expect to escape regulation. What makes informalization a distinct process today is not these small cracks in the institutional framework, but rather the informalization of activities generally taking place in the formal economy."

39. Moreover, the formal and informal sectors are also linked through individual workers (Zlolniski, 1994): a garment employee working in a regulated facility may also bring material home to work on over the weekends and during the evenings.

40. The original data set drew a slightly different boundary around who was to be included by labor force experience. Working directly with Marcelli, we drew a sample that included any individual reported as either working or looking for work (in the civilian sector of the economy) on the grounds that we were seeking to estimate the economic outcomes not just for the employed but for the entire labor supply. We also drew data sets only for those who were employed at the time of the census, thereby affording a better estimate of labor demand.

41. The procedure involves a logistic regression given that the independent variable is zero or one, that is, documented or undocumented.

42. The results in the text focus on unauthorized Mexicans as this is the population for which our estimates are most accurate. We also used the coefficient estimates from the logit procedure to calculate the number of undocumented non-Mexican non-Cuban Latino immigrants (Cubans were excluded since until recently nearly any Cuban immigrant making it to this country was automatically granted residency status) and used discordant pairs analysis to verify that applying the coefficients was permissible. The resulting estimate of all Latino-origin unauthorized workers is naturally larger, but the relative ranking of the industries remains similar. We did not include Asian immigrants since the discordant pairs analysis between Asians and Mexicans indicated that the fit was less appropriate.

43. Such estimates usually include those who are also not of working age; even accounting for likely age structure, the estimates here are low. See the early estimates by McCarthy and Valdez (1986).

44. Less formal analysis than that discussed here also suggests that our measure may be a good proxy for informality. For example, the garment industry, which ranks high in our measure of employing undocumented workers, is also plagued with the sort of violations of safety and other regulations considered characteristic of the informal economy: a 1996 sample taken by state and federal regulators found that nearly 75 percent of Southern California's garment-sewing shops had serious workplace health or safety problems, a rate at least half again as much as the state average, while 43 percent violated the minimum wage law and 55 percent violated overtime pay regulations (see Stuart Silverstein and George White, "Hazards Found in Nearly 75% of Garment Shops," *Los Angeles Times*, May 8, 1996, A1).

45. Our experts examined a list of 485 occupations and 235 industries, ranking each as "likely to be" formal or informal. To group their answers into the more compact occupational and industrial list shown in tables 2.2 and 2.3, we set the "probably informal" ranking as one and the "probably formal" as zero and took employment-weighted means to reflect the expert-determined probability that a particular industrial or occupation grouping was informal.

46. Indeed, the data suggest that the relationship between informality and poverty by industry is less pronounced than by occupation.

47. An alternative test checked the distribution of undocumented workers across occupations with the distribution of the poor across occupations. This yielded a correlation coefficient of .9458 with a significance level of .001.

48. For more, see the extensive methodological discussion in Pastor (forthcoming).

49. To derive the percent of regional income, we took all wage, salary, and net self-employment earnings, summed by the designated occupations, and divided by the sum of all earnings for workers in our sample. A similar procedure was used for determining the proportion of the labor force in largely informal occupations. All data from PUMS CD-ROM, 1990.

50. The interviewing method was qualitative, using an instrument consisting largely of open-ended questions that were then recoded for some quantitative analysis. The sample was collected between 1993 and 1996 by teams of students from both California State University, Los Angeles, and Occidental College, led by Professor Marta López-Garza. For a fuller report on this effort, focusing specifically on the Latino respondents, see López-Garza (forthcoming).

51. See James Flanigan, "Two Cheers for DreamWorks and a Resurgent L.A.," *Los Angeles Times*, December 17, 1995, D1. The news that DreamWorks would be built in Los Angeles was not without controversy, particularly because of the $70 million in subsidies provided by the Riordan administration to an already wealthy group of investors.

52. On the Alameda Corridor loan, see Bill Boyarsky, "Alameda Corridor Could Be Our Biggest Boon—or Boondoggle," *Los Angeles Times*, March 20, 1996, B1, and Jean Meri, "Officials Celebrate Promised Loan for Alameda Corridor Project," *Los Angeles Times*, March 20, 1996, B10. The federal government also

awarded a $1 billion contract to Lockheed Martin for the construction of a new space shuttle prototype at its Skunk Works plant in Palmdale; see Patrice Apodaca, "Shuttle Deal Will Benefit Scores of Firms," *Los Angeles Times*, July 4, 1996, D2. Of course, not all the news from the federal government was good: in September 1996, Congress awarded the Metropolitan Transportation Authority (MTA) less than half the funding requested for the next year of construction on its problem-plagued subway project; see Richard Simon and Jon D. Markman, "Congress Leaves MTA with Less Subway Funding," *Los Angeles Times*, September 12, 1996, A1.

53. The recovery continued in part because the steep decline in housing prices through the early 1990s recession made the L.A. area more attractive to employees and workers. See "California's U-Haul Meter Points South," *Los Angeles Times*, November 15, 1998, A1.

54. This process continued through the recovery. For example, even areas where job growth was high, such as the San Gabriel Valley, saw real earnings decline. See Don Lee, "A Mountain of Jobs," *Los Angeles Times*, June 19, 1998, D2.

3. Disconnected Futures

1. Data is from the Los Angeles Economic Development Corporation. Total employment refers to total nonagricultural employment; service employment does not include finance, insurance, real estate, or the government sector.

2. The apparel and textile industry was also in a modest upswing but this was mostly because fashion design, an allied service sector, was located in the Los Angeles basin.

3. One key element in this process was the Housing Act of 1949, which formed much of the legal basis for federal involvement in urban renewal activities from 1949 to 1974. See Frieden and Sagalyn (1989) and Beatty et al. (1991).

4. Boston and Chicago both produced innovative alternative strategies in the 1980s. For more on Boston, see chapter 6. For more examples and policies, see Sanyika (1986, 1987).

5. This partly reflected the philosophical position of the administration that simply helping the private sector to generate "a healthy economy . . . is our most powerful tool for revitalizing our cities" (Stegman, 1996: 242). In any case, the effect was to shift resources away from the cities, a trend that also fit neatly with demographic trends: because of significant population shifts from urban to suburban areas, many newly elected congressional members came increasingly from suburban areas, and their political and programmatic agendas were quite different from those of their urban colleagues.

6. See Schrag (1998) and Fulton (1997).

7. While the HUD budget has increased slightly during the Clinton administration, it has not come close to reaching the funding levels of the pre-Reagan era.

8. This seems to be part of the motivation behind HUD's new commitment to what it calls "metropolitan" strategies (see U.S. Department of Housing and Urban Development, 1996).

9. On the other hand, much of the housing stock eliminated by the Bunker Hill project had been deemed unsafe and unsound, and through the next three decades the Community Redevelopment Agency (CRA) created over 10,000

affordable housing units throughout the city (see Grigsby and Hruby, 1991). This record did not eliminate the outcry and concern over the CRA, particularly since the displacement was localized, visible, and immediate while the replacement housing was scattered and occurred over a much longer period.

Another redevelopment effort of the era that drew the ire of critics occurred at Chavez Ravine (a semirural setting close to downtown), now the location of the Dodger Stadium. A well-established Mexican-American community had been living in this area for some time when it was decided in the early 1950s that the residents would be displaced to make way for a proposed public housing project. After the site was cleared, however, the housing project was derailed by opponents, including the *Los Angeles Times,* who labeled state involvement in housing as "creeping socialism." Eventually, the city granted large subsidies to attract the Dodgers to the vacant site. In short, the poor were driven away, affordable housing was not created, and a regional attraction was built. Perhaps even more dramatically than at Bunker Hill, "urban renewal" plans had brought grief to lower-income residents. See Thomas S. Hines, "The Battle of Chavez Ravine," *Los Angeles Times,* April 20, 1997, M1.

10. This analysis draws from Davis (1987: 69–70). See also Sonenshein (1993).
11. Tax increment revenues generated by the two downtown projects, Bunker Hill and the central business district (CBD), totaled $1.01 billion between 1960 and 1997 (Grigsby and Caltabiano, 1998).
12. See, for example, Pastor and Hayling (1990). Several important documents and efforts fueled this rising critique of the Bradley administration's redevelopment efforts, including Ong et al. (1989), the "Remaking L.A." conference (sponsored by an alternative paper, the *LA Weekly*), and the "New Majority" conference (sponsored by a coalition of minority leaders) in 1989.
13. In some sense, the Los Angeles Community Development Bank was not explicitly regional but rather focused on poorer communities. Still, as we note later in the text, it was featured by HUD in its own evaluation of the Los Angeles regional strategies (U.S. Department of Housing and Urban Development, 1996), and like RLA, it hoped to have an effect on low-income communities throughout the region.
14. Funding for the agency comes from several different sources. While the Department of Transportation provides the majority of the monies, the agency also receives funding from the State of California and the City of Los Angeles as a result of bond issues passed by the voters. Additional revenues are derived from fees charged to transit users.
15. Metropolitan Transportation Authority (1997).
16. The one possible exception to this criticism was the proposed line from Pasadena to downtown Los Angeles, a route that would run through densely populated and mostly Latino Northeast Los Angeles. Unfortunately, this project was delayed due to the MTA's financial problems and the effects of public protest based on earlier rail projects.
17. The bus riders group was represented by the NAACP Legal Defense Fund. See Mike Davis, "L.A.'s Transit Apartheid: Runaway Train Crushes Buses," *The Nation,* September 18, 1995, pp. 271–74.

18. See Richard Simon, "MTA Pledges Better Bus Service in Suit Accord," *Los Angeles Times*, September 26, 1996, A1. As of 1998, the MTA was still out of compliance with the decree and organizing and protests by bus riders continued. See Daniel Wood, "No-Seat, No-Fare Campaign Moves L.A. Buses into Gear," *Christian Science Monitor*, 14 September 1998, p. 3, and Jeffrey L. Rabin, "Negotiations on MTA Bus Overcrowding Break Down," *Los Angeles Times*, September 10, 1998, B1.

19. See Jeffrey L. Rabin, "Backing for Anti-Subway Measure Equally Strong in All Areas of City," *Los Angeles Times*, November, 1998, B1. As a result of a number of problems encountered by the agency, in 1998 Congress threatened to withhold future federal funding for the project until the agency could develop a plan to demonstrate how it could better manage its activities. In July 1998, Congress approved the agency's recovery plan and authorized $61.5 million for continued rail construction. The majority of these funds were to be used to finish the Hollywood-to-North Hollywood segment of the subway; eight million dollars were used to continue to study mass transit alternatives for Los Angeles's Eastside and the Mid-City area, and three million were set aside for new bus purchases.

20. Ohland believes that the rail versus bus debate is a bit miscast, pointing to the benefits of transit-oriented development and making a distinction between commuter and inner-city rail. She argues that the real problem is the MTA's spending on highway support (Gloria Ohland, "What's Missing in the 'Rail vs. Bus' Debate," *Los Angeles Times*, July 22, 1998, B9). Still, public debate has focused on subsidies to rail.

21. See Dave Lesher, "Golden and Global California," *Los Angeles Times*, January 8, 1998, A1, and Erie (1996: 1). The pace of growth in transshipment has relaxed somewhat since 1995.

22. The project also envisions widening and improving the truck route paralleling the rail facility to expedite port truck traffic.

23. See Alameda Corridor Transportation Authority (1994).

24. See "Alameda Corridor Project Gets $59 Million From Congress," *Los Angeles Times*, October 1, 1996, B4.

25. The suit was dismissed in October 1996, a decision that was allowed to stand by the state supreme court in July 1997.

26. The quote is from UCLA planning professor Goetz Wolff, as cited in Gloria Ohland, "The Economic Engine That Couldn't," *LA Weekly*, June 9–15, 1995, pp. 15, 17.

27. The corridor has exceeded its goal of awarding 22 percent of contract dollars to small "disadvantaged" firms; see Marla Dickerson, Lee Romney, and Vicki Torres, "Despite Wilson Order, Goals for Diversity Thrive Elsewhere," *Los Angeles Times*, March 13, 1998, A1.

28. See Steve Eric, "A Regional Report: The Status of Expanding Southern California's Global Ports and Gateways," *Metro Investment Report*, January 1996, pp. 8, 16, 17.

29. There are now efforts to help corridor-based and minority enterprises to better expand their export potential. For example, Mayor Richard Riordan's office and the Los Angeles Minority Business Opportunity Committee cohosted an

International Trade Forum in October 1997 that focused on how minority-owned and small businesses could take advantage of new global opportunities. The mayor followed up in early 1998 by taking small and medium-sized entrepreneurs, many minority, on a trade delegation to Asia; see James Flanigan, "Small Firms See Opportunity in Mayor's Trip," *Los Angeles Times,* February 25, 1998, D1.

30. Given its attempt to utilize the human and other resources of the downsizing aerospace industry in a new economic role, it is perhaps appropriate that CALSTART is located in the former Lockheed headquarters in Burbank.

31. Massachusetts and New York soon adopted California's mandate while many other states in the northeast (as well as the District of Columbia) approved similar regulations.

32. Indeed, estimates by the Lewis Center at UCLA suggest that the potential electrification of transit could indeed generate more than 24,000 jobs in Southern California.

33. See Marla Cone, "1990 Vote Was the Spark That Drove Electric Cars," *Los Angeles Times,* December 8, 1996, A3, and "CARB Begins Work on Finalizing ZEV Rule Changes," ENN Daily News, at http://www.aloha.net/~sos/news40.html.

34. See Hugo Martin, "$6 Million Awarded for Electric Cars," *Los Angeles Times,* September 2, 1992, B1, and Patrice Apodaca, "Plugging Parts for Plug-In Cars," *Los Angeles Times,* November 10, 1992, D4.

35. The Advanced Research Projects Agency (Department of Defense) and the Federal Transit Administration (Department of Transportation) promised $12.7 million in 1994. See *CALSTART Connection,* vol. 3, no. 1, January/February 1995, p. 1. See also the CALSTART web page: www://calstart.org. For an earlier evaluation of the CALSTART effort, see Jill Leovy, "Thinking Ahead; CALSTART: The Development of a Research Consortium," *Los Angeles Times,* February 11, 1996, B2.

36. In a session on the regional economy Pastor conducted for the Los Angeles Community Development Technologies Center in Pacoima, about ten miles north of the CALSTART headquarters, none of the Pacoima community members had heard about CALSTART, despite the fact that Pacoima has many industrial workers with potentially transferable skills.

37. There is also some question about how much of a regional gainer CALSTART has truly been. While many businesses have been involved in the CALSTART incubator, few have hatched and the effort was undercut by both the aforementioned change in state regulations and the entry into the electric vehicle industry of companies outside of Southern California.

38. As noted earlier, parts of this assessment of the New Economy Project were originally written by Goetz Wolff for Wolff and Grigsby (1995).

39. One contradiction was that some of Los Angeles's emerging industries, such as alternative vehicles and environmental engineering, were actually triggered by regulations.

40. See Nancy Rivera Brooks, "Southern California Enterprise," *Los Angeles Times,* October 24, 1994, D1.

41. Fulton (1997) contends that SCAG was actually formed to preclude a stronger form of regionalism, suggesting that its relative lack of power is intentional. For a review of SCAG and the limits to its authority, see Bollens (1997a).

42. Unlike chapters on transportation and the environment, this section of the plan was not mandated by the federal or state regulations; it was an organizational choice and reflected the desire of SCAG leadership to participate in the public policy debate about how to steer the economy out of the deep regional recession of the early 1990s.

43. Like the New Economy Project, SCAG suggests streamlining public bureaucracy, including the reduction of the number of agencies that firms must deal with to acquire permits, as an important element of increasing regional competitiveness. Perhaps due to its largely public sector membership, the RCP seems somewhat less vehement than the New Economy Project about the obstacles such regulations present to the goal of balanced growth.

44. Another example is the Arroyo-Verdugo cluster containing Burbank, Glendale, and Pasadena, as well as the two residential communities of La Cañada–Flintridge and South Pasadena. These cities have hosted a joint economic conference, produced a marketing video, and collaborated on other elements of their economic strategies, recognizing that by doing so they can attract industries such as multimedia and entertainment even as they maintain the usual city-level competition for retail sales taxes.

45. See Jim Newton, "With Los Angeles's Image Restored, Agency Disbands," *Los Angeles Times,* November 28, 1998, A1.

46. The final version of the RCP, however, was much better than the initial drafts, which made almost no mention of equity issues.

47. The RCP also listed general goals like providing basic human services to families and individuals to foster human dignity; promoting opportunities for all individuals to achieve self-sufficiency; and encouraging safe, vital communities with cultural, educational, and recreational opportunities, but offered few specifics on how to achieve these.

48. One avenue for participation by the private citizenry was SCAG's Regional Advisory Council; however, outreach was limited during the drafting of the RCP.

49. SCAG itself notes that the agency's recommendations in the economic arena "do not create new legal mandates for local governments or other regional organizations."

50. "The Renaissance of Los Angeles: How Rebuild LA and the Visionaries of the Private Sector Are Reshaping and Revitalizing Los Angeles's Neglected Communities" (special advertising section), *Fortune,* May 17, 1993, 103–20.

51. For a more detailed discussion of RLA in its early Ueberroth period, see Grigsby (1993) and Johnson and Farrell (1996).

52. After some debate about whether to focus just on those areas where the unrest had occurred, RLA decided to work with all neglected areas, defined as census tracts in which poverty rates exceeded 20 percent. Eventually, this was narrowed down to a focus area that included much of South Central Los Angeles and Mid-City.

53. Even RLA's official closing document (RLA, 1997: 13) notes that Ueberroth "added four co-chairs in response to public pressure for a more diverse leadership." Moreover, board expansion came in the wake of conflicts over the awarding of rebuilding contracts, particularly tension between African-American

and Latino representatives and businesses. See the discussion in Pastor (1993); see also the general review of RLA in Johnson, Farrell, and Jackson (1994).

54. Early on, RLA co-chair Peter Ueberroth claimed that sixty-eight companies (and over 400 other organizations) were planning to invest $1 billion "to encourage economic development and job creation in neglected areas," but a *Los Angeles Times* article reported that more than one-fourth of the companies RLA identified had no such plans (see Nancy Rivera Brooks and Henry Weinstein, "19 of 68 Firms Question Listings by Rebuild LA," *Los Angeles Times*, November 18, 1992, A1).

55. For a review of RLA that suggests that the shift in direction under Linda Griego was due to pressure from Mayor Richard Riordan, see Hula, Jackson, and Orr (1997). It is true that Griego's direction was more compatible with the outlines of the New Economy Project sponsored by the mayor's office.

56. Rebuild LA (RLA), *Progress Report*, March 9, 1995, p. 1. Given the difficulty of assembling large land parcels in South Los Angeles, RLA developed a concept of creating "shopping clusters" anchored by small full-service grocery stores (ranging in size from 8,000 to 14,000 square feet). These small stores were encouraged to belong to grocers' cooperatives in order to lower the usual costs of insurance and inventory; one of the smaller stores that opened with RLA's help quickly grew to have a sales volume 50 percent higher than anticipated, a fact that induced larger chains to look into the possibility of fitting themselves into the smaller store model. Interview with Linda Griego, May 1995, and James Flanigan, "Capital Offensive: Inner Cities Make Headway in Search for Growth Funds," *Los Angeles Times*, October 25, 1995, D1.

57. RLA tends to blame part of the rebuilding difficulty on the small size of the available land parcels. See RLA (1996).

58. RLA (1997:16) suggests that by the end of 1996, 17 stores were created in the larger set of "neglected" or high-poverty tracts, a scattered population that included 2.5 million people. However, the numbers were lower in RLA's focus area, the high-poverty belt of South Central and Mid-City that included over 900,000 individuals. See RLA (1996).

59. The restrictions on HUD assistance for land purchase are quite stringent, leading some observers to believe this will be a minor part of bank operations.

60. See Jean Merl, "Community Development Bank Takes Important Step," *Los Angeles Times*, May 26, 1996, B1.

61. See Lee Romney, "Community Bank Failing to Achieve Inner-City Goals," *Los Angeles Times*, December 8, 1998, A1. The bank received special criticism for having financed a garment firm that folded in late 1998 amid accusations of operating under sweatshop conditions (see also Patrick J. McDonnell, "Industry Woes Help Bury Respected Garment Maker," *Los Angeles Times*, December 1, 1998, A1). For an earlier critique of the slow start-up of the Community Development Bank, see David Friedman, "Power in Name Only," *Los Angeles Times*, February 8, 1998, M1; for a defense of the bank's activities, see the comment of C. Robert Kemp, the bank's president (in Ronald D. White, Interview with Robert Kemp, "On the Slow But Steady Progress Lending to L.A.'s Poor Communities," *Los Angeles Times*, February 15, 1998, B7).

62. See Lee Romney, "Banking on a New Strategy, Community Lender Looks to Strengthen Industries as Whole," *Los Angeles Times,* August 15, 1998, B1.

63. As C. Robert Kemp put it, "The community development bank will be more flexible than commercial banks. We'll consider borrowers with fewer assets, higher debt, a shorter profit history, a shorter time in business or a weaker credit record" (see "The Man in Charge of Putting Jobs Where the Jobless People Are," *Los Angeles Times,* June 8, 1996, B7). The idea, however, was not to lose money on risky creditors but rather to demonstrate to the private sector that risks were warranted; the eventual hope was that private institutions, once acquainted with the particularities of lending in higher-poverty areas, would cease what is effectively redlining and help meet the business needs of these neighborhoods. For more on the problem of redlining in Los Angeles, see Dymski and Veitch (1996).

64. For more on the economic challenges facing Pacoima, which not only suffered recession and downsizing (particularly the closing of a 500-employee plant owned by faucet maker Price Pfister) but was also deeply affected by the 1994 earthquake, see Lee Romney, "Toughing It Out," *Los Angeles Times,* January 2, 1998, D1.

65. See Don Lee, "A Mountain of Jobs," *Los Angeles Times,* June 19, 1998, D2.

66. The survey instrument, utilized in face-to-face interviews, asked community leaders about their organizations' activities, strategies, and goals. We then surveyed the leaders about the major problems facing their neighborhoods. This section included questions about the major problems facing the neighborhoods and the major types of economic activity in each neighborhood, including where people worked (both the type of industry and whether they worked in the informal sector); how they got to work; how they found out about jobs; what significant economic changes had taken place in recent years; and the direction in which their neighborhood was headed. The third section of the interview focused on questions about regional initiatives. This section included questions about the regional economy, how the neighborhoods were being affected by regional trends, what the people in the neighborhoods needed to do to benefit from the growing sectors of the economy, and how each organization was being affected by the major regional initiatives discussed in this chapter. Finally, we asked about economic improvement efforts outside of the organization. Specifically, we asked what private businesses, other nonprofit organizations, and local and county government offices were doing to assist development in the neighborhoods. The survey instrument used in these interviews can be obtained by contacting one of the authors.

67. Of course, there was some correlation between the industry identified, such as health care or ethnic foods, and the location of such firms in the respondent's own location. This may explain why only one respondent identified tourism as an emerging sector; many of the neighborhoods studied were well off the usual tourist path through Los Angeles.

68. RLA also served as an information clearinghouse, providing some organizations with demographic data on their communities (Belvedere) and offering tips to others on how to run effective local governments (Southeast Pomona),

including the initiation of "one-stop" permitting and the opening of an Economic Development Department.

69. Some respondents did express optimism about the project's future impact. A South Vermont respondent noted that a major street linked his neighborhood to the Alameda Corridor; Pacoima respondents suggested that an extended rail system might tie their manufacturing firms to the corridor and its ports; and Inglewood and Westlake respondents thought that their residents might be able to get jobs and business contracts as a result of the project.

70. At the time of our interviews, Huntington Park was putting in place a shuttle system to transport commuters in the Southeast area to the City of Commerce Metro Link station, the Blue Line stations, and other places of business. In Watts, another organization had secured a $280,000 contract to pursue a tele-village project that would offer long distance learning via a remote hookup with the California State University system, helping to reduce commuter travel and encourage the use of, and business clustering around, fixed rail.

71. The other affiliations included government boards, think tanks, and social clubs. This analysis of boards was conducted under a separate grant awarded to Peter Dreier by the Haynes Foundation; actual data collection was done by a team of undergraduates and processed by Manuel Pastor as part of this project.

4. Community Builders and Concentrated Poverty

1. Data from U.S. Department of Housing and Urban Development (1998b: 4). The 1996 city-suburban disparity was actually reduced from 1995 when central-city poverty hovered at 20.6 percent and suburban poverty was at 9.1 percent; the improvement in 1996 reflected the strong national economy.

2. For example, 87 percent of new low-skilled jobs in the service and retail sectors during 1991 to 1994—and 66 percent during 1994 to 1995—were created in the suburbs. See U.S. Department of Housing and Urban Development (1998b: 4).

3. For one of the most recent studies on sprawl, see Burchell et al. (1998).

4. See also Mollenkopf (1983) and Hirsch (1983).

5. See Minerbrook (1992). A study by HUD found, however, that there are few census tracts in suburbs with extremely high (i.e., 40 percent and more) poverty rates; see U.S. Department of Housing and Urban Development (1998a).

6. However, the most sizable increase in poverty concentration occurred among whites, with the percent of white poor living in extreme-poverty tracts increasing by 145 percent between 1970 and 1990 (Jargowsky, 1997: 41). Still, racial disparities are evident in terms of poverty concentration. If we lower our standard to "poverty neighborhoods" (those where at least 20 percent of the residents live below the poverty line), a Census Bureau study using 1990 data found that 60 percent of poor black residents of metropolitan areas, compared with 26 percent of poor whites, lived in such areas (U.S. Bureau of the Census, 1991).

7. See Gillmor and Doig (1992), Massey and Denton (1993), Taeuber and Taeuber (1965), and Harrison and Weinberg (1992).

8. One study of thirty metropolitan areas found that in 1980 black families with incomes below $2,500, between $25,000 and $27,000, and over $50,000 were almost equally segregated from whites (Massey and Denton, 1993: 86); see also Fainstein (1993: 397). Moreover, blacks who move out of areas of concentrated

poverty end up in areas with lower average incomes and lower levels of home ownership than would otherwise be predicted given their individual characteristics; see Alba and Logan (1992), Logan, Alba, and Leung (1996), and Logan et al. (1996). Other studies suggest that blacks moving into suburban areas trigger those areas into a rapid demographic shift via "white flight" (see Galster, 1991). On racial "steering" (in which real estate agents direct minorities toward particular locations), see Galster (1990).

9. See the arguments in Jargowsky (1997) and the review of the general evidence in Ellen and Turner (1997).

10. For a review of disproportionate exposure to environmental hazards, see Szasz and Meuser (1997); for more specifics on the debate, see Boer et al. (1997). On the issue of sexually transmitted diseases, see Sheryl Gay Stolberg, "U.S. Wakes to Epidemic of Sexual Diseases," *New York Times,* March 9, 1998, A1, A14.

11. The economic impacts also show up in consumption patterns: because the poor are also physically isolated from many retail markets, "the poor pay more," as the title of a classic book on the subject put it, for a whole range of goods and services (Caplovitz, 1963).

12. This "spatial mismatch" perspective was initially formulated by Kain (1968); both he and Kasarda (1983, 1989) have stressed how the movement of entry-level and other low-skill jobs to the suburbs and the expansion of high-skill information processing jobs in central cities has had a negative impact on the economic prospects of the central-city poor, particularly since residential segregation hampers them from moving to areas with job openings more suited to their educational level. See also Ihlanfeldt (1994), Ellwood (1986), Fainstein (1986), and Ross (1998).

13. The literature on redlining is voluminous. For an introduction, see Squires (1992).

14. We take the phrase from Galster and Killen (1995); see also Hughes (1991, 1995).

15. For two excellent reviews of the debate, see Gottlieb (1997) and Briggs (1997).

16. See Rochelle Stanfield, "The Reverse Commute," *National Journal,* November 23, 1996, pp. 2546–49; Penelope Lemov, "The Impossible Commute," *Governing,* June 1993, 32–35; Rick Wartzman, "Good Connections: New Bus Lines Link the Inner-City Poor with Jobs in Suburbia," *Wall Street Journal,* September 24, 1993, A1.

17. Moreover, many CDCs grew out of the attempts of minority communities to ensure some control over their environment (see Gottlieb, 1997). As Fernandez (1997: 93) suggests, some minority politicians might resist housing mobility, or "dispersal," strategies because this could dilute a hard-won political base.

18. Nonprofit housing groups also exist in many rural areas and in some suburban areas, but the focus here is on their activities in cities.

19. This study excluded housing units without federal subsidies. While the numbers for the 1960s and 1970s look impressive, they can be misleading. Many of the nonprofits engaged in housing sponsorship during these years were set up exclusively to build housing for the elderly under the federal Section 202 program. Indeed, about one-third of these units were part of this program, which is targeted exclusively to nonprofit sponsors (Walker, 1993). In most cases, these were not community-based groups, but rather social service agencies

that *sponsored* projects built and managed by for-profit contractors. Since 1991, CDCs produced 90,000 new units in the twenty-three major cities studied in Walker and Weinheimer (1998).

20. Indeed, federal policies continue to "shape the conditions under which community-based housing organizations work" (Koschinsky, 1998).

21. See Center for National Policy and Local Initiatives Support Corporation (1997).

22. In Newark, for example, the New Community Corporation (NCC) brought a Pathmark supermarket into the Central Ward, a low-income neighborhood where NCC had been developing housing, child care facilities, and other activities for several decades. See Vidal (1995).

23. One estimate suggests that CDCs have developed more than 23 million square feet of commercial, office, and industrial space through 1993 (Walker and Weinheimer, 1998).

24. See Clavel and Wiewel (1991), DeLeon (1992), Dreier and Ehrlich (1991), Dreier and Keating (1990), Krumholz and Forester (1990), Medoff and Sklar (1994), and Calavita, Grimes, and Reynolds (1994).

25. See Bockmeyer (1996).

26. For discussion of these efforts, see Gittell and Vidal (1998), Brown (1996), Kingsley, McNeely, and Gibson (1997), Stone (1996), Walsh (1997), Mattressich and Monsey (1997), Committee for Economic Development (1995), and Kretzmann and McKnight (1993).

27. For an examination of how many CDCs emerged from the local activism of the 1960s and 1970s, see Boyte (1980, 1987), Delgado (1994), and Dreier (1996a).

28. Walker and Weinheimer (1998) express some concern that the comprehensive community-building approach, while theoretically appropriate, may be straining the capacity of CDCs and so suggest caution in embracing this strategy.

29. This program is a joint effort between HUD and Harvard University's Kennedy School of Government that is part of HUD's new "management reform plan." For more information, see HUD's website at http://www.hud.gov/pressrel/pr98-123.html.

30. For a critique of the CDC movement on this and other grounds, see Koschinsky (1998) and Stoecker (1997).

31. See also the arguments in Schill and Wachter (1995) with regard to federal housing policy and concentrated poverty.

32. This figure does not include construction jobs produced by CDC-sponsored projects or seasonal/temporary employment. See National Congress for Community Economic Development (1995).

33. See Porter (1995) for an elaboration of the limited contributions of such social service programs to neighborhood development. On the other hand, Porter is too optimistic in his view that inner-city areas can be revitalized by unleashing the private sector; for a more extensive critique of his views, see Boston and Ross (1997).

34. Short summaries of Rusk's finding are cited in Katz (1997) and Orfield (1998). See also the full discussion in Rusk (1999).

35. This discussion draws primarily on Harrison and Weiss (1998), Harrison (1995: viii), and Zdenek (1998).

36. For more on the Center for Employment Training, see Melendez (1996); for more on Project Quest, see Jay Walljasper, "A Quest for Jobs in San Antonio," *The Nation*, July 21, 1997, pp. 30–33. Other pioneering efforts to do regionally oriented job development are profiled in chapter 7.

37. Lenz (1998); Rusk (1998).

38. Descriptions of these regional housing efforts can be found in Peterson and Williams (1994).

39. Such intermediaries provide technical assistance, channel private, philanthropic, and government funding (including federal HOME/Community Housing Partnership money and Low Income Housing Tax Credits), and help package financing for affordable housing construction. Intermediaries that work primarily at the local and regional levels include the Telesis Corporation, the Development Training Institute, Community Builders, and Community Economics. LISC and the Enterprise Foundation have also been managing the multifunder National Community Development Initiative; Walker and Weinheimer (1998: 48) argue that such intermediaries have had a big impact on CDC capacity.

40. Training and capacity building along these lines is provided, for example, by the Community Development Technology Center in Los Angeles and the Center for Neighborhood Technology in Chicago.

41. See Ladd (1994) and Bartik (1994) for fuller discussions of the people- and place-based approaches. As noted in the text, community builders draw from each strategy to pursue comprehensive community development.

5. Only as Strong as the Team

1. For an analysis of this new policy mood from the perspective of one big-city mayor, see McEnery (1994).

2. See Myron Levin, "'90s a Rude Awakening from Suburban Dream," *Los Angeles Times*, June 9, 1996, A1. Boding ill for the future is the fact that the poverty rate among children in the San Fernando Valley is twice that of the population as a whole.

3. For further reviews of the relevant literature and critiques of the usual empirical methods, see Hill, Wolman, and Ford (1994) and Ihlanfeldt (1995). The best recent review is Gottlieb (1998).

4. In an earlier 1992 study, Ledebur and Barnes note that the quintile of metropolitan areas with the least central city/suburb income disparity in 1989 experienced the most robust employment growth while the two most disparate quintiles experienced employment recessions. However, this result is problematic since the static income disparity measure is taken from during the middle of the period and could reflect an outcome rather than a cause.

5. Much of this previous research by Barnes and Ledebur is summarized in their 1998 book, *The New Regional Economies.*

6. The study estimates that for every dollar increase in central-city household incomes, suburban household incomes increased by $1.12; conversely, where central-city incomes declined, so did suburban incomes. Note that a larger dollar increase in suburban income can be consistent with improving equality if the initial income level for the suburb is significantly higher (i.e., an increase by

$112 in the suburb and $100 in the city will narrow the percentage difference between these two parts of a region if the suburb's initial income was $200 and the city's initial income was $100).

7. Brooks and Summers (1998) also find that the links between central-city and suburban fortunes have grown over time. In careful tests, including a simultaneous equations approach, they find city and suburban employment growth were essentially independent in the 1970s, but interdependent in the 1980s; in that latter era, central-city growth had positive and significant impacts on suburban prospects while the reverse direction was positive but insignificant.

8. There are also a series of interesting studies looking at the reverse direction: the impact of metropolitan restructuring on poverty neighborhoods (see Galster, Mincy, and Tobin, 1997; Jargowsky, 1997). Here, we are focusing on the effect of poverty and equity on growth, even as we try to control for possible reverse causal direction explored by these authors.

9. Hill et al. (1994) also cite a specification error with the regression used by Savitch et al. (1993) to examine central-city/suburban income relationships: the inappropriate combination of central-city income and population density to form an index of central-city vitality.

10. Brooks and Summers (1998) also offer a simultaneous model, using three-stage least squares on city and suburban employment growth.

11. Voith (1998) is the exception because of his deployment of an alternative method parallel to that used in this research. However, he focuses on the growth of city and suburban incomes (as well as housing values and populations) and uses a far richer model. The parsimony of our approach is driven in part by the desire to have a series of parallel regressions with different dependent variables measuring equity.

12. Obviously, another important reason is that a poor and poorly trained central-city labor force might lead investors to look elsewhere. The general pattern of our results holds even when we control for the level of resident education, suggesting that the impact goes beyond human capital per se and instead includes the influence of social capital.

13. See also Wallis (1995) on regional governance.

14. Voith (1998) uses a broader sample and finds that the central city–suburban relationship is positive and strong only for larger cities. Our initial focus was on the larger MSAs and we did not explore the sensitivity of our findings beyond this set of eighty-five MSAs.

15. For instance, in 1980 Oakland was included in San Francisco's MSA. In 1990, the two cities were separate statistical entities, making temporal comparisons problematic.

16. We specifically used version 2.11A (September 22, 1997).

17. The formula for the dissimilarity index is derived by summing over i (from 1 to n) the expression $t_i|p_i-P|/2TP(1-P)$ where t_i and p_i are the total population and proportion poor, respectively, of neighborhood i, and T and P are the total population and proportion poor of the entire MSA, which is divided into 'n' neighborhoods; see Abramson, Tobin, and VanderGoot (1995: 45).

18. See Kain (1968), Wilson (1987), and Garreau (1991) and our discussion in chapter 3 on the general trends toward the suburbanization of manufacturing and other forms of employment. As we note below, dropping this rough measure of competitive advantage does not change our basic results; including it may be warranted since it squares with our presumptions and generally attains significance in the regressions considered.

19. This sort of criticism of our method is suggested in Harrison (1998).

20. Note that this formulation allows for the fact that central-city poverty is generally higher than suburban poverty. Suppose, for example, that the poverty rates in 1980 for any particular MSA were 10 percent in the central city and 5 percent outside the central city. If each rises by 50 percent (to 15 percent and 7.5 percent, respectively), then central-city poverty is still twice as high and *Change in City/Suburb Poverty Ratio, 1980–90* over the period equals 100 (i.e., [(10/5)/ (15/7.5)]).

21. Our measure of the change in central-city poverty is constructed such that a reduction in poverty of five percentage points has the same effect on growth regardless of whether the starting point for central-city poverty was 10 percent or 20 percent. Reconfiguring this variable as a percentage change—so that a five percentage point reduction yields a 50 percent improvement for the 10 percent city and a 25 percent improvement for the 20 percent city—does not alter the pattern of signs and significance, although the coefficients naturally change. We stick with the specification of regressions (3a) and (3b) because they are a bit simpler to understand, particularly when we "model" the system graphically in the next section.

22. The relative size of the central city also had an unexpected, albeit insignificant sign. We have no ready explanation for the "flip" in signs but take comfort in the fact that it was not significant.

23. Note that we are using here an MSA-wide measure of minority presence, rather than the city-suburb comparison, primarily because the dependent variable measures inequality at the level of the MSA as a whole.

24. Brooks and Summers (1998) also tried an educational measure but dropped it due to colinearity with our economic variables.

25. All of these specifications were suggested by individuals commenting on earlier drafts of our statistical work. The alternative specification of minority concentration we tested directly compared percentages in the central city to those in the suburb; to use it required that we drop the control for the relative size of the central city (to see why, multiply out the divisors of such a relative percentage term and note that the resulting right-side expression is nearly identical to the relative weight of the central city). In any case, the results for these sorts of runs are very similar for the key variables of interest.

26. As a result of another suggestion, we also tried a measure of lagged growth; the sign in the resulting growth equation was negative, indicating a possible process of income convergence across regions. Such income convergence is consistent with a general notion of markets steering investment and growth to those areas still playing catch-up in the national context. Introducing a measure of lagged MSA per capita income growth did reduce the significance of

other variables, but while such lags are often standard in the instrumental variables approach underlying two-stage least squares, the procedure lacks much theoretical justification. Further, the drop in significance could be explained by the fact that equity and poverty measures themselves are correlated with their own lags that predict past growth.

27. We thank Paul Gottlieb for comments that pushed us in the direction of exploring the role of elasticity.

28. Rusk (1995) has an elasticity measure that is even more variable but we decided to use the simple ranking measure offered in the appendices to his book.

29. However, introducing elasticity does reduce the significance of the change in poverty on growth (when the regional dummies are dropped), suggesting some trade-off between the two variables.

30. Gottlieb (1998) also draws the comparison with the international development literature.

31. The most important author in this regard was Kuznets (1955), who found that income inequality first rose as economic development proceeded, then declined after various measures of such development (for example, per capita GDP) reached a sort of threshold; see Ahluwalia (1976), Paukert (1973), and Lecaillon et al. (1984) for various confirmations of this finding. While Kuznets did not mean to imply that it was the inequality driving the growth, one standard policy interpretation was that altering the "natural" regressive pattern could slow economic progress.

32. The connections between this international and domestic literature are also made in Partridge (1997), but the results there do not support the notion of a positive relationship between inequality and growth at the state level.

33. We "set" the intercepts of each relationship close to the (unreported) estimates of the constant from each regression. However, since we are not accounting for the other exogenous factors, the positions of the lines are arbitrary and chosen only for purposes of easily illustrating the behavior of the model.

34. The stability of our estimated system lends an extra degree of confidence to our earlier regression results.

35. This approach of identifying viable business clusters already located in poor areas and helping them "network" to build an industry presence was taken by RLA in the last few years of its existence (see chapter 3). We discuss other strategies to improve the growth-equity relationship in chapter 7.

36. Obviously, the circle ends as you drift from the first equilibrium, E1, to the second, E2.

37. Recall that central-city elasticity seems to dampen geographic disparity measures such as residential segregation or city-suburb poverty differentials.

38. See Theodore Williams and Michael Leum, "Paying a Living Wage Is Good for Business," *Los Angeles Times*, August 4, 1996, M5. Williams, chairman and CEO of Bell Industries Inc., and Leum, vice president of Pioneer Foods Inc., also noted that a "study commissioned by the Council of State Governments found that the most important factors in choosing a business location included quality of life, education and skills of the work force, proximity to markets and access to infrastructure. The ability to pay substandard wages was not on the list."

6. Regions That Work

1. The urban distress measure used to determine whether a city was in need of revitalization is an evenly weighted average of n scores over various cities for the 1980 unemployment rate, the 1980 poverty rate, the 1980 median household income, per capita income growth between 1970 and 1980, and the 1970–80 population growth. The urban improvement measure calculates the percentage change in median household income, the percentage change in per capita income, the percent point change in persons below the poverty line, the percentage change in unemployment, and the percentage change in labor force participation (with the last intending to reflect improved job prospects for discouraged workers).

2. This group of experts included "members of the editorial boards of the leading American academic journals concerned with urban affairs and economic development . . . [and] members of the Executive Boards of two leading economic development practitioner organizations, the American Economic Development Council and the Council on Urban Economic Development" (Wolman, Ford, and Hill, 1994: 837).

3. Of course, there were some agreements between the data and the experts: Baltimore, Atlanta, and Boston (which also show up in our data as strong performers) were successful both in the subjective expert views and by the objective criteria developed by Wolman, Ford, and Hill (1994).

4. We are using here the actual reduction in the poverty rate. If we used instead the percentage reduction in poverty (so that a five percentage point reduction would be twice as important for a region with an initial poverty rate of 10 percent as for a region with an initial poverty rate of 20 percent), we might theoretically have a different ranking. However, such an alternative ranking system yields roughly the same list of "above-median" cities in about the same order. Recall from chapter 5 that our basic regression results are also similar regardless of whether we use change in percentage point of poverty or percentage change in poverty.

5. Recall from chapter 5 that the inequality data are not available for all our regions and hence figure 6.5 includes only eighteen of the initial twenty-seven high performance observations. We also considered a range of other variables, such as the differential in city and suburban unemployment, changes in relative poverty rates and equity, and other relevant measures. These examinations also pointed to the cases we selected; in the text, we focus on a subset of these charts to simplify the presentation and the logic.

6. Newark (NW) was also a strong performer on the growth and poverty reduction fronts but exhibited a significant level of residential segregation, midrange central-city/suburban differentials, and a relatively high level of inequality.

7. Our other possible case, Atlanta, was barely in the top third of this ranking. Los Angeles fell into the middle third according to this cumulative ranking system on the first three indicators and in the bottom half when we also used a measure of metropolitan equity.

8. We thank Paul Gottlieb for raising this point.

9. For technical reasons having to do with the availability of tract-level data,

mapping across the decades was done at the whole tract level; where there were partial tracts, the whole tract assumed the place designation of the partial with the highest population.

10. While Charlotte was visited only once, Boston received two visits, and San Jose three. Follow-up phone calls and information gathering continued after the field visits. In conducting the San Jose case study, we were able to secure interviews with a wide range of leaders and analysts and were provided key data and contacts by others. For their cooperation, we thank Annalee Saxenian, UC Berkeley; Leslie Parks, Office of Economic Development, City of San Jose; Becky Morgan, CEO and president of Joint Venture: Silicon Valley Network; Don Rothblatt, chair, Urban Planning, San Jose State University; Max Martinez, Center for Employment Training; Esther Medina, executive director, Mexican American Community Services Agency, Inc.; Jose Vasquez, Mexican American Community Services Agency, Inc.; Richard Rios, deputy director, San Jose Redevelopment Agency; Leslie Coleman, Santa Clara Valley Manufacturing Group; Amy Dean, South Bay Labor Council; Lisa Hoyos, Working Partnerships, USA; Chris Benner, Working Partnerships, USA; William V. Flores, dean of social and behavioral sciences at California State University at Northridge; Elaine Romero Luksus, Growth and Opportunity, Inc.; Debra Trent, Literacy Alliance for the South Bay; Ann Danner, Non-profit Development Center Corporation; Tony Estremeda, Legal Aid Society; Kenneth Kamei, Asian Americans for Community Involvement; Margarita Luna Robles, longtime San Jose activist; Jesus Martinez, Political Science, Santa Clara University; and Vilma Guerrero Ruben, East San Jose Community Law Center.

In understanding Charlotte, we were helped by interviews with Mel Watt, Congressman, U.S. House of Representatives; Isaac Heard, Jr., AICP, executive director, Northwest Corridor Community Development Corporation; Harvey Gantt, former mayor of Charlotte; Martin R. Cramton, Jr., AICP, planning director, Charlotte-Mecklenburg Planning Commission; Lawrence J. Tolliver, group vice president for community development, Charlotte Chamber of Commerce; Terry Orell, group vice president for business growth, Charlotte Chamber of Commerce; Lynette Fox, assistant professor, School of Business, Johnson C. Smith University; Tom Warshauer, manager, commercial and industrial development, Neighborhood Development Key Business; Tony Crumbley, vice president for research, customer response, Charlotte Chamber of Commerce; George T. Lathrop, deputy director, Department of Transportation; Ed Henegar, vice president, Carolinas Partnership; Alfred W. Stuart, Ph.D., professor, Department of Geography and Earth Sciences, University of North Carolina at Charlotte.

For the Boston case study, we benefited from interviews with a wide range of analysts and leaders. For providing interviews and data, we thank Gregory Perkins, Boston Redevelopment Authority; Doug Carnahan, Metropolitan Area Planning Council; Thomas Quattromani, Metropolitan Area Planning Council; and Judy Alland, Metropolitan Area Planning Council; Chris Tilly, University of Massachusetts, Lowell; William Edgerly, former chairman, State Street Bank, and founding chairman, Boston Housing Partnership; Evelyn Vargas, Nuestra Communidad Development Corporation; Jack Delaney, Hale and Dorr; Ed Sidman, Beacon Properties; Mossik Hacobian, Urban Edge Housing Corporation; Richard Thal, Jamaica Plain Neighborhood Development Corporation; Paul

O'Brien, former CEO, New England Telephone Company; Phil Moss, University of Massachusetts, Lowell; Steve Landau, Metropolitan Area Planning Council; Jerome Rubin, Massachusetts Manufacturing Partnership; Neil Sullivan, Boston Private Industry Council; Randy Albelda, University of Massachusetts, Boston; Katherine Bradbury, Federal Reserve Bank of Boston; Paul Harrington, Center for Labor Market Studies, Northeastern University; John Riordan, Massachusetts Blue Cross; Michael Gondek, Community Economic Development Assistance Corporation; Peg Barringer, Community Economic Development Assistance Corporation; Fletcher (Flash) Wiley, Goldstein and Manello; Phil Clay, MIT; and Jerome Grossman, New England Medical Center.

11. Data on city and county population from the U.S. Bureau of the Census.

12. Segregation indices by tract indicate that residential concentration of Latinos and Asians rose between 1980 and 1990, suggesting that segregation may be heightened *within* cities and suburbs, respectively. Data from Douglas Massey, University of Pennsylvania, as reported in "A Valley Divided," *San Jose Mercury News*, Mercury Center (http://cgi.sjmercury.com, June 25, 1996).

13. All data taken from the Public Use Microdata Sample, 1990, for Santa Clara County. The service industry in this case excludes protective services and includes household occupations, food preparation, health services, cleaning, and personal services. The figure for Latinos is not distorted by the inclusion of household services: the presence of Latinos is virtually the same if we exclude this occupation from the service category. We should note that the occupational pyramid has been getting worse in the high-tech industry itself. The proportion of Anglos in the industry holding managerial and professional jobs rose from 49 percent to 72 percent between 1983 and 1993, with the percentage holding clerical and operator jobs falling from 28 percent to 15 percent over the same period. The percentage of Latinos in the industry who held professional jobs also rose, reflecting the overall shift in the industry; however, this shift went from 14 percent to 28 percent while the proportion of Latinos holding clerical and operator jobs decreased only slightly, from 58 percent to 51 percent. Data on the high-tech industry from the Equal Employment Opportunity Commission, as reported in "A Valley Divided," *San Jose Mercury News*, Mercury Center (http://cgi.sjmercury.com, June 25, 1996).

14. For example, Anglo per capita income in Santa Clara County in 1990 was $23,222 compared to $10,917 for Latinos; the comparable national figures were $15,687 to $8,400. The data on income differentials comes from "A Valley Divided," *San Jose Mercury News*, Mercury Center (http://cgi.sjmercury.com, June 25, 1996), and is originally from the 1990 Census.

15. As a paradigmatic example, the janitorial industry expanded in terms of numbers but plummeted in terms of working conditions. This was partly because in the early 1980s many firms began to subcontract cleaning, a phenomenon that pitted long-term resident and largely unionized janitors of San Jose against recent immigrants who were willing to accept nonunion positions in the new outsourced firms. See Cooper (1996).

16. In line with this bifurcation of opportunities, the bottom 20 percent of the Silicon Valley's residents earn only 3.6 percent of the area's income (see Cooper, 1996: 12).

17. This education linkage was stressed frequently in our interviews, as well as those conducted and reported by Saxenian (1996). The importance of educational institutions to research and technology, and of workforce development to metropolitan success, is highlighted in general terms in U.S. Department of Housing and Urban Development (1996).

18. As Saxenian notes (1996: 42), "In the 1970s San Jose State University trained as many engineers as either Stanford or Berkeley and the region's six community colleges offered technical programs that were among the best in the nation. Foothill College in Los Altos Hills, for example, offered the nation's first two-year A.S. degree in semiconductor processing, and the mandate of Mission Community College in Santa Clara was to coordinate programs with the neighboring electronics complex . . . . The community colleges were particularly responsive to the needs of local businesses: they contracted with local companies to teach private courses for their employees, even holding courses at company plants to enable employees to attend after hours."

19. The record of collaboration by the Santa Clara Valley Manufacturing Group (SCVMG) has drawn high praise from seemingly unlikely quarters, including Amy Dean, leader of the South Bay AFL-CIO Labor Council, who is quoted as saying, "Whether the issue has been land use, housing, transportation or education, the Manufacturing Group deserves four stars and an A+ for effectiveness in building partnerships with organized labor and the community." See Callie Gregory, "SCVMG-17 Years of Success," in *Bay Business,* June 1995, pp. 10–14.

20. The balance between public and private in this partnership is reflected in the statement of a high-ranking official of Joint Venture that "in our case, business leads and government follows." The risk, as we see in the text, is that while such arrangements may produce growth, they may not reduce poverty; for this, one needs an organized and participatory community sector as well as new creative policies.

21. See Miguel Helft, "CEO Fills a Void in Silicon Valley," *San Jose Mercury News,* April 15, 1999, 1A, 20A.

22. Even East San Jose's designation as an enterprise zone and the creation of a Neighborhood Business District have failed to encourage much private investment.

23. One exception to this trend is Touché Manufacturers, a Latino-owned firm that makes encasements for computers and has made a point of hiring from the east side community in which the business resides.

24. While some of our information on the downtown strategy comes from interviews with personnel of the Redevelopment Agency and the Economic Development Department, an account of the genesis of the downtown "renaissance" strategy is available in McEnery (1994). McEnery was mayor of San Jose from 1983 to 1990 and so the book has something of a self-congratulatory tone; nonetheless, it offers both a useful history and a set of lessons to other mayors hoping to ensure that their own central cities will continue to anchor an economic region.

25. Indeed, San Jose itself has long carried the reputation of a nondescript and uncentered city that might as well have been the "northernmost suburb of Los Angeles" (McEnery, 1994: 72).

26. Some of our respondents, hard-pressed to point to any specific antipoverty poli-
     cies, suggested that the relatively superior performance on poverty reduction
     was a statistical artifact resulting from an exodus out of the area by low-income
     residents in the face of high housing prices. While there is some merit to this
     argument, high housing prices were common in other areas, including Los
     Angeles, which experienced a sharper increase in the poverty population. In our
     view, San Jose's poverty record reflects a real phenomenon: robust growth tight-
     ened the regional labor markets, allowing many to find employment.

27. Benner (1996b: 45) reports that of over 600 labor councils in the United States,
     the South Bay Central Labor Council, covering the San Jose MSA, "represents
     the 15th highest per capita level of unionization in the country." However, the
     union presence is higher in older and now downsized defense-reliant assembly
     industries (see the following note), as well as the public sector and the building
     trades, with newer recruitment efforts concentrating on lower-wage service
     workers.

28. As a result, while many defense contractors were unionized in the immediate
     postwar period, "no high technology firm has been organized by a labor union
     in Silicon Valley during the past twenty years" (Saxenian, 1996: 55).

29. This was a multiunion effort in 1993–94 to organize low-wage, often immi-
     grant workers in the service and manufacturing sectors of the Silicon Valley.
     Called the Campaign for Justice, the effort was innovative in several ways,
     including its attempt to push for industrywide agreements and its desire to
     broaden political support for labor through community-based organizing. It
     was, however, derailed by competing union agendas and other factors. See
     Hoyos (1994), as well as David Bacon, "High Tech's Low-wage Workers Try New
     Labor Tactics," *Pacific News Service,* February 7–11, 1994: 2, and Sherri Eng, "Is
     It Labor's Day?" *San Jose Mercury News,* January 30, 1994, 1E.

30. In two national studies, in one case looking at single mothers and in another
     case at youth, San Jose's CET was the only program reviewed that showed sta-
     tistically significant improvement in income for trainees. As a result, the
     Department of Labor encouraged other areas to adopt the CET model, partly
     through providing funding to CET to do training for other organizations and by
     having CET set up satellite offices. While CET's success is partly due to a model
     that integrates educational and vocational skills and allows for individualized
     instruction, two other key components are the center's historical ties to the
     community (which helps its credibility) and its ongoing connection with
     regional business needs via an advisory council and technical advisory com-
     mittees. CET's place in the local social ecology may explain why replication of
     the model has not been as successful as once hoped: these sorts of programs
     needed to be rooted in the region and emerge from community dynamics.
     Information culled from interviews as well as from Conrad (1994), Lee (1995),
     Tershy (1995), Melendez (1996), and Fred R. Bleakley, "Center's Mix of Study
     and Skills Is a Hot Job-Training Model," *The Wall Street Journal,* October 4,
     1994, B1.

31. There are positive signs that a more holistic development approach may be
     gaining ground. In October 1996, the Community Foundation of Santa Clara
     County received a $255,000 neighborhood revitalization planning grant from

the Hewlett Foundation for the East San Jose neighborhood of Mayfair, which led to an extensive outreach process and the production of a comprehensive strategic plan by late 1997. City officials have been working creatively and flexibly with this effort in the intervening years.

32. It is noteworthy that the concepts of social capital and network formation, usually considered academic notions, are explicitly recognized by Joint Venture: Silicon Valley Network (1995: i / 18) as contributing to the region's competitive advantage. The actual steps in organizing Joint Venture are detailed in Joint Venture: Silicon Valley Network (1995). The recognition that the region's social capital needed to be strengthened is reflected in an earlier document, *Blueprint for a 21st Century Community: The Phase II Report, June 1993*, in which it is argued that while Silicon Valley was traditionally technologically driven, its future will be relationship-driven (that is, dependent on dynamic interfirm and public-private sector partnerships).

33. Growth, of course, brings its own problems, including skyrocketing housing prices and increasing traffic congestion. See "Silicon Valley: Victim of Its Own Success," *San Jose Mercury News*, January 13, 1997, 1E, 6E, and Robert D. Hof, "Too Much of a Good Thing?" in *Business Week*, August 18, 1997, pp. 134–35. The latter is part of a special issue on the Silicon Valley.

34. Cooper (1996: 12) reports that "since 1989 the rate of local children living in poverty went from 10 percent to 13 percent." Rising inequality is indicated by the increasing divergence between average and median incomes (see Joint Venture 1998: 8) and most recently by a sharp increase in the ratio of median incomes of the top 20 percent to the bottom 20 percent of households (see Charles Piller, "High-Tech Model of Inconsistency," *Los Angeles Times*, January 9, 1999, C1). Benner (1996a) argues that one reason is the sharp increase in contingent (contract and part-time) labor; while this allows companies to respond more easily to market trends, it leads to declines in both wages and job security.

35. For example, officials at the Mexican-American Community Service Agency (MACSA), a social service and advocacy group that has been in operation in East San Jose for more than thirty years, have bemoaned the lack of city and business interest in their problems on the east side and suggested that efforts such as Joint Venture have paid little attention to incorporating the poor. MACSA, however, has worked with the San Jose Redevelopment Agency to develop a Mexican Heritage Center in East San Jose.

36. See Benner (1998).

37. Raleigh, a city identified as "elastic" and successful in David Rusk's *City Without Suburbs*, was also favorably affected by the same North Carolina law. See Rusk (1995).

38. The annexation of Charlotte's suburbs also changed the area's political dynamics, bringing into the electorate some voters who were less connected to Charlotte's traditional political coalitions. Smith (1997) argues that this introduction of new voters was partly responsible for the defeat of Harvey Gantt in the 1987 mayoral election.

39. As Charlotte matures in its development process, it is likely to attract more immigrant Latino and Asian labor. For example, in Monroe, North Carolina, the

state's largest poultry producer already has a workforce that is over 80 percent Latino. In the city of Charlotte itself, several of our respondents observed that construction and landscaping crews are increasingly composed of Latino workers. Still, respondents suggested that there were no identifiable Latino neighborhoods and the area's racial dynamics, as noted in the text, remain largely black-white.

40. As noted in chapter 5, part of the city of Charlotte's poverty reduction came simply from annexing wealthier areas. However, we still see a reduction in poverty even if we exclude the annexed areas, and Charlotte retains its ranking as one of the nation's top performers on this front.

41. Between 1970 and 1993 the region lost some 55,000 jobs in the textile and apparel manufacturing industries. Nearly 34,000 of these jobs were lost between 1982 and 1993. However, during the same period other kinds of manufacturing added over 25,000 jobs, thus reducing the net loss of factory jobs to just over 8,000, or a 4 percent decline. Recall, however, that the regional population and workforce were growing throughout this period; thus, the small absolute loss in manufacturing implied a sharply falling share of employment in this sector. This restructuring hit the outlying counties particularly hard. Indeed, Mecklenburg County actually experienced a net gain of over 4,800 factory jobs while seven of the twelve counties in the region saw a decline in total manufacturing employment.

42. The key freeways in this regard are I-85, which was completed in the mid 1960s, and I-77, completed in 1972. In 1987, construction began on an outer-ring road that is likely to dramatically affect development patterns within Charlotte after its expected completion in 2010.

43. We use Bureau of Labor Statistics figures for 1979 and 1989, the actual years for which we have MSA per capita income; recall that it is the growth in this latter variable that put Charlotte in the "best-performing" quadrant.

44. Rusk (1995: 37) argues that consolidated city-county districts in the South have helped school integration be more successful and more stable precisely because "middle class Whites cannot flee to other public school systems."

45. In the early 1980s, the city council fortified the scattered-site approach by declaring that no new low-income housing consisting of over fifty units would be built. This allowed for such projects to be better integrated into existing residential communities.

46. The picture is, of course, hardly rosy for public housing residents. While the poverty threshold for a family of three in 1993 was $11,522, the average income of public housing residents was only 59 percent of that, or $6,789. Moreover, residents within public housing units may not have benefited much from the boom growth of the 1980s because low skills and poor networks reduced their access to employment in the expanding economy (see Charlotte Housing Authority (undated), *A Demographic Profile of Residents 1995–1996*, Charlotte, North Carolina: 38–39).

47. This scattered-site and small-scale approach also minimized tensions surrounding African-Americans (who make up 87 percent of public housing residents) moving into predominantly white residential neighborhoods.

48. See Peirce et al. (1995: 10). One aspect of the City Within a City's approach is coordinating the efforts of the public sector, private business, and nonprofits. Since 1993, the gap between growth in the northeast and southern sections of the city has narrowed.

49. One reason for this enthusiastic embrace of regionalism is that a number of Charlotte's old elite have been involved in enterprises—such as cotton and tobacco farming, power development along the state's major rivers, supermarkets linked to statewide farming, and banking—that historically have depended on a regional distribution system in order to work. Charlotte continues to serve as the hub for many of these activities.

50. Strictly speaking, the annexation laws have governed only the Charlotte-Mecklenburg County portion of the MSA. Charlotte and Mecklenburg County have also consolidated city and county planning functions, providing area leaders, grassroots organizations, and business with uniform and unified demographic and economic information.

51. In part this was pure politics; the African-American vote was critical and the needs of this poor population could not be ignored. African-American alliances with business were a political necessity and help explain Harvey Gantt's election in a city that was nearly 70 percent white.

52. The smallest of our case studies, Charlotte's 1990 central city population of nearly 400,000, is about half the size of San Jose's and 70 percent the size of Boston's. The MSA population of 1.2 million is around three-quarters that of the San Jose/Santa Clara MSA and 40 percent of the larger Boston MSA.

53. The speech was given to a meeting of the International Council on Shopping Centers in Charlotte on March 30, 1999. McColl did stress the need to use incentives instead of market constraining controls, but he was very supportive of the general themes of the Smart Growth movement and urged the shopping center developers to work against sprawl. See Neal Peirce, "Bank of America Chief Champions Smart Growth," syndicated column, Washington Post Writer's Group, April 18, 1999, http://www.citistates.com/columns.htm.

54. We focus here on the 1980–90 time frame used to select the cases. In this period, the Boston economy was booming and the key question was whether and how this prosperity would be shared with the region's low-income population and neighborhoods. Beginning in 1989, the region's economy began to falter. Henderson (1990) and others account for much of the region's economic slump with the impact of federal defense cuts. Case (1991) argues that economic hard times can be explained in large part by the bursting of the speculative real estate bubble.

55. "Boston's Economy," City of Boston bond statement, September 1994.

56. "Boston's Economic History," Boston Redevelopment Authority, January 1995, draft.

57. In 1993, the U.S. Census Bureau and the federal Office of Management and Budget revised the definition of metropolitan areas in greater Boston. The Boston Primary Metropolitan Statistical Area (PSMA) was enlarged and now consists of Suffolk, Essex, Middlesex, Plymouth, and Norfolk Counties.

58. The city's population increased by 2 percent, from 562,994 to 574,283; the metropolitan area grew by 1.1 percent, from 2,763,257 to 2,794,280.

59. Physically, Boston is a relatively small city of about forty-eight square miles. In *Cities Without Suburbs*, David Rusk (1995) identifies Boston as a city with "zero elasticity"—one that is trapped within a larger metropolitan area with no room to expand its borders. Such cities, Rusk argues, are generally less likely to experience either economic or population growth.

60. Several Boston neighborhoods, including Jamaica Plain, Dorchester, and the South End, were particularly affected by this demographic transition. Percentage minority in the region is taken from our seventy-four-region data set (see appendix 5.1); most other numbers in these paragraphs are taken from Judd and Swanstrom (1994: 160–61), or calculated from "Population by Race and Hispanic Origin 1980–1990" (compiled by the Metropolitan Area Planning Council, undated) and "Population and Housing Composition by 69 Neighborhoods and 16 Planning Districts" (Boston Redevelopment Authority, February 1995). Recent data also suggests an increasing suburbanization of the minority population.

61. The Vault was dominated by bankers and the insurance and medical sectors; only one major manufacturing firm, Gillette, was represented. This may help to explain the group's support for the central city; while manufacturing had both declined and moved to the suburbs, the downtown remained the key location of high-end service industries. See the Boston Urban Study Group (1984), Mollenkopf (1983), and Dreier (1983).

62. The importance of informal leadership structures for regions is stressed in U.S. Department of Housing and Urban Development (1996: 1–19).

63. See "Boston's Economic History," Boston Redevelopment Authority, January 1995, draft.

64. In 1980, 13 percent of workers in the Boston metropolitan area utilized public transit to get to work, placing Boston fourth behind New York City, Chicago, and Washington, D.C. (Judd and Swanstrom, 1994). In 1990, 32 percent of Boston residents who worked used public transportation to get to work, 11 percent used car pools, and 40 percent regularly drove alone. The average time was only 25 minutes and 36 percent were able to get to work in less than 20 minutes (Goetz, 1992), making for a relatively easy commute.

65. By 1988, the gap between wages and housing prices was wider in the Boston metropolitan area than in any other area in the country (see Dreier, Schwartz, and Greiner, 1988) and rent-to-income ratios in Boston were also the highest in the nation. As Case notes, however, this run-up in housing costs also severely reduced in-migration to the Boston area from outside the region. This helped exacerbate the labor shortage, giving most workers more bargaining power over jobs and wages (see Leonard and Lazere, 1992).

66. Henderson (1990) notes that prime contracts do not include subcontracts, suggesting that firms headquartered in Massachusetts may have received prime contracts and then subcontracted much of the work to firms outside the state. In fact, this is not the case. As Henderson notes (p. 6), New England (of which Massachusetts is by far the largest state economy) "receives almost as large a share of total defense work as it does of prime contracts. In 1989, 9.9 percent of goods and services purchased directly by the Defense Department came from New England."

67. Between 1965 and 1993, the MBTA received $3.8 billion in federal funds. In addition, between 1983 and 1994, the MBTA undertook capital projects totaling $3.5 million, most of which came from state bond issues. See "Boston's Economy," City of Boston bond statement, September 1994.

68. Case (1991) argues that this dramatic increase in home prices cannot be explained primarily by the improvement of the region's economy. Controlling for the combined effects of employment growth, population growth, interest rate, income, construction costs, and other variables, Case's model would have predicted a 15 percent increase in housing prices between 1983 and 1986. He suggests that home sellers and buyers were "significantly influenced by psychology," or real estate speculation, in anticipation of continued housing price inflation.

69. While these trends were concentrated in Boston, other cities and suburbs in the metropolitan area faced similar conditions (see Clay, 1988; Case and Shiller, 1994; Collins and White, 1994; Dreier and Keating, 1990).

70. For example, the city linked a prime downtown site with a publicly owned site in Roxbury where the state built its new headquarters for the Registry of Motor Vehicles, the city constructed its new police headquarters, and a private developer built an office complex.

71. A particularly interesting community-building effort, the Dudley Street Neighborhood Initiative (DSNI), received significant municipal support, including the delegation of eminent domain authority from the Boston Redevelopment Authority (see Medoff and Sklar, 1994; Dreier, 1997).

72. Horan and Jonas (1998) disagree, arguing that regional governance was fragmented in the greater Boston area and that Boston's community policies often involved "enclave" or neighborhood-specific agendas.

73. While we focus here on the 1980s, it is important to note that the Boston economy was hard-hit by the defense cuts and other structural shifts in the early 1990s.

74. Annexation is not the only way to create "ties that bind." Lang and Hornburg (1997), for example, argue that Portland achieved much the same results with its urban growth boundaries and metropolitan governance structures, suggesting further that the resulting compact urban form—in which "even the edge of the region still looks, feels, and correspondingly thinks like the center"—reinforced a sense of a regional common identity and destiny.

7. Growing Together

1. In coming up with some of the examples used throughout this chapter, we benefited from interviews with Lester Bens of Sustainable Milwaukee; Scott Bollens of the University of California at Irvine; David Dahlstrom of the Southern Florida Regional Council; Bill Dempsy of Sustainable Milwaukee; David Donahoe of the Allegheny Regional Assets District; Sheril Francis of Bethel New Life–Chicago; Ana Guerrero of the Center for Community Change; Steve Holt of the Milwaukee Jobs Initiative; Jeremy Nowak of the Delaware Valley Community Reinvestment Fund; Gloria Ohland of the Surface Transportation Policy Project; John Pawasara of the Employment and Training Institute, University of Wisconsin, Milwaukee; and Benetta Johnson, community organizer, Greater Bethany Economic Development Corporation, Los Angeles.

2. On civic leadership, see also Abbot (1997) and Henton, Melville, and Walesh (1997).

3. On the issue of regional governance, see Orfield (1997), Summers (1997), and Hamilton (1999).

4. For case studies of regional governments and authorities, see Savitch and Vogel (1996).

5. As noted in chapter 1, such agencies have been most effective when they have focused their efforts on major infrastructure issues such as transit systems, waste disposal, water systems, and airports, areas where they can persuade disparate players that each has a stake in working together. They have been least effective when they have tried to address issues of social equity (Grigsby, 1996; Bollens, 1997).

6. The various governments have attempted to redirect development and investment to older urbanized areas in the eastern parts of these counties, developed a joint approach to the Environmental Protection Agency's Brownfields Program, and articulated a new vision of how to extend Dade County's existing rail system to the other counties (see Parzen, 1997; information also taken from an interview with David Dahlstrom of the Southern Florida Regional Planning Council).

7. See the Irvine Foundation (1988); the framework for such an effort is laid out in Henton, Melville, and Walesh (1997).

8. For example, the Irvine Foundation hosts an annual summit for civic, business, community, labor, and environmental leaders to discuss successes and failures at consensus building and regional planning.

9. See Greene (1999).

10. Cleveland even compares its performance with that of thirteen other regions.

11. See http://www.narc.org/1999.htm.

12. See Neal R. Peirce, "Gore Rx: Fight Sprawl with Billions + Coalitions," syndicated column, Washington Post Writer's Group, January 17, 1999, http://www.citistates.com/columns.htm.

13. One interesting measure for many regions is the geographic spread of poverty from the inner cities to the suburbs, a point that has been stressed by Myron Orfield in both his 1997 book and a series of reports done for metro areas such as Chicago and Portland.

14. While progress in Silicon Valley resulted from a sort of battle of competing indicators, in San Luis Obispo, the Foundation for Community Design brought together constituents from business, government, and the community sector to jointly identify community benchmarks for success. See also the recent alternative indicator attempt in San Diego (Marcelli and Joassart, 1998).

15. Working in collaboration with the city, other colleges and schools, and the local Private Industry Councils (PICs), the university conducts surveys of the unemployed and underemployed, analyzes the adequacy of existing services, monitors local job openings, and attempts to match the workforce with the needs of employers. The data is given back to local nonprofits to help them develop intervention strategies and is regularly updated and available on the internet.

16. Calvin Sims, "Corporate Vows to Aid Poor Produce Little in Los Angeles," *New York Times*, April 19, 1993, A1; Matthew Smith, "All the Best Intentions: Why

Rebuild LA Didn't," *LA Weekly,* April 27, 1997, 22–27; Calvin Sims, "Who Said Los Angeles Could Be Rebuilt in a Day?" *New York Times,* May 22, 1994, F5; Joseph Nocera, "City of Hype," *Gentleman's Quarterly,* April 1993, 86–89.

17.   In San Jose, for example, the Metropolitan Chamber of Commerce appointed as its chair Tommy Fulcher Jr., head of the county's largest antipoverty agency. See Scott Thurm, "The Chamber's Unenigmatic Leader," *San Jose Mercury News,* March 24, 1997, 1E.

18.   The Southern California Association of Governments' (SCAG's) Regional Advisory Council (RAC) has been moving in this direction over the past few years; since the RAC's power is quite limited—it advises a COG that itself has little power—this should be viewed mostly as a way to begin intersectoral conversations.

19.   This initiative recognizes the importance of local industry clusters, focusing its efforts on specific sectors in the regional economy, including health care and manufacturing. Jobs are expected to pay at least $10 per hour (Abt Associates and New School for Social Research, 1997). DVCRF also works with the Pittsburgh Jobs Initiative, providing training and referrals for employees.

20.   For more information, see Connolly and Daddario (1995), Jacobson (1996), Peirce (1996), and Ruben (1995).

21.   Not all such clusters are "industrial" in the traditional sense. Many entertainment firms, for example, have clustered successfully, including in their immediate proximity graphic artists, software developers, computer programmers, art and graphic material suppliers, and so on.

22.   WIRE-Net has established training networks that link institutions, manufacturers, and residents; assisted firms in researching new markets and technology; and facilitated the organization of small-firm clusters to combine resources, encourage knowledge transfer, and achieve scale economies (Indergaard, 1997).

23.   Currently, the CRA covers only residential lending, and community organizations have used this information effectively to combat redlining. With a new information base on commercial loans available, communities could work to improve banker performance in lending to retail and other businesses in distressed neighborhoods. Banks and other financial institutions could also institute executive seminars and/or mentor programs that provide minority business owners with access to credit. For example, Operation Hope in Los Angeles operates banking centers that help individuals and entrepreneurs understand the credit system; it also provides the opportunity for banking executives to come into regular contact with local minority executives and business owners.

24.   In Montgomery County, Ohio, Economic Development/Government Equity (ED/GE) fosters cooperative economic development among twenty-nine of the county's thirty jurisdictions, redistributing a portion of increases in tax revenue generated as a result of economic growth to nongrowth jurisdictions. In New Jersey, the Hackensack Meadowlands Development Commission was established to redistribute property tax revenue to fourteen cities based on a per capita basis. In Pennsylvania, the Allegheny County Assets District

(around Pittsburgh) allocates half of a 1 percent countywide sales tax to fund regional assets such as the zoo, libraries, and parks; the other half of the sales tax revenue is divided between the county and 130 local jurisdictions and goes to support interjurisdictional cooperative and development programs. Data from Hollis (1997), Parzen (1997), Summers (1997), and personal interviews.

25. An earlier version of this was outlined in Wolff and Grigsby (1995). Gottlieb (1997) develops a similar framework for analyzing general development strategies such as central business district expansion, growth management policies, school reform, and metrowide job training programs.

26. For more on the Maryland effort, as codified in the 1997 Smart Growth Areas Act, see *Managing Maryland's Growth: Smart Growth and Neighborhood Conservation Initiatives,* available from the Maryland Office of Planning, Baltimore, Maryland, and Gurwitt (1999).

27. Services to job seekers should also be integrated. In Sacramento, California, for example, a collection of neighborhood groups and religious organizations called the Sacramento Valley Organizing Committee (SVOC) has initiated a one-stop job center as a "seamless web" of services for individuals transitioning from welfare to work, including job readiness training and child-care services. Graduates will then move on to other SVOC training programs created through partnerships with local industries.

28. See Jack Norman, "Jobs Initiative Off to Strong Start; Program Links Urban Workers, Outlying Firms," *Milwaukee Journal Sentinel,* June 8, 1998, pp. 1, 8, and Pete Millard, "This Jobs Program Really Works," *Milwaukee Business Journal,* May 29, 1998, p. 50.

29. Another way to create employment networks involves explicit public policies to encourage "linkage" between employers and residents; see Molina (1998).

30. See Harrison and Weiss (1998) and Abt Associates (1997); information on these programs also taken from interviews with Sheril Francis of Bethel New Life, Steve Holt of the Milwaukee Jobs Initiative, and Bill Dempsy and Lester Bense of Sustainable Milwaukee.

31. Under the Section 8 program, families pay 30 percent of their income to landlords who agree to participate. HUD covers the rest, up to a "fair market rent" ceiling.

32. We use the terms housing voucher, certificate, and allowance interchangably here.

33. Legally, families can use Section 8 certificates outside the local jurisdiction but in practice this is discouraged. Indeed, since it is easier administratively to simply place clients in apartments whose owners are already experienced with taking vouchers, "Section 8 ghettoes"—concentrations of certificate holders— have developed in many cities.

34. The Metropolitan Boston Housing Partnership, a consortium of business, government, and community leaders, offers an example of a metropolitan-wide housing allowance program.

35. Information based on ongoing evaluations of the MTO program; see also Larry Gordon, "A Social Experiment in Pulling Up Stakes," *Los Angeles Times,* September 23, 1997, A1, as well as Dreier and Moberg's (1996) general

230 • *Notes to Chapter 7*

discussion of mobility. In 1998, HUD secretary Andrew Cuomo announced that HUD was setting aside 50,000 housing vouchers specifically for city families to move closer to suburban jobs (see Neal R. Peirce, "Sustainability Takes Wing," syndicated column, Washington Post Writer's Group, March 22, 1998, http://www.citistates.com/columns.htm).

36. See Hughes (1992, 1995) and Stanfield (1996) on "reverse commuting" programs that focus on making connections between employers and community organizations and on supplementing the existing public transit systems with new connections in the form of buses, vans, jitneys, car pools, and other means of transportation. For an early review of the Bridges to Work program, see Palubinsky and Watson (1997).

37. See also Peter Dreier, "Low-Wage Workers Miss a Tax Break," *Los Angeles Times,* January 24, 1999, M5, which estimates that full participation in the EITC among eligible workers would add $200 million to the Los Angeles area economy.

38. For example, the living wage law passed in San Jose in late 1998 involved the highest target wage of any such ordinance thus far, reflecting the vibrancy of the local Silicon Valley economy.

39. Living wage laws can also help community development directly as higher-paid workers spend additional dollars in the low-income communities where they live, supporting neighborhood grocery stores, restaurants, laundromats, and clothing and other retail establishments. See Peter Dreier and Manuel Pastor, "It's Business as Usual for Living-Wage Opponents," *Los Angeles Times,* December 8, 1996, M6.

40. Microlending programs that lend not on existing collateral but rather on an individual's business plan and history of work effort are key. The model for such programs is the well-known Grameen Bank in Bangladesh; over the past twenty years, this innovative mix of lenders' circles, business training, and modest credit has been copied in numerous places around the world.

41. As noted in chapter 3, RLA attempted to address this issue in Los Angeles by developing a strategy to bring smaller, but full-service, markets into low-income neighborhoods. The Local Initiatives Support Corporation (LISC), which works with CDCs around the country, has developed a national plan to help bring new supermarkets to low-income areas.

42. Another important force propelling suburbanization was the mortgage interest deduction that made housing relatively cheaper. Gyourko and Voith (1997) show that when such a tax policy interacts with the typical suburban practice of zoning for larger lots, this creates incentives for both low-density development and income sorting, which concentrates poverty in the central city.

43. Distribution of the tax benefits is taken from Dreier, forthcoming, with the calculations based on data provided in the Joint Committee on Taxation (1995).

44. See Neal R. Peirce, "Sustainability Takes Wing," *Washington Post,* March 22, 1998, http://www.citistates.com/columns.htm.

45. For a discussion of how the federal government can limit bidding wars, see Melvin Burstein and Arthur Rolnick, "Congress Should End the Economic War for Sports and Other Business," in *The Region* (June 1996), pp. 35–36, a publication sponsored by the Federal Reserve Bank of Minneapolis.

46. See Neal R. Peirce, "Maryland's 'Smart Growth' Law: A National Model?" syndicated column, Washington Post Writer's Group, April 20, 1997, http://www.citistates.com/column.htm.

47. See "Speaker Villaraigosa Announces New Blue-Ribbon Commission on State-Local Fiscal and Tax Policy," *Metro Investment Report,* September 1998, p. 5.

48. For critiques of how the recent period of economic growth has not touched all sectors, see Schwarz (1998) and Schwarz (1997).

49. For more on LAANE and other labor-community initiatives, see Soja, forthcoming, and Harold Myerson, "No Justice, No Growth," *LA Weekly,* July 17–23, 1998.

50. See the following reports: *Beyond Sprawl: New Patterns of Growth to Fit the New California,* San Francisco: Bank of America, California Resources Agency, Greenbelt Alliance, Low Income Housing Fund, n.d.; *Land Use and the California Economy: Principles For Prosperity and Quality of Life,* San Francisco: Californians and the Land, William and Flora Hewlett Foundation, James Irvine Foundation, David and Lucile Packard Foundation, Environment Now, Bank of America, n.d.; and *Building a Legacy for the Next Generation,* Sacramento: California Business Roundtable, n.d.

51. Johnson is quoted in Lora Engdahl, "What Is . . . Regionalism?" *Neighborhood Works,* vol. 20, no. 6, 1997, pp. 8–9, 36.

52. For news articles on the growing debate about sprawl and Smart Growth, see Todd Purdum, "Suburban 'Sprawl' Takes Its Place on the Political Landscape," *New York Times,* February 6, 1999, A1, A12; Neal Peirce, "Sprawl Control: A Political Issue Comes of Age" syndicated column, Washington Post Writer's Group, November 15, 1998, http://www.citistates.com/columns.htm); Margaret Kriz, "The Politics of Sprawl," *National Journal,* February 6, 1999, p. 332; Steve Chawkins, "Homes Sprouting, Farms Dying," *Los Angeles Times,* February 7, 1999, A1, A22–23; and "Urban Sprawl: To Traffic Hell and Back," *The Economist,* May 8, 1999, p. 23. The antisprawl movement has actually gained enough political traction to encourage a series of critical responses; see, for example, George F. Will, "Al Gore Has a New Worry," *Newsweek,* February 15, 1999, p. 76; Steven Hayward, "Suburban Legends," *National Review,* March 22, 1999, p. 35; and Greg Easterbrook, "The Suburban Myth," *New Republic,* March 15, 1999, p. 18. For a more academic approach to the resurgence of sprawl as a political issue, see also Leo (1998).

References

Abbot, Carl. 1997. "The Portland Region: Where the City and Suburbs Talk to Each Other and Agree." *Housing Policy Debate*, vol. 8, issue 1, pp. 1–73.

Abramson, Alan J., Mitchell S. Tobin, and Matthew R. VanderGoot. 1995. "The Changing Geography of Metropolitan Opportunity: The Segregation of the Poor in U.S. Metropolitan Areas, 1970 to 1990." *Housing Policy Debate*, vol. 6, no. 1, pp. 45–72.

Abt Associates & New School for Social Research. 1997. *Evaluation of the Annie E. Casey Foundation's Jobs Initiatives.* Baltimore: Annie E. Casey Foundation.

Advisory Commission on Intergovernmental Relations. 1969. *Urban America and the Federal System.* Washington, DC: Advisory Commission on Intergovernmental Relations.

———. 1967. *Fiscal Balance in the American Federal System.* Washington, DC: Advisory Commission on Intergovernmental Relations.

AFL-CIO Human Resources Development Institute. 1998. "Economic Development: A Union Guide to the High Road." Washington, DC: AFL-CIO, May.

Ahluwalia, Montek S. 1976. "Income Distribution and Development: Some Stylized Facts." *American Economic Review*, vol. 66, pp. 128–35.

Alameda Corridor Transportation Authority. 1994. "The National Economic Significance of the Alameda Corridor." Los Angeles: Alameda Corridor Transportation Authority, February, p. iii.

Alba, Richard D., and John R. Logan. 1992. "Analyzing Locational Attainments." *Sociological Methods and Research*, vol. 20, no. 3, pp. 367–97.

Alesina, Alberto, and Allan Drazen. 1991. "Why Are Stabilizations Delayed?" *American Economic Review*, vol. 8, no. 5, pp. 1170–88.

Alesina, Alberto, and Roberto Perotti. 1993. *Income Distribution, Political Instability, and Investment.* Working Paper No. 4486. Cambridge, MA: National Bureau of Economic Research.

Allen, James P., and Eugene Turner. 1997. *The Ethnic Quilt: Population Diversity in Southern California.* Northridge, CA: The Center for Geographical Studies.

Angelides, Philip. 1999 (June). *Smart Investments: A Special Edition of California's Debt Affordability Report.* Sacramento: California State Treasurer's office.

Aron, Joan B. 1969. *The Quest for Regional Cooperation: A Study of the New York Metropolitan Regional Council.* Berkeley: University of California Press.

Aschaer, David Alan. 1993. *Public Infrastructure Investment: A Bridge to Productivity Growth?* Public Policy Brief No. 4. Annandale-on-Hudson, New York: Jerome Levy Economics Institute of Bard College.

Atlas, John, and Peter Dreier. 1997. "Courting Racial Justice." *Tikkun,* vol. 12, no.1, pp. 68–69.

Baker, Dean, and Todd Schafer. 1995. *The Case for Public Investment.* Washington, DC: Economic Policy Institute.

Baldassare, Mark, ed. 1994. *The Los Angeles Riots: Lessons for the Urban Future.* Boulder, CO: Westview Press.

Barnes, William, and Larry C. Ledebur. 1998. *The New Regional Economies: The U.S. Common Market and the Global Economy.* Thousand Oaks, CA: Sage Publications.

Bartik, Timothy. 1994. "What Should the Federal Government Be Doing About Urban Economic Development?" *Citiscape,* vol. 1, no. 1, pp. 267–92.

Bean, Frank D., Jennifer V. W. Van Hook, and Jennifer Glick. 1994. *Poverty and Welfare Recipiency Among Immigrants in California.* Claremont, CA: The Tomás Rivera Center.

Beatty, David F., Joseph E. Coomes Jr., Brent T. Hasking, Edward J. Quinn Jr., and Iris P. Yang. 1991. *Development in California.* Point Arena, CA: Solano Press Books.

Benner, Chris. 1998. *Growing Together or Drifting Apart? Working Families and Business in the New Economy.* San Jose: Working Partnerships USA.

———. 1996a. *Shock Absorbers in the Flexible Economy: The Rise of Contingent Employment in Silicon Valley.* San Jose: Working Partnerships USA.

———. 1996b. "Computer Workers Feel the Byte: Temp Jobs in Silicon Valley." *Dollars and Sense,* September/October, pp. 23–25, 44–45.

Berg, Andrew, and Jeffrey Sachs. 1988. "The Debt Crisis: Structural Explanations of Country Performance." *Journal of Development Economics,* vol. 29, pp. 271–306.

Bernstein, Michael A., and David E. Adler. 1994. *Understanding American Economic Decline.* New York: Cambridge University Press.

Bernstein, Scott. 1997. "Community Based Regionalism Key for Sustainable Future." *The Neighborhood Works,* vol. 20, no. 6, p. 10.

Birdsall, Nancy, and Richard Sabot. 1994. "Inequality as a Constraint on Growth in Latin America." *Development Policy: Newsletter on Policy Research.* Washington, DC: Inter-American Development Bank, Office of the Chief Economist.

Blair, John P., and Zhongcai Zhang. Forthcoming. "Ties That Bind Revisited." *Economic Development Quarterly.*

Blank, Rebecca M. 1997. *It Takes a Nation: A New Agenda for Fighting Poverty.* New York: Russell Sage Foundation, pp. 72–75.

Bluestone, Barry, and Bennett Harrison. 1982. *The Deindustrialization of America: Plant Closings, Community Abandonment, and the Dismantling of Basic Industry.* New York: Basic Books.

Bockmeyer, Janice. 1996. "Community Coup: CDC Activism in Detroit's Empowerment Zone." Paper presented to the annual meeting of the American Political Science Association, San Francisco, California, September.

Boer, J. Tom, Manuel Pastor, James L. Sadd, and Lori D. Snyder. 1997. "Is There Environmental Racism? The Demographics of Hazardous Waste in Los Angeles County." *Social Science Quarterly,* vol. 78, no. 4, December, pp. 793–810.

Bollens, Scott. 1997a. "Fragments of Regionalism: The Limits of Southern California Governance." *Journal of Urban Affairs,* vol. 19, no. 1, pp. 105–22.

———. 1997b. "Concentrated Poverty and Metropolitan Equity Strategies." *Stanford Law & Policy Review,* vol. 8, no. 2, pp. 11–23.

Bonacich, Edna, Lucie Cheng, Norma Chinchilla, Nora Hamilton, and Paul Ong, eds. 1994. *Global Production: The Apparel Industry in the Pacific Rim.* Philadelphia: Temple University Press.

Boston Urban Study Group. 1984. *Who Rules Boston? A Citizen's Guide.* Boston: Boston Urban Study Group.

Boston, Thomas, and Catherine Ross, eds. 1997. *The Inner City: Urban Poverty and Economic Development in the Next Century.* New Brunswick, NJ: Transaction Publishers.

Bowles, Samuel, David M. Gordon, and Thomas E. Weisskopf. 1983. *Beyond the Waste Land: A Democratic Alternative to Economic Decline.* Garden City, NY: Anchor Press/Doubleday.

Boyte, Harry. 1987. *Commonwealth: A Return to Citizen Politics.* New York: Free Press.

———. 1980. *The Backyard Revolution: Understanding the New Citizen Movement.* Philadelphia: Temple University Press.

Bratt, Rachel. 1989. *Rebuilding a Low-Income Housing Policy.* Philadelphia: Temple University Press.

Briggs, Xavier de Souza. 1997. "Moving Up Versus Moving Out: Neighborhood Effects in Housing Mobility Programs." *Housing Policy Debate,* vol. 8, issue 1, pp. 195–234.

Brooks, Nancy, and Anita A. Summers. 1998. "Does the Economic Health of America's Largest Cities Affect the Economic Health of Their Suburbs?" Working Paper No. 263. Wharton Working Paper Series, University of Pennsylvania.

Brown, Prudence. 1996. "Comprehensive Neighborhood-Based Initiatives." *Cityscape,* vol. 2, no. 2, May, pp. 161–76.

Browne, Lynn E. 1989. "Shifting Regional Fortunes: The Wheel Turns." *New England Economic Review,* May/June, pp. 27–40.

Burchell, Robert W., David Listokin, Naveed A. Shad, Hilary Phillips, Anthony Downs, Samuel Seskin, Judy S. Davis, Terry Moore, David Helton, and Michelle Gall. 1998. *Costs of Sprawl Revisited: The Evidence of Sprawl's Negative and Positive Impacts.* Washington, DC: Transportation Research Board, National Research Council, March.

Calavita, Nico, Kenneth Grimes, and Susan Mallach. 1997. "Inclusionary Housing in California and New Jersey: A Comparative Analysis." *Housing Policy Debate,* vol. 8, no. 1, pp. 109–42.

Calavita, Nico, Kenneth Grimes, and Susan Reynolds. 1994. "Zigzagging Toward Long-Term Affordability in the Sunbelt: The San Diego Housing Trust Fund." In John Davis, ed., *The Affordable City.* Philadelphia: Temple University Press.

California Economic Strategy Panel. 1996. *Collaborating To Compete in the New Economy: An Economic Strategy for California.* Sacramento: California Trade and Commerce Agency, February.

Campbell, Brett. 1994. *Investing in People: The Story of Project QUEST.* San Antonio: Communities for Public Services and Metro Alliance. Also at www.cpn.org.

Caplovitz, David. 1963. *The Poor Pay More: Consumer Practices of Low-Income Families.* Glencoe, IL: Free Press, chapter 6.

Case, Karl E. 1991. "The Real Estate Cycle and the Economy: Consequences of the Massachusetts Boom of 1984–1987." *New England Economic Review*, September/October, pp. 37–46.

Case, Anne, and Lawrence Katz. 1991. *The Company You Keep: The Effects of Family and Neighborhood on Disadvantaged Youths.* Cambridge, MA: National Bureau of Economic Research.

Case, Karl, and Robert J. Shiller. 1994. "A Decade of Boom and Bust in the Prices of Single-Family Homes: Boston and Los Angeles, 1983 to 1993." *New England Economic Review*, pp. 40–51.

Center for National Policy and Local Initiatives Support Corporation. 1997. *Life in the City: A Status Report on the Revival of Urban Communities in America.* Washington, DC: Center for National Policy and Local Initiatives Support Corporation.

Chernick, Howard, and Andrew Reschovsky. 1997. "Urban Fiscal Problems: Coordinating Actions Among Governments." In Burton A. Weisbrod and James C. Worthy, eds., *The Urban Crisis.* Evanston, IL: Northwestern University Press, pp. 131–75.

Cisneros, Henry. 1996. "Community Colleges and Urban Development." *Cityscape*, special issue, December, pp. 127–53.

———. 1995. *Regionalism: The New Geography of Opportunity.* Washington, DC: U.S. Department of Housing and Urban Development, March.

Clavel, Pierre, and Wim Wiewel, eds. 1991. *Harold Washington and the Neighborhoods.* New Brunswick, NJ: Rutgers University Press.

Clay, Phil. 1988. *Housing in Boston: A Five Year Retrospective.* Boston: McCormack Institute of Public Affairs, University of Massachusetts.

Coalition of Neighborhood Developers (CND). 1994. *From the Ground Up: Neighbors Planning Neighborhoods.* Los Angeles: Coalition of Neighborhood Developers.

Coase, Ronald H. 1937. "The Nature of the Firm." *Economica*, vol. 4, pp. 386–405.

Cole, Rick, Trish Kelly, and Judy Corbett, with Sharon Sprowls. 1998. *The Ahwahnee Principles for Smart Economic Development: An Implementation Guidebook.* Sacramento: Local Government Commission, Center for Livable Communities.

Collins, Chuck, and Kirby White. 1994. "Boston in the 1980s: Toward a Social Housing Policy." In John Davis, ed., *The Affordable City.* Philadelphia: Temple University Press, pp. 201–25.

Committee for Economic Development. 1995. *Rebuilding Inner-City Communities: A New Approach to the Nation's Urban Crisis.* New York: Committee for Economic Development, Research and Policy Committee.

Community Redevelopment Agency (CRA), City of Los Angeles. 1995. "Draft Project Description and Alternatives for the Vermont Manchester Recovery Study Area." Los Angeles: Community Redevelopment Agency.

Connely, Kathleen, and David Daddario. 1995. "How to Find the Green in Your City's Brownfields." *American City & County*, vol. 110, no. 12, pp. 28–35.

Conrad, Katherine. 1994. "San Jose CET Trains the Hard-Core Poor." *Youth Today,* vol. 3, no. 2, pp. 1, 24, 25.

Cooper, Marc. 1996. "Class.War @ Silicon.Valley: Disposable Workers in the New Economy." *The Nation,* May 27, pp. 11–16.

Coulton, Claudia, Julian Chow, Edward C. Want, and Marily Su. 1996. "Geographic Concentration of Affluence and Poverty in 100 Metropolitan Areas, 1990." *Urban Affairs Review,* vol. 32, no. 2, pp. 186–216.

Davis, Mike. 1987. "Chinatown, Part Two? The 'Internationalization' of Downtown Los Angeles." *New Left Review,* no. 164, July/August, pp. 65–86.

Delgado, Gary. 1999. "Race and Regionalism." *GRIPP (Grass Roots Innovative Policy Program) News & Notes,* vol. 1, spring, pp. 3–4, 6–7, 10–11.

Delgado, Gary. 1994. *Beyond the Politics of Place: New Directions in Community Organizing in the 1990s.* Oakland, CA: Applied Research Center.

DeLeon, Richard. 1992. *Left Coast City: Progressive Politics in San Francisco, 1975–1991.* Lawrence, KS: University of Kansas Press.

Dreier, Peter. Forthcoming. *Housing Policy for the 21st Century.* New York: The Century Foundation.

———. 1997. "Urban Politics and Progressive Housing Policy: Ray Flynn and Boston's Neighborhood Agenda." In W. Dennis Keating, Norman Krumholz, and Philip Star, eds., *Revitalizing Urban Neighborhoods.* Lawrence, KS: University Press of Kansas.

———. 1996. "Community Empowerment Strategies: The Limits and Potential of Community-Based Organizing in Urban Neighborhoods." *Cityscape,* vol. 2, no. 2, pp. 121–59.

———. 1991. "Redlining Cities: How Banks Color Community Development." *Challenge,* vol. 34, no. 6, pp. 15–23.

———. 1983. "The Vault Comes Out of the Darkness." *Boston Business Journal,* October l0, pp. 1–3.

Dreier, Peter, and Bruce Ehrlich. 1991. "Downtown Development and Urban Reform: The Politics of Boston's Linkage Policy." *Urban Affairs Quarterly,* vol. 26, no. 3, pp. 354–73.

Dreier, Peter, and Dennis Keating. 1990. "The Limits of Localism: Progressive Municipal Housing Policies in Boston." *Urban Affairs Quarterly,* vol. 26, no. 2, pp. 191–216.

Dreier, Peter, and David Moberg. 1996. "Moving from the 'Hood': The Mixed Success of Integrating Suburbia." *The American Prospect,* winter, pp. 75–79.

Dreier, Peter, and Richard Rothstein. 1994. "Seismic Stimulus: The California Quake's Creative Destruction." *The American Prospect,* summer, pp. 40–46.

Dreier, Peter, David Schwartz, and Ann Greiner. 1988. "What Every Business Can Do About Housing." *Harvard Business Review,* September/October, pp. 52–58.

Drennen, Matthew, Emanuel Tobier, and Jonathan Lewis. 1996. "The Interruption of Income Convergence and Income Growth in Large Cities in the 1980s." *Urban Studies,* vol. 33, no. 1, pp. 63–82.

Dresser, Laura, and Joel Rogers. 1997. "Rebuilding Job Access and Career Advance-ment Systems in the New Economy." Madison: University of Wisconsin, Center on Wisconsin Strategy Briefing Paper, December.

Dressner, Julianne, Wendy Fleischer, and Kay E. Sherwood. 1998. *Next Door: A Concept Paper for Place-Based Employment Initiatives.* A Report to the Rockefeller Foundation. New York: The Corporation for Supportive Housing.

DRI/McGraw-Hill. 1998. *The Role of Metropolitan Areas in the National Economy.* Report prepared for the Joint Center for Sustainable Communities of the United States Conference of Mayors and the National Association of Cities, March 19.

Dymski, Gary A., and John M. Veitch. 1996. "Financing the Future in Los Angeles: From Depression to 21st Century." In Michael J. Dean, H. Erick Schockman, and Greg Hise, eds., *Rethinking Los Angeles.* Thousand Oaks, CA: Sage Publications, pp. 35–55.

Edin, Kathryn, and Laura Lein. 1997. *Making Ends Meet: How Single Mothers Survive Welfare and Low-Wage Work.* New York: Russell Sage Foundation.

Ehrenhalt, Alan. 1993. "The Underclass and the Suburban Solution." *Governing,* July, pp. 6–7.

Ellen, Ingrid Gould, and Margery Austin Turner. 1997. "Does Neighborhood Matter? Assessing Recent Evidence." *Housing Policy Debate,* vol. 8, issue 4, pp. 833–66.

Ellwood, David T. 1986. "The Spatial Mismatch Hypothesis: Are There Teenage Jobs Missing in the Ghetto?" In Richard B. Freeman and Harry J. Holzer, eds. *The Black Youth Employment Crisis.* Chicago: University of Chicago Press, pp. 147–87.

Erie, Steven. 1992. "How the Urban West Was Won: The Local State and Economic Growth in Los Angeles, 1880–1932." *Urban Affairs Quarterly,* vol. 27, no. 4, pp. 519–54.

Erie, Stephen P., with Harold Brackman and James E. Rauch. 1996. *International Trade and Job Creation in Southern California: Facilitating Los Angeles/Long Beach Port, Rail, and Airport Development.* Berkeley: California Policy Seminar.

Estrada, Leobardo F., and Sylvia Sensiper. 1993. "Mending the Politics of Division in Post-Rebellion L.A." In Allen J. Scott and E. Richard Brown, eds., *South-Central Los Angeles: Anatomy of an Urban Crisis.* Working Paper No. 6. Los Angeles: Lewis Center for Regional Policy Studies, University of California, Los Angeles.

Fainstein, Norman. 1986. "The Underclass/Mismatch Hypothesis as an Explanation for Black Economic Deprivation." *Politics and Society,* vol. 15, pp. 403–51.

———. 1983. "Race, Class, and Segregation: Discourses About African Americans." *International Journal of Urban and Regional Research,* special issue, vol. 7, no. 3, pp. 384–404.

Fernandez, Roberto M. 1997. "Spatial Mismatch: Housing, Transportation, and Employment in Regional Perspective." In Burton A. Weisbrod and James C. Worthy, eds., *The Urban Crisis: Linking Research to Action.* Evanston, IL: Northwestern University Press.

Fernandez, Roberto M., and Nancy Weinberg. 1997. "Sifting and Sorting: Personal Contacts and Hiring in a Retail Bank." *American Sociological Review,* vol. 62, pp. 883–902.

Fernandez-Kelly, Maria Patricia, and Saskia Sassen. 1992. "Immigrant Women in the Garment and Electronic Industries in the New York–New Jersey Region and in Southern California." Final research report presented to the Ford, Revson, and Tinker Foundations, New York, June.

Fernandez-Kelly, Maria Patricia, and Anna M. Garcia. 1989. "Informalization at the Core: Hispanic Women, Homework, and the Advanced Capitalist State." In

Alejandro Portes, Manuel Castells, and Lauren A. Benton, eds., *The Informal Economy.* Baltimore: The Johns Hopkins University Press, pp. 247–64.

Fix, Michael, and Jeffrey S. Passel. 1994. *Immigration and Immigrants: Setting the Record Straight.* Washington, DC: The Urban Institute.

Fogelson, Robert. 1967. *The Fragmented Metropolis: Los Angeles 1850–1930.* Cambridge, MA: Harvard University Press.

Ford Foundation. 1989. *Affordable Housing: The Years Ahead.* New York: The Ford Foundation.

Fossett, James W., and Janet D. Perloff. 1995. *The New Health Reform and Access to Care: The Problem of the Inner City.* Washington, DC: Kaiser Commission on the Future of Medicaid.

Frey, William, and Douglas Geverdt. 1998. "Changing Suburban Demographics: Beyond the 'Black-White, City-Suburb' Typology." Paper prepared for the conference "Suburban Racial Change" sponsored by the Harvard Civil Rights Project and the Taubman Center on State and Local Government, Cambridge, Massachusetts, March 28.

Frieden, Bernard J., and Lynn B. Sagalyn. 1989. *Downtown, Inc.* Cambridge, MA: Massachusetts Institute of Technology Press.

Friedman, David (project director). 1994. *The New Economy Project: Final Report.* Los Angeles: The New Vision Business Council of Southern California.

Friedman, David. 1992. *Getting Industry to Stick: Enhancing High Value-Added Production in California.* Working Paper. Cambridge, MA: Japan Program, Center for International Studies, Massachusetts Institute of Technology.

Fulton, William. 1997. *The Reluctant Metropolis: The Politics of Urban Growth in Los Angeles.* Point Arena, CA: Solano Press Books.

———. 1996. *The New Urbanism: Hope or Hype for American Communities?* Cambridge, MA: Lincoln Institute of Land Policy.

Galster, George. 1991. "Black Suburbanization: Has It Changed the Relative Location of Races?" *Urban Affairs Quarterly,* vol. 26, pp. 621–28, n.4.

———. 1990. "Racial Steering in Urban Housing Markets: A Review of the Audit Evidence." *Review of Black Political Economy,* vol. 18, no. 3, pp. 105–29.

Galster, George, and Sean P. Killen. 1995. "The Geography of Metropolitan Opportunity: A Reconnaissance and Conceptual Framework." *Housing Policy Debate,* vol. 6, no. 1, pp. 10–47.

Galster, George, Ronald Mincy, and Mitchell Tobin. 1997. "The Disparate Racial Neighborhood Impacts of Metropolitan Restructuring." *Urban Affairs Review,* vol. 32, no. 6, pp. 797–824.

Garland, Susan, and Peter Galuszka. 1997. "The 'Burbs Fight Back." *Business Week,* no. 3529, June 2, pp. 147–48.

Garreau, Joel. 1991. *Edge City.* New York: Doubleday.

Gillmor, Dan, and Stephen Doig. 1992. "Segregation Forever?" *American Demographics,* vol. 14, no. 1, pp. 48–51.

Gitell, Ross, and Avis Vidal. 1998. *Community Organizing: Building Social Capital as a Development Strategy.* Thousand Oaks, CA: Sage Publications.

Goetz, Edward, Hin Kin Lam, and Anne Heitlinger. 1996. *There Goes the Neighborhood? The Impact of Subsidized Multi-Family Housing on Urban Neighborhoods.* Minneapolis: University of Minnesota, Center for Urban and Regional Affairs.

Goetze, Rolf. 1992. *Income, Employment, and Housing Changes Revealed by the 1990 U.S. Census.* Boston: Boston Redevelopment Authority, July.

Gortmaker, Steven L., and Paul H. Wise. 1997. "The First Injustice: Socioeconomic Disparities, Health Services Technology, and Infant Mortality." In John Hagan and Karen S. Cook, eds., *Annual Review of Sociology,* vol. 23. Palo Alto: Annual Reviews, Inc., pp. 147–70.

Gottlieb, Paul D. 1998. *The Effects of Poverty on Metropolitan Area Economic Performance: A Policy-Oriented Research Review.* Washington, DC: National League of Cities.

———. 1997. "Neighborhood Development in the Metropolitan Economy: A Policy Review." *Journal of Urban Affairs,* vol. 19, no. 2, pp. 163–82.

Grigsby, J. Eugene. 1993. "Rebuild Los Angeles: One Year Later." *National Civic Review,* fall, pp. 348–53.

Grigsby, J. Eugene, and Jeffrey J. Caltabiano. 1998. "An Assessment of Fifty Years of Redevelopment in Los Angeles." Paper prepared for the Community Redevelopment Agency of Los Angeles by the UCLA Advanced Policy Institute, August.

Grigsby, J. Eugene, and Mary Hruby. 1991. "Recent Changes in the Housing Status of Blacks in Los Angeles." *The Review of Black Political Economy,* vol. 19, nos. 3–4, pp. 210–40.

Grobar, Lisa Morris. 1996. "Comparing the New England and Southern California Regional Recessions." *Contemporary Economic Policy,* vol. 14, no. 3, pp. 71–84.

Gurwitt, Rob. 1998. "The Quest for Common Ground." *Governing,* June, pp. 16–22.

Gyourko, Joseph, and Anita Summers. 1997. *A New Strategy for Helping Cities Pay for the Poor.* Brookings Policy Brief. Washington, DC: The Brookings Institution.

Halpern, Robert. 1995. *Rebuilding the Inner City: A History of Neighborhood Initiatives to Address Poverty in the United States.* New York: Columbia University Press.

Hamilton, David K. 1999. *Governing Metropolitan Areas: Response to Growth and Change.* New York: Garland Publishing, Inc.

Harr, Charles. 1996. *Suburbia Under Siege.* Princeton: Princeton University Press.

Harris, Kathleen Mullan. 1993. "Work and Welfare Among Single Mothers in Poverty." *American Sociological Review,* vol. 61, pp. 207–46.

Harrison, Roderick, and Daniel Weinberg. 1992. "Racial and Ethnic Residential Segregation in 1990." Washington, DC: U.S. Bureau of the Census, April.

Harrison, Bennett. 1998. "It Takes a Region (Or Does It?): The Material Basis for Metropolitanism and Metropolitics." Paper prepared for the Twentieth Annual Research Conference, Association for Public Policy and Management, New York City, October 29–31.

Harrison, Bennett, with Marcus Weiss and Jon Gant. 1995. *Building Bridges: Community Development Corporations and the World of Employment Training.* New York: The Ford Foundation, January.

Harrison, Bennett, and Marcus Weiss. 1998. *Workforce Development Networks: Community-Based Organizations and Regional Alliances.* Thousand Oaks, CA: Sage Publications.

Henderson, Yolanda. 1990. "Defense Cutbacks and the New England Economy." *New England Economic Review,* July/August, pp. 3–24.

Henton, Douglas, Sharon Huntsman, Tom Lewcock, Kathy Maag, Beck Morgan, and Kim Walesh. 1998. *Silicon Valley 2010: A Regional Framework for Growing Together.* Palo Alto: Joint Venture: Silicon Valley Network.

Henton, Douglas, John Melville, and Kimberly Walesh. 1997. *Grassroots Leaders for a New Economy: How Civic Entrepreneurs Are Building Prosperous Communities.* San Francisco: Jossey-Bass Publishers.

Hill, Edward W., and Harold L. Wolman. 1997. "City-Suburban Income Disparities and Metropolitan Area Employment: Can Tightening Labor Markets Reduce the Gaps?" *Urban Affairs Review,* vol. 32, no. 4, pp. 558–82.

Hill, Edward W., Harold L. Wolman, and Coit Cook Ford III. 1995. "Can Suburbs Survive Without Their Central Cities?" *Urban Affairs Quarterly,* vol. 31, no. 2, pp. 147–74.

———. 1994. "Do Cities Lead and Suburbs Follow? Examining Their Economic Interdependence." Paper prepared for the conference "Rethinking the Urban Agenda," sponsored by the Sydney C. Spivack Program, American Sociological Association, Belmont Conference Center, Maryland, May 20–22.

Hirsch, Arnold. 1983. *Making the Second Ghetto: Race and Housing in Chicago, 1940–1960.* New York: Cambridge University Press.

Hiss, Tony. 1997. "Outlining the New Metropolitan Initiative." Posted at the website of the Center for Neighborhood Technology (www.cnt.org).

Hollis, Linda E. 1997. *Regionalism Today: Background, Timelines, and Current Practice.* Washington, DC: Urban Land Institute, September 15.

Horan, Cynthia, and Andrew C. Jonas. 1998. "Governing Massachusetts: Uneven Development and Politics in Metropolitan Boston." *Economic Geography,* special issue, March, pp. 83–95.

Hossfeld, Karen J. 1990. "'Their Logic Against Them': Contradictions in Sex, Race, and Class in Silicon Valley." In Kathryn Ward, ed., *Women Workers and Global Restructuring.* Ithaca: Cornell University ILR Press.

Hoyos, Lisa. 1994. "Worker at the Center." *Crossroads,* July/August, pp. 24–26.

Hughes, Mark Alan. 1995. "A Mobility Strategy for Improving Opportunity." *Housing Policy Debate,* vol. 6, no. 1, pp. 271–97.

———. 1991. "Employment Decentralization and Accessibility." *Journal of the American Planning Association,* vol. 57, pp. 288–99.

Hughes, Mark Alan, with Julie Sternberg. 1992. *The New Metropolitan Reality: Where the Rubber Meets the Road in Anti-Poverty Policy.* Washington, DC: The Urban Institute, December.

Hula, Richard C., Cynthia Y. Jackson, and Marion Orr. 1997. "Urban Politics, Governing Nonprofits, and Community Revitalization." *Urban Affairs Review,* vol. 32, no. 4, pp. 459–89.

Ihlanfeldt, Keith R. 1995. "The Importance of the Central City to the Regional and National Economy: A Review of the Arguments and Empirical Evidence." *Cityscape,* vol. 1, no. 2, pp. 125–50.

———. 1994. "The Spatial Mismatch Between Jobs and Residential Locations Within Urban Areas." *Cityscape,* vol. 1, no. 1, pp. 219–44.

———. 1992. *Spatial Mismatch and the Commutes, Employment, and Wages of Young Puerto Ricans Living in New York.* Atlanta: Policy Research Center, Georgia State University.

Ihlanfeldt, Keith R., and David L. Sjoquist. 1990a. "The Effect of Residential Location on the Probability of Black and White Teenagers Having a Job." *The Review of Regional Studies,* vol. 20, Winter, pp. 10–20.

———. 1990b. "Job Accessibility and Racial Differences in Youth Employment Rates." *The American Economic Review,* vol. 80, March, pp. 267–76.

Immergluck, Daniel, and Marti Wiles. 1998. *A Rising Tide . . . But Some Leaky Boats: The 1990s Economic Expansion and Job Sprawl in the Chicago Region.* Chicago: Woodstock Institute, November.

Indergaard, Michael. 1997. "Community-Based Restructuring? Institution Building in the Industrial Midwest." *Urban Affairs Review,* vol. 32, no. 5, pp. 662–82.

Jackson, Kenneth. 1985. *Crabgrass Frontier: The Suburbanization of the United States.* New York: Oxford University Press.

Jacobson, Louis. 1996. "Out Here, the Rough Is Really Rough." *National Journal,* vol. 28, no. 47, pp. 2251–52.

Jargowsky, Paul A. 1997. *Poverty and Place: Ghettos, Barrios, and the American City.* New York: Russell Sage Foundation.

———. 1996. "Take the Money and Run: Economic Segregation in U.S. Metropolitan Areas." *American Sociological Review,* vol. 61, December, pp. 984–98.

Jencks, Christopher, and Kathryn Edin. 1995. "Do Poor Women Have a Right to Bear Children?" *The American Prospect,* no. 20, winter, pp. 43–52.

Johnson, James H., Jr., and Walter C. Farrell Jr. 1996. "The Fire This Time: The Genesis of the Los Angeles Rebellion of 1992." In John Charles Boger and Judith Welch Wegner, eds., *Race, Poverty, and American Cities.* Chapel Hill, NC: University of North Carolina Press.

Johnson, James H., Jr., Walter C. Farrell Jr., and Maria-Rosario Jackson. 1994. "Los Angeles One Year Later: A Prospective Assessment of Responses to the 1992 Civil Unrest." *Economic Development Quarterly,* vol. 8., no. 1, pp. 19–27.

Johnson, James H., Jr., Cloyzelle K. Jones, Walter C. Farrell Jr., and Melvin L. Oliver. 1992a. *The Los Angeles Rebellion, 1992: A Preliminary Assessment from Ground Zero.* Working Paper. Los Angeles: Center for the Study of Urban Poverty, University of California, Los Angeles, May.

———. 1992b. "The Los Angeles Rebellion: A Retrospective View." *Economic Development Quarterly,* vol. 6, no. 4, pp. 356–72.

Joint Venture: Silicon Valley Network. 1999. *Joint Venture's 1999 Index of Silicon Valley.* San Jose: Joint Venture: Silicon Valley Network.

———. 1998. *Joint Venture's 1998 Index of Silicon Valley: Measuring Progress Toward a 21ˢᵗ Century Community.* San Jose: Joint Venture: Silicon Valley Network.

———. 1995. *The Joint Venture Way: Lessons for Regional Rejuvenation.* San Jose: Joint Venture: Silicon Valley Network.

Judd, Dennis, and Todd Swanstrom. 1994. *City Politics.* New York: Harper Collins.

Kain, John. 1968. "Housing Segregation, Negro Employment, and Metropolitan Decentralization." *Quarterly Journal of Economics,* vol. 25, pp. 110–30.

Kasarda, John D. 1993. "Inner City Concentrated Poverty and Neighborhood Distress: 1970–1990." *Housing Policy Debate,* vol. 4, no. 3, pp. 253–302.

———. 1989. "Urban Industrial Transition and the Underclass." *Annals, AAPSS,* vol. 50, pp. 26–47.

———. 1983. "Entry-Level Jobs, Mobility, and Urban Minority Unemployment." *Urban Affairs Quarterly,* vol. 19, pp. 21–40.

Kasarda, John D., Stephen J. Appold, Stuart Sweeney, and Elaine Sieff. 1997. "Central City and Suburban Migration Patterns: Is a Turnaround on the Horizon?" *Housing Policy Debate,* vol. 8, no. 2, pp. 307–58.

Katz, Bruce. 1998. "Reviving Cities: Think Metropolitan." Brookings Policy Brief, no. 33, June, http://www.brook.edu/comm/policybriefs.

———. 1997. "Give Community Institutions a Fighting Chance." *Brookings Review,* vol. 15, no. 4, pp. 32–35.

Keating, Dennis W. 1994. *The Suburban Racial Dilemma: Housing and Neighborhoods.* Philadelphia: Temple University Press.

Kenney, Genevieve M., and Douglas A. Wissoker. 1994. "An Analysis of the Correlates of Discrimination Facing Young Hispanic Job-Seekers." *The American Economic Review,* vol. 84, no. 3, pp. 674–83.

Keyes, Langley, Alex Schwartz, Avis Vidal, and Rachel Bratt. 1996. "Networks and Nonprofits: Opportunities and Challenges in an Era of Federal Devolution." *Housing Policy Debate,* vol. 7, no. 2, pp. 201–30.

Kingsley, Thomas G., Joseph B. McNeely, and James O. Gibson. 1997. *Community Building Coming of Age.* Washington, DC: The Development Training Institute, Inc., The Urban Institute.

Kirp, David, John Dwyer, and Larry Rosenthal. 1996. *Our Town: Race, Housing, and the Soul of Suburbia.* New Brunswick, NJ: Rutgers University Press.

Kirschenman, Joleen, Philip Moss, and Chris Tilly. 1996. "Space as a Signal, Space as a Barrier: How Employers Map and Use Space in Four Metropolitan Labor Markets." Working Paper No. 89. New York: Russell Sage Foundation.

Kirschenman, Joleen, and Kathryn M. Neckerman. 1991. " 'We'd Love to Hire Them, but . . . ': The Meaning of Race for Employers." In Christopher Jencks and Paul E. Peterson, eds., *The Urban Underclass.* Washington, DC: The Brookings Institution.

Koschinsky, Julia. 1998. "Challenging the Third Sector Housing Approach: The Impact of Federal Policies (1980–1996)." *Journal of Urban Affairs,* vol. 20, no. 2, pp. 203–32.

Kotkin, Joel, and David Friedman. 1993. *The Los Angeles Riots: Causes, Myths and Solutions.* Washington, DC: The Progressive Policy Institute.

Kozol, Jonathan. 1991. *Savage Inequalities: Children in America's Schools.* New York: Crown Publications.

Kretzmann, John P., and John L. McKnight. 1993. *Building Communities from the Inside Out: A Path Toward Finding and Mobilizing a Community's Assets.* Evanston, IL: Center for Urban Affairs and Policy Research, Northwestern University.

Krumholz, Norman, and John Forester. 1990. *Making Equity Planning Work.* Philadelphia: Temple University Press.

Kuznets, Simon. 1955. "Economic Growth and Income Inequality." *American Economic Review,* vol. 45, March, pp. 1–28.

Ladd, Helen F. 1994. "Spatially Targeted Economic Development Strategies: Do They Work?" *Citiscape,* vol. 1, no. 1, pp. 193–218.

Lang, Robert, and Steven Hornburg. 1997. "Planning Portland Style: Pitfalls and Possibilities." *Housing Policy Debate,* vol. 8, issue 1, pp. 1–73.

Leavitt, Jacqueline. 1997. "Los Angeles Neighborhoods Respond to Civil Unrest: Is Planning an Adequate Tool?" In W. Dennis Keating, Norman Krumholz, and Philip Star, eds., *Revitalizing Urban Neighborhoods*. Lawrence, KS: University Press of Kansas.

Lecaillon, Jacques, Felix Paukert, Christian Morrisson, and Dimitri Germidis. 1984. *Income Distribution and Economic Development: An Analytical Survey*. Geneva: International Labour Office.

Ledebur, Larry C., and William R. Barnes. 1993. *All in It Together: Cities, Suburbs, and Local Economic Regions*. Washington, DC: National League of Cities, February.

———. 1992. *Cities' Distress, Metropolitan Disparities, and Economic Growth*. Washington, DC: National League of Cities, September.

Lee, Chris. 1995. "Out of the Maze: Can the Federal Job-Training Mess Be Fixed?" *Training*, vol. 32, no. 2, February, pp. 29–37.

Lenz, Thomas. 1998. "Building a Force for the Common Good." *Shelterforce*. September/October, http://www.uhi.org/online/issues/101/lenz.html.

Leo, Christopher, with Mary Ann Beavis, Andrew Carver, and Robyne Turner. 1998. "Is Urban Sprawl Back on the Political Agenda?" *Urban Affairs Review*, vol. 34, no. 2, pp. 179–211.

Leonard, Paul, and Edward Lazere. 1992. *A Place to Call Home: The Low Income Housing Crisis in 44 Major Metropolitan Areas*. Washington, DC: Center on Budget and Policy Priorities, November.

Light, Ivan. 1987. "Los Angeles." In Mattei Dogan and John D. Kasagarda, eds., *Mega-Cities: The Metropolis Era, Volume Two*. Newbury Park, CA: Sage Publications, pp. 56–96.

Logan, John R., Richard D. Alba, and Shu-Yin Leung. 1996. "Minority Access to White Suburbs: A Multiregional Comparison." *Social Forces*, vol. 74, no. 3, pp. 851–81.

Logan, John R., Richard D. Alba, Tom McNulty, and Brian Fisher. 1996. "Making a Place in the Metropolis: Locational Attainment in Cities and Suburbs." *Demography*, vol. 33, no. 4, pp. 443–53.

López-Garza, Marta. Forthcoming. "A Study of the Informal Economy and Latino/a Immigrants in Greater Los Angeles." In David Diaz and Marta López-Garza, eds., *Asian and Latino Immigrants in a Restructuring Economy: The Metamorphosis of Southern California*. Palo Alto: Stanford University Press.

———. 1989. "Immigration and Economic Restructuring: The Metamorphosis of Southern California." *California Sociologist*, vol. 12, no. 2, pp. 93–110.

Los Angeles 2000 Committee. 1988. *Los Angeles 2000: A City for the Future*. Los Angeles: Los Angeles 2000 Committee.

Luria, Daniel D., and Joel Rogers. 1997. "A New Urban Agenda." *Boston Review*, February/March, http://www.bostonreview.mit.edu/BR22.1.

Lynch, Kevin. 1960. *The Image of the City*. Cambridge, MA: Cambridge Technology Press.

Madden, Janice. 1996. "Changes in the Distribution of Poverty Across and Within the U.S. Metropolitan Areas, 1979–1989." *Urban Studies*, vol. 33, no. 9, pp. 1581–600.

Marcelli, Enrico A., and David M. Heer. 1997. "Unauthorized Mexican Workers in the 1990 Los Angeles County Labour Force." *International Migration*, vol. 35, no. 1, pp. 59–83.

Marcelli, Enrico A., and Pascale M. Joassart. 1998. "Prosperity and Poverty in the New Economy: A Report on the Social and Economic Status of Working People in San Diego County." San Diego: Center on Policy Initiatives, December.

Marcelli, Enrico A., Manuel Pastor, and Pascale Joassart-Marcelli. 1999. "Estimating the Effects of Informal Economic Activity: Evidence from Los Angeles." *Journal of Economic Issues,* vol. XXXIII, no. 3., pp. 579–607.

Marglin, Stephen A., and Juliet B. Schor. 1991. *The Golden Age of Capitalism: Reinterpreting the Postwar Experience.* Oxford, U.K.: Clarendon Press.

Markusen, Ann, Peter Hall, Scott Campbell, and Sabina Dietrich. 1991. *The Rise of the Gunbelt: The Military Remapping of Industrial America.* New York: Oxford University Press.

Massey, Douglas S., and Nancy A. Denton. 1993. *American Apartheid: Segregation and the Making of the Underclass.* Cambridge, MA: Harvard University Press.

Massey, Douglas S., and Mitchell L. Eggers. 1993. "The Spatial Concentration of Affluence and Poverty During the 1970s." *Urban Affairs Quarterly,* vol. 29, no. 2, pp. 299–315.

Mattressich, Paul, and Barbara Monsey. 1997. *Community Building: What Makes It Work.* St. Paul, MN: Amherst H. Wilder Foundation.

McCarthy, Kevin F., and Robert B. Valdez. 1986. *Current and Future Effects of Mexican Immigrants in California.* Santa Monica: The Rand Corporation.

McEnery, Tom. 1994. *The New City-State: Change and Renewal in America's Cities.* Niwot, CO: Roberts Rinehart Publishers.

Medoff, Peter, and Holly Sklar. 1994. *Streets of Hope: The Fall and Rise of an Urban Neighborhood.* Boston: South End Press.

Melendez, Edwin. 1996. *Working on Jobs: The Center for Employment Training.* Boston: Mauricio Gastón Institute, University of Massachusetts, Boston.

———. 1993. "Understanding Latino Poverty." *Sage Relations Abstracts,* vol. 18, no. 2, pp. 31–42.

Metropolitan Transportation Authority. 1997. *Long Range Transportation Plan: 1997 Update.* Los Angeles: Metropolitan Transportation Authority.

Metzger, John. 1998. "Remaking the Growth Coalition: The Pittsburgh Partnership for Neighborhood Development." *Economic Development Quarterly,* vol. 12, no. 1, pp. 12–29.

Mier, Robert, and Joan Fitzgerald. 1991. "Managing Local Economic Development." *Economic Development Quarterly,* vol. 5, fall, pp. 268–79.

Minerbrook, Scott. 1992. "A Tale of Two Suburbias: The Decline of Blue-Collar Suburbs and Growth of 'Edge Cities' Create a New Kind of Isolation." *U.S. News and World Report,* November 9, pp. 32–40.

Mishel, Lawrence, and Jared Bernstein. 1995. *The State of Working America.* Armonk, NY: M.E. Sharpe Inc.

Molina, Frieda. 1998. *Making Connections: A Study of Employment Linkage Programs.* Washington, DC: Center for Community Change.

Mollenkopf, John. 1983. *The Contested City.* Princeton: Princeton University Press.

Morales, Rebecca, and Paul Ong. 1993. "The Illusion of Progress—Latinos in Los Angeles." In Rebecca Morales and Frank Bonilla, eds., *Restructuring and the New Inequality.* Thousand Oaks, CA: Sage Publications, pp. 55–84.

Morales, Rebecca, and Manuel Pastor. 2000. "Can't We All Just Get Along? Interethnic Organizing for Economic Development." In John J. Betancur and Douglas C. Gills, eds., *The Collaborative City: Opportunities and Struggles for Blacks and Latinos in U.S. Cities.* New York: Garland Publishing.

Moss, Philip, and Chris Tilly. 1993. "'Soft Skills' and Race: An Investigation of Black Men's Employment Problems." Paper presented at the Eastern Economic Association meetings, Washington, DC, March 19.

National Academy of Public Administration. 1998. *Building Stronger Communities and Regions: Can the Federal Government Help?* Washington, DC: National Academy of Public Administration.

National Association of Counties. 1997. "Innovative City/County Partnerships." Washington, DC: Joint Center for Sustainable Partnerships.

National Congress for Community Economic Development. 1995. *Tying It All Together: The Comprehensive Achievements of Community Based Development Organizations.* Washington, DC: National Congress for Community Economic Development.

Nowak, Jeremy. 1997. "Neighborhood Initiative and the Regional Economy. *Economic Development Quarterly,* vol. 11, no. 1, pp. 3–10.

Nunn, Samuel, and Mark Rosentraub. 1997. "Dimensions of Interjurisdictional Cooperation." *Journal of the American Planning Association,* vol. 63, no. 2, pp. 205–19.

O'Regan, Katherine M. 1993. "The Effect of Social Networks and Concentrated Poverty on Black and Hispanic Youth Unemployment." *The Annals of Regional Science,* vol. 27, pp. 327–42.

Odland, John, and Blanche Balzer. 1979. "Localized Externalities, Contagious Processes, and the Deterioration of Urban Housing: An Empirical Analysis." *Socio-Economic Planning Science,* vol. 13, pp. 87–93.

Oliver, Melvin L., and Michael Lichter. 1996. "Social Isolation, Network Segregation, and Job Search Among African Americans." University of California, Los Angeles, January. Mimeographed.

Oliver, Melvin L., and Thomas M. Shapiro. 1995. *Black Wealth, White Wealth: A New Perspective on Racial Inequality.* New York: Routledge.

Ong, Paul, with Evelyn Blumenberg and Jainling Li. 1993. "Poverty and Employment Issues in the Inner Urban Core." In Allen J. Scott and E. Richard Brown, eds., *South-Central Los Angeles: Anatomy of an Urban Crisis.* Working Paper No. 6. Los Angeles: Lewis Center for Regional Policy Studies, University of California, Los Angeles.

Ong, Paul, and Evelyn Blumenberg. 1998. "Job Access, Commute and Travel Burden Among Welfare Recipients." *Urban Studies,* vol. 35, no. 1, pp. 73–93.

Ong, Paul, et al. 1989. *The Widening Divide: Income Inequality and Poverty in Los Angeles.* Los Angeles: Graduate School of Architecture and Urban Planning, University of California, Los Angeles.

Ong, Paul M., and Janette R. Lawrence. 1995. "Race and Employment Dislocation in California's Aerospace Industry." *Review of Black Political Economy,* vol. 23, no. 3, pp. 91–101.

Orfield, Gary. 1993. *The Growth of Segregation in American Schools: Changing Patterns of Segregation and Poverty Since 1968.* Washington, DC: National School Boards Association.

Orfield, Myron. 1998. "Conflict or Consensus: Forty Years of Minnesota Metropolitan Politics." *Brookings Review,* vol. 16, no. 4, pp. 31–34.

———. 1997. *Metropolitics: A Regional Agenda for Community and Stability.* Washington, DC: The Brookings Institution.

Osterman, Paul. 1991. "Gains from Growth? The Impact of Full Employment on Poverty in Boston." In Christopher Jencks and Paul Peterson, eds., *The Urban Underclass.* Washington, DC: The Brookings Institution.

Pack, Janet Rothenberg. 1998. "Poverty and Urban Public Expenditures." *Urban Studies,* vol. 35, no. 11, pp. 1995–96.

Paget, Karen, and Amy Burke. 1998. "Can Cities Escape Political Isolation?" *The American Prospect,* January/February, pp. 54–62.

Palley, Thomas I. 1994. "Capital Mobility and the Threat to American Prosperity." *Challenge,* vol. 37, no. 6, pp. 31–37.

Palubinsky, Beth Z., and Bernardine H. Watson. 1997. *Getting from Here to There: The Bridges to Work Demonstration, First Report to the Field.* Philadelphia: Public/Private Ventures.

Partridge, Mark D. 1997. "Is Inequality Harmful to Growth? Comment." *American Economic Review,* vol. 87, no. 5, pp. 600–21.

Parzen, Julia. 1997. "Innovations in Metropolitan Cooperation." Chicago: Center for Neighborhood Technology (www.cnt.org).

Passel, Jeffrey. 1994. *Immigrants and Taxes: A Reappraisal of Huddle's "The Costs of Immigrants."* Claremont, CA: The Tomás Rivera Center.

Pastor, Manuel, Jr. Forthcoming. "Economics and Ethnicity: Poverty, Race, and Immigration in Los Angeles." In Marta López-Garza and David R. Diaz, eds. *Asian and Latino Immigrants in a Restructuring Economy: The Metamorphosis of Los Angeles.* Palo Alto: Stanford University Press.

———. "Advantaging the Disadvantaged Through International Trade." Paper funded by the Pacific Council on International Policy (PCIP) and the John Randolph Haynes and Dora Haynes Foundation. Can be obtained from the Latin American & Latino Studies Department, University of California, Santa Cruz.

———. 1995. "Economic Inequality, Latino Poverty, and the Civil Unrest in Los Angeles." *Economic Development Quarterly,* vol. 9, no. 3, pp. 238–58.

———. 1993. *Latinos and the Los Angeles Uprising: The Economic Context.* Claremont: The Tomás Rivera Center.

Pastor, Manuel, Jr., with Crystal Hayling. 1990. *Economic Development: The New Majority in Los Angeles.* Los Angeles: Occidental College.

Pastor, Manuel, Jr., and Ana Robinson Adams. 1996. "Keeping Down with the Joneses: Neighbors, Networks, and Wages." *Review of Regional Economics,* vol. 26, no. 2, pp. 115–45.

Pastor, Manuel, Jr., and Enrico Marcelli. 1998. "Social, Spatial, and Skill Mismatch in Los Angeles." Paper presented for a meeting of the Latin American Studies Association, Chicago, Illinois, September.

Paukert, Felix. 1973. "Income Distribution at Different Levels of Development: A Survey of Evidence." *International Labor Review,* vol. 108, pp. 97–125.

Peirce, Neal. 1996. "New Life for Lightly Polluted Lands." *National Journal,* vol. 28, no. 37, p. 1970.

Peirce, Neal R., with Curtis W. Johnson and John Stuart Hall. 1993. *Citistates: How Urban America Can Prosper in a Competitive World.* Washington, DC: Seven Locks Press.

Peirce, Neal, and Curtis Johnson. 1997. *Boundary Crossers: Community Leadership for a Global Age.* College Park, MD: The Academy of Leadership.

Peirce, Neil R., Curtis Johnson, and staff. 1995. "The Peirce Report," taken from *The Charlotte Observer,* September 17, 1995, to October 8, 1995.

Persson, Torsten, and Guido Tabellini. 1994. "Is Inequality Harmful for Growth?" *American Economic Review,* vol. 84, no. 3, pp. 600–21.

Peterson, George E., and Kale Williams. 1994. *Housing Mobility: What Has It Accomplished and What Is Its Promise?* Washington, DC: The Urban Institute, October.

Phillips, Heith R. 1992. "Regional Wage Divergence and National Wage Inequality." *Economic Review.* Federal Reserve Board of Dallas, Fourth Quarter, pp. 31–44.

Piore, Michael, and Charles Sabel. 1984. *The Second Industrial Divide: Possibilities for Prosperity.* New York: Basic Books.

Piven, Francis Fox, and Richard A. Cloward. 1993. *Regulating the Poor: The Functions of Public Welfare.* New York: Random House.

Polednak, Anthony P. 1997. *Segregation, Poverty, and Mortality in Urban African Americans.* New York: Oxford University Press.

Polikoff, Alexander, ed. 1995. *Housing Mobility: Promise or Illusion?* Washington, DC: The Urban Institute.

Pollin, Robert, and Stephanie Luce. 1998. *The Living Wage: Building a Fair Economy.* New York: The New Press.

Porter, Michael, 1995. "The Competitive Advantage of the Inner-City." *Harvard Business Review,* May–June, pp. 55–71.

Portes, Alejandro, Manuel Castells, and Lauren A. Benton, eds. 1989. *The Informal Economy: Studies in Advanced and Less Developed Countries.* Baltimore: The Johns Hopkins University Press.

Portes, Alejandro, and Saskia Sassen. 1987. "Making It Underground: Comparative Material on the Informal Sector in Western Market Economies." *American Journal of Sociology,* vol. 3, no. 1, pp. 30–61.

powell, john a. 1998. "Race and Space: What Really Drives Metropolitan Growth." *Brookings Review,* vol. 16, no. 4, pp. 20–22.

Putnam, Robert, with Robert Leonardi and Rafaella Y. Nanetti. 1993. *Making Democracy Work: Civic Traditions in Modern Italy.* Princeton: Princeton University Press.

Rabrenovic, Gordana. 1996. *Community Builders: A Tale of Neighborhood Mobilization in Two Cities.* Philadelphia: Temple University Press.

Regalado, Jaime. 1994. "Community Coalition-Building." In Mark Baldassare, ed., *The Los Angeles Riots: Lessons for the Urban Future.* Boulder, CO: Westview Press.

Reich, Robert. 1991. *The Work of Nations: Preparing Ourselves for 21st-Century Capitalism.* New York: Alfred A. Knopf.

Richmond, Henry R. 1997. "Comment on Carl Abbott's 'The Portland Region: Where the City and Suburbs Talk to Each Other and Agree.'" *Housing Policy Debate,* vol. 8, issue 1, pp. 53–64.

RLA. 1997. *Rebuilding LA's Urban Communities: A Final Report from RLA.* Santa Monica, CA: The Miliken Institute.

———. 1996. *Rebuilding LA's Neglected Communities.* Los Angeles: RLA.

———. 1995. *Detailed Progress Report: May 23, 1995.* Los Angeles: RLA.

Robinson, Carla J. 1989. "Municipal Approaches to Economic Development Growth and Distribution Policy." *APA Journal,* Summer, pp. 283–95.

Rodrik, Dani. 1994. "King Kong Meets Godzilla: The World Bank and the East Asian Miracle." In A. Fishlow, ed., *Miracle or Design: Lessons from the East Asian Experience.* Washington, DC: Overseas Development Council, pp. 13–53.

Roisman, Florence, and Hilary Botein. 1993. "Housing Mobility and Life Opportunities." *Clearinghouse Review,* special issue, pp. 335–51.

Rosenbaum, James E. 1995. "Changing the Geography of Opportunity by Expanding Residential Choice: Lessons from the Gautreaux Program." *Housing Policy Debate,* vol. 6, no. 1, pp. 231–69.

Rosenbaum, James, Nancy Fishman, Alison Brett, and Patricia Meaden. 1993. "Can the Kerner Commission's Housing Strategy Improve Employment, Education, and Social Integration for Low-Income Blacks?" *North Carolina Law Review,* vol. 71, no. 5, pp. 1519–56.

Ross, Stephen L. 1998. "Racial Differences in Residential and Job Mobility: Evidence Concerning the Spatial Mismatch Hypothesis." *Journal of Urban Economics,* vol. 43, pp. 112–35.

Rusk, David. 1999. *Inside Game, Outside Game: Winning Strategies for Saving Urban America.* Washington, DC: The Brookings Institution.

———. 1998. "St. Louis Congregations Challenge Urban Sprawl." *Shelterforce,* no. 97, January/February, pp. 21–22, 26.

———. 1995. *Cities Without Suburbs.* Baltimore: The Johns Hopkins University Press.

Ryscavage, Paul. 1996. *A Perspective on Low-Wage Workers.* Washington, DC: Current Population Reports, Household Economic Studies, U.S. Department of Commerce, Economics and Statistics Administration, pp. 57–70.

Sabel, Charles. 1988. "Flexible Specialization and the Re-emergence of Regional Economies." In Paul Hirst and Jonathan Zeitlin, eds., *Reversing Industrial Decline.* Oxford, U.K.: Berg, pp. 17–70.

Sanyika, Matangulizi. 1987. "Balancing Downtown and Neighborhood Development. Part III: A Study of Two Triangular Equity Partnerships." *Economic Development & Law Center Report,* Spring, pp. 25–31.

———. 1986. "Balancing Neighborhood and Downtown Development: Issues for Local Government and CBOs." *Economic Development & Law Center Report,* Summer, pp. 12–15.

Sassen, Saskia. 1994a. *Cities in a World Economy.* Thousand Oaks, CA: Pine Forge Press.

———. 1994b. "The Informal Economy: Between New Developments and Old Regulations." *Yale Law Journal,* vol. 103, pp. 2289–304.

———. 1991. *The Global City: New York, London, Tokyo.* Princeton: Princeton University Press.

———. 1989. "New York City's Informal Economy." In Alejandro Portes, Manuel Castells, and Lauren A. Benton, eds., *The Informal Economy.* Baltimore: The Johns Hopkins University Press, pp. 60–77.

Savitch, H. V., and Ronald K. Vogel, eds. 1996. *Regional Politics: America in a Post-City Age.* Thousand Oaks, CA: Sage Publications.

Savitch, H.V., David Collins, Daniel Sanders, and John Markham. 1993. "Ties That Bind: Central Cities, Suburbs, and the New Metropolitan Region." *Economic Development Quarterly,* vol. 7, no. 4, pp. 341–57.

Saxenian, Annalee. 1996. *The Regional Advantage: Culture and Competition in Silicon Valley and Route 128.* Cambridge, MA: Harvard University Press.

Schill, Michael H., and Susan M. Wachter. 1995. "The Spatial Bias of Federal Housing Law and Policy: Concentrated Poverty in Urban America." *University of Pennsylvania Law Review,* vol. 143, no. 5, pp. 1285–342.

Schrag, Peter. 1998. *Paradise Lost: California's Experience, America's Future.* New York: The New Press.

Schwarz, John E. 1997. *Illusions of Opportunity: The American Dream in Question.* New York: W. W. Norton & Company.

Scott, Allen J. 1993. "The New Southern California Economy: Pathways to Industrial Resurgence." Lewis Center for Regional Policy Studies, University of California, Los Angeles.

———. 1988. *Metropolis: From the Division of Labor to Urban Form.* Berkeley: University of California Press.

Sexton, Edwin A. 1991. "Residential Location, Workplace Location, and Black Earnings." *The Review of Regional Studies,* vol. 21, spring, pp. 11–20.

Shuman, Michael. 1998. "Going Local: Devolution for Progressives." *The Nation,* October 12, pp. 11–15.

Sirola, Paula M. 1991a. "Conceptualizing Microentreprenuership in an Industrialized Economy: The Case of Los Angeles." Paper prepared for a conference of the Association of Women in Development, Washington, DC, November.

———. 1991b. "Economic Survival Alternatives for Urban Immigrants: Informal Sector Strategies in Los Angeles." Paper prepared for the seventeeth Pacific Science Congress, Honolulu, Hawaii.

Smith, Stephen Samuel. 1997. "Hugh Governs? Regime and Educational Policy in Charlotte, North Carolina." *Journal of Urban Affairs,* vol. 19, no. 3, pp. 247–74.

Soja, Edward W. Forthcoming. *Postmetropolis: Critical Studies of Cities and Regions.* Oxford, U.K.: Blackwell.

———. 1989. *Postmodern Geographies: The Reassertion of Space in Critical Social Theory.* New York: Verso.

Sonenshein, Raphael J. 1993. *Politics in Black and White: Race and Power in Los Angeles.* Princeton: Princeton University Press.

Southern California Association of Governments (SCAG). 1996. *Regional Comprehensive Plan and Guide.* Los Angeles: Southern California Association of Governments.

Southern California Edison (SCE). 1995. *Southern California's Apparel Industry: Building a Path to Prosperity.* Report prepared by SCE with the assistance of DRI/McGraw Hill, February.

Squires, Gregory. 1999. "The Indelible Color Line: The Persistence of Housing Discrimination." *The American Prospect,* no. 42, January–February, p. 67.

———., ed. 1992. *From Redlining to Reinvestment: Community Responses to Urban Disinvestment.* Philadelphia: Temple University Press.

Stack, Carol B. 1974. *All Our Kin: Strategies for Survival in a Black Community.* New York: Harper & Row.

Stanfield, Rochelle. 1997. "Splitsville." *National Journal,* May 3, pp. 862–65.

———. 1996. "The Reverse Commute." *National Journal,* November 23.

Stegman, Michael. 1996. "National Urban Policy Revisited: Policy Options for the Clinton Administration." In John Charles Boger and Judith Welch Wegner, eds., *Race, Poverty, and American Cities.* Chapel Hill, NC: University of North Carolina Press, pp. 228–69.

Stegman, Michael, and Margery Austin Turner. 1996. "The Future of Urban America in the Global Economy." *Journal of the American Planning Association,* vol. 62, no. 2 , pp. 157–64.

Steinmo, Sven. 1994. "The End of Redistribution? International Pressures and Domestic Policy Choices." *Challenge,* vol. 37, no. 6, pp. 9–17.

Stepick, Alex. 1989. "Miami's Two Informal Sectors." In Alejandro Portes, Manuel Castells, and Lauren A. Benton, eds., *The Informal Economy.* Baltimore: The Johns Hopkins University Press, pp. 111–34.

Stoecker, Randy. 1997. "The CDC Model of Urban Redevelopment: A Critique and an Alternative." *Journal of Urban Affairs,* vol. 19, no. 1, pp. 1–22.

Stone, Rebecca, ed. 1996. *Core Issues in Comprehensive Community-Building Initiatives.* Chicago: Chapin Hall Center for Children at the University of Chicago.

Storper, Michael. 1997. *The Regional World: Territorial Development in a Global Economy.* New York: Guilford Press.

Stuart, Alfred W. 1995a. *Growth and Development Trends in the Greater Charlotte Region Since 1990.* Charlotte: Centralina Council of Governments.

———. 1995b. "The Role of the Textile Industry in Shaping the Charlotte Region." Department of Geography & Earth Sciences, The University of North Carolina, Charlotte.

Summers, Anita A. 1997. *Major Revitalization Efforts Between Cities and Suburbs in the United States.* Working Paper 46. Philadelphia: Wharton School Real Estate Center, University of Philadelphia, March.

Swanstrom, Todd. 1996. "Ideas Matter: Reflections on the New Regionalism." *Cityscape,* vol. 2, no. 2, pp. 5–21.

Swanstrom, Todd, and Richard Sauerzkopf. 1993. "The Urban Electorate in Presidential Elections." Conference paper for the Urban Affairs Association, Indianapolis, Indiana, April.

Szasz, Andrew, and Michael Meuser. 1997. "Environmental Inequalities: Literature Review and Proposals for New Directions in Research and Theory." *Current Sociology,* vol. 45, no. 3, pp. 99–120.

Taeuber, Karl, and Alma Taeuber. 1965. *Negroes in Cities: Residential Segregation and Neighborhood Change.* Chicago: Aldine.

Tershy, Russell. 1995. Testimony before the Subcommittee on Postsecondary Education, Training, and Life-long Learning, Committee on Economic and Educational Opportunities, United States Congress, March 7.

Tienda, Marta, and Haya Stier. 1991. "Joblessness and Shiftlessness: Labor Force Activity in Chicago's Inner City." In Christopher Jencks and Paul E. Peterson, eds., *The Urban Underclass.* Washington, DC: The Brookings Institute, pp. 135–54.

Torto, Raymond, and William Wheaton. 1994. *Downtown/Suburban Competition for Jobs in the 1990s: Economic Policy and Implications for Boston.* Boston: John W. McCormack Institute of Public Affairs.

U.S. Bureau of the Census. 1991. *Poverty in the United States: 1990.* Washington, DC: U.S. Bureau of the Census.

U.S. Department of Housing and Urban Development (HUD). 1998a. *Hunting for Troubled Suburbs.* Washington, DC: U.S. Department of Housing and Urban Development.

———. 1998b. *State of the Cities.* Washington, DC: U.S. Department of Housing and Urban Development.

———. 1997. *State and Metropolitan Administration of Section 8: Current Models and Potential Resources: Final Report.* Washington, DC: Office of Policy Development and Research, April.

———. 1996. *America's New Economy and the Challenge of the Cities: A HUD Report on Metropolitan Economic Strategy.* Washington, DC: U.S. Department of Housing and Urban Development, October.

———. 1995. *Promoting Housing Choice in HUD's Rental Assistance Programs: A Report to Congress.* Washington, DC: Office of Policy Development and Research, April.

———. 1994a. *Regional Housing Mobility Opportunities for Lower Income House-holds: A Resource Guide to Affordable Housing and Regional Mobility Strategies.* Washington, DC: Office of Policy Development and Research, March.

———. 1994b. *Residential Mobility Programs.* Washington, DC: Office of Policy Development and Research, September.

Vidal, Avis C. 1995. "Reintegrating Disadvantaged Communities into the Fabric of Urban Life: The Role of Community Development." *Housing Policy Debate,* vol. 6, no. 1, pp. 169–230.

———. 1992. *Rebuilding Communities: A National Study of Urban Community Development Corporations.* New York: Community Development Research Center, The New School for Social Research.

———. 1989. *Community Economic Development Assessment: A National Study of Urban Community Development Corporations.* New York: Community Development Research Center, The New School for Social Research.

Vogel, Carl, Linda Lutton, Karen Sheets, Christine McConville, and Ed Finkel. 1997. "Forums Bring Together Diverse Regional Voices." *The Neighborhood Works,* vol. 20, no. 6, pp. 22–35.

Voith, Richard. 1998. "Do Suburbs Need Cities?" *Journal of Regional Science,* vol. 38, no. 3, pp. 445–65.

———. 1992. "City and Suburban Growth: Substitutes or Complements?" *Business Review,* September/October, pp. 445–64.

Waldinger, Roger, and Mehdi Bozorgmehr, eds. 1996. *Ethnic Los Angeles.* New York: Russell Sage Foundation.

Walker, Christopher. 1993. "Nonprofit Housing Development: Status, Trends, and Prospects." *Housing Policy Debate,* vol. 4, no. 3, pp. 369–414.

Walker, Christopher, and Mark Weinheimer. 1998. *Community Development in the 1990s.* Washington, DC: The Urban Institute.

Wallis, Allan. 1995. "Regional Governance and the Post-Industrial Economy." *The Regionalist,* vol. 1, no. 3, pp. 1–11.

Walsh, Joan. 1997. *Stories of Renewal: Community Building and the Future of Urban America.* New York: The Rockefeller Foundation.

Weir, Margaret. 1995. "In the Shadows: Central Cities' Loss of Power in State Politics." *Brookings Review,* vol. 13, no. 2, pp. 16–19.

Williams, E. Douglass, and Richard H. Sander. 1997. *An Empirical Analysis of the Proposed Los Angeles Living Wage Ordinance: Final Report.* Prepared under contract for the City of Los Angeles, January 17.

Wilson, William Julius. 1996. *When Work Disappears: The World of the New Urban Poor.* New York: Alfred A. Knopf, Inc.

———. 1987. *The Truly Disadvantaged: The Inner City, the Underclass, and Public Policy.* Chicago: University of Chicago Press.

Wolff, Goetz. 1992. "The Making of a Third World City? Latino Labor and the Restructuring of the L.A. Economy." Draft paper for the Seventeenth International Congress of the Latin American Studies Association, Los Angeles, California, September.

Wolff, Goetz, and J. Eugene Grigsby. 1995. *Making Economic Development Work in LA's Low-Income Communities: MCC's Strategic Approach.* Report prepared for the Multicultural Collaborative, Los Angeles, California, January.

Wolman, Harold L., Coit Cook Ford III, and Edward W. Hill. 1994. "Evaluating the Success of Urban Success Stories." *Urban Studies,* vol. 31, no. 6, pp. 835–50.

Wolman, Harold L., and Lisa Marckini. 1998. "Changes in Central-City Representation and Influence in Congress Since the 1960s." *Urban Affairs Review,* vol. 34, no. 2, pp. 291–312.

Wong, Linda J. 1996. "The Role of Immigrant Entrepreneurs in Urban Economic Development." *Stanford Law & Policy Review,* vol. 7, no. 2, pp. 75–87.

Wood, Robert, with Vladimir V. Almendinger. 1961. *1400 Governments: The Political Economy of the New York Metropolitan Region.* Cambridge, MA: Harvard University Press.

Yin, Jordan. 1998. "The Community Development Industry System: A Case Study of Politics and Institutions in Cleveland, 1967–1997." *Journal of Urban Affairs,* vol. 20, no. 2, pp. 137–57.

Zdenek, Robert O. 1998. "Connecting People to Jobs: Capitalizing on Regional Economic Development Opportunities." *Shelterforce,* no. 97, January/February, pp. 13–15.

Zlolniski, Christian. 1994. "The Informal Economy in an Advanced Industrialized Society: Mexican Immigrant Labor in Silicon Valley." *Yale Law Journal,* vol. 103, no. 8, pp. 2305–35.

Index

activists. *See* community leaders

AFL-CIO, 172

African-Americans: in Boston, 145, 149; in Charlotte, 140, 143, 224n.51; and concentrated poverty, 83–84, 210n.6; demographics, 194n.7; in Los Angeles, 22–23, 24 *figure 2.6* (*see also* poverty [Los Angeles]); in San Jose, 133, 137

agencies, regional planning, 158

AGENDA (Los Angeles), 179

Alameda Corridor (Los Angeles), 51, 55, 59, 61, 71, 77, 167, 202n.52, 205n.22, 205–6n.29; Alameda Corridor Jobs Coalition (ACJC), 180; Alameda Corridor Transportation Authority (ACTA), 62, 180; and community leaders, 74, 75, 210n.69; defined, 62; economic impact, 62, 63; impact on low-income communities, 63, 72; support for, 62

Angelides, Phil, 180

Anglos: and concentrated poverty, 83, 210n.6; demographics, 194n.7; in Los Angeles, 22–23, 99 (*see also* poverty [Los Angeles]); in San Jose, 133, 134, 219nn.13–14

Annie E. Casey Foundation, 163, 168

antipoverty efforts. *See* community-building movement; community

development; poverty reduction, arguments for; urban revitalization

Asians: in Boston, 146; demographics, 194n.7; in Los Angeles, 22–23; in San Jose, 133, 134, 137, 138

Atlanta, 128, 160, 167

Barnes, William C., 4, 100, 101, 103, 213nn.5–6

Bedford Stuyvesant Restoration Corporation (New York), 87

Benner, Chris, 221n.27

bidding wars, 166–67

Boston, City of, 145, 146, 147

Boston Compact, 150, 151

Boston Housing Partnership (Metropolitan Boston Housing Partnership), 151, 161

Boston Jobs Policy, 148, 150

Boston (MSA), 5, 15, 89, 93, 94, 126, 128, 130, 132, 161, 173, 194n.15; business leadership in, 151, 153, 161; community development in, 149, 150, 151, 153; demographics, 130, 145–46; economy and workforce, 146–47; growth and poverty reduction in, 125–26, 147–50; housing development, 149, 150, 151, 153; lessons from, 151–52, 153, 154; minorities in, 145–46; poverty performance, 152,

San Jose, City of, 132, 137, 138
San Jose (MSA), 15, 125, 128, 130, 131;
   business leadership, 136, 137, 153;
   community development, 138;
   demographics, 130, 132–33; differential outcomes, by race, 134,
   219nn.13–14; economy and workforce, 133–35; growth and poverty,
   125–26, 135–37, 139; lessons from,
   137–39, 152, 154; poverty performance, 137, 152; poverty rate, 133,
   135; residential segregation, 133;
   social capital, 136, 138, 139
Santa Clara County. *See* San Jose (MSA)
Santa Clara Valley Manufacturing
   Group, 136, 153, 220n.19
Sassen, Saskia, 201n.38
Savitch, H. V., 100, 101
Saxenian, Annalee, 5, 136, 194–95n.15,
   220n.18
schools. *See* education, public
Section 8 voucher program, 169,
   229n.31, n.33
segregation: class, 82, 85, 91; racial, 83,
   146, 181; residential, 6, 20, 102, 103,
   104, 108, 128, 152, 219n.12 (*see also*
   concentrated poverty)
service sector: employment, 6; in Los
   Angeles, 21, 53 *figure 3.1*, 54; in San
   Jose, 134
Silicon Valley, 5–6, 131, 134, 135, 136,
   137, 138, 161, 167, 194–95n.15. *See
   also* San Jose (MSA)
Silicon Valley Manufacturing Group,
   136
Smart Growth, 16, 145, 159, 177, 180,
   182, 231n.52
Smith, Stephen, 144
social capital, 6, 7, 80, 90, 98, 155, 181,
   195n.19, n.23; bonding and bridging,
   14, 95; in Boston, 152; and concentrated poverty, 102; defined, 6, 102;
   in San Jose, 136, 138, 139
Social/Economic Impact Reports
   (SIRs), 167
social networks. *See* networks, social;
   social capital

South Central Los Angeles, 17, 58, 69,
   196n.1, 198n.17
Southern California Association of
   Governments (SCAG), 18, 54,
   59, 62, 65, 71, 180, 96n.34, 206n.41,
   207n.43, nn.48–49; and community
   leaders, 74, 75, 76; economic
   strategy, 66–67, 206–7n.42; impact
   on low-income communities,
   67–68; purpose of, 66; Regional
   Advisory Council, 76, 228n.18;
   Regional Comprehensive Plan,
   66–68, 76, 207nn.46–47; Regional
   Economic Strategies Consortium
   (RESC), 67
Southern California, 19, 122, 127. *See
   also* Los Angeles (County)
"spatial mismatch," 6, 27, 84, 137, 168,
   195n.20, 211n.12
"State of the Nations Cities, The," 103,
   194n.7
State of the Region, 160
Stories of Renewal (Walsh), 7
strategies, regional (Los Angeles
   County), 55–78; view of community
   leaders, 72, 74–76
strategies for community-based
   regionalism: clustering, 157,
   164–66; enhance labor mobility,
   169–70; making work pay, 171–72;
   neighborhood building, 173–74;
   promote infrastructure and equity,
   167; reduce bidding wars, 166–67;
   regional workforce development,
   168–69; regularizing the informal
   sector, 172–73;
subsidies, federal, 174, 175; to cities, 2,
   97; promoting suburbanization, 2,
   82, 230n.42
suburbanization, 81, 82, 97, 121–23,
   174, 175, 176, 193nn.4–5; of
   electorate, 97; of employment, 168;
   racial composition of, 3, 194n.7
suburbs: relation to central cities, 3, 81,
   97–101, 121–22
Surface Transportation Policy Project
   (STPP), 177

Manuel Pastor Jr. is professor of Latin American and Latino studies and director of the Center for Justice, Tolerance, and Community at the University of California, Santa Cruz.

Peter Dreier is E. P. Clapp Distinguished Professor of Politics at Occidental College and director of the Urban and Environmental Policy Program.

J. Eugene Grigsby III is director of the Advanced Policy Institute and professor of urban planning at UCLA's School of Public Policy and Social Research.

Marta López-Garza is an assistant professor and holds a joint position in the Women's Studies Department and the Chicano/Chicana Studies Department at California State University, Northridge.